UNDERSTANDING STATISTICAL CONCEPTS USING S-PLUS

UNDERSTANDING STATISTICAL CONCEPTS USING S-PLUS

Randall E. Schumacker
Allen Akers

University of North Texas

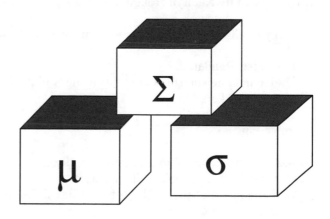

LEA
2001

LAWRENCE ERLBAUM ASSOCIATES, PUBLISHERS
Mahwah, New Jersey   London

Lawrence Erlbaum Associates, Inc., Publishers
10 Industrial Avenue
Mahwah, NJ 07430

Cover design by Kathryn Houghtaling Lacey

Library of Congress Cataloging-in-Publication Data

Schumacker, Randall E.
  Understanding statistical concepts using S-plus / Randall E. Schumacker
  and Allen Akers.

     p.   cm.

Includes bibliographical references and indexes.
ISBN 0-8058-3623-3 (pbk. : alk. paper)
1. Mathematical statistics—Data processing. 2. S-Plus.   I. Akers,
  Allen.   II. Title.

QA276.4 .S366   2001
519.5´0285—dc21   00-065444
                                                                      CIP

Printed in the United States of America
10 9 8 7 6 5 4 3 2 1

DEDICATED TO OUR CHILDREN

Rachel and Jamie

Joshua

TABLE OF CONTENTS

PART V: HYPOTHESIS TESTING IN RESEARCH

PART VI: REPLICABILITY OF FINDINGS

PREFACE

This book was written as a supplemental text for use with introductory or intermediate statistics books. The content of each chapter is appropriate for any undergraduate or graduate level statistics course. The chapters are ordered along the lines of many popular statistics books so it should be easy to supplement the chapter content and exercises with your statistics book and lecture materials. Each chapter lists a set of objectives and a summary of what the student should have learned from the chapter. The content of each chapter was written to enrich a students' understanding of statistical concepts as well as S-PLUS due to the inclusion of exercises that use S-PLUS script programs. The chapter exercises reinforce an understanding of the statistical concepts and the S-PLUS script programs in the chapters.

Computational skills are kept to a minimum in the book by including S-PLUS script programs that can be run for the exercises in the chapters. Students are not required to master the writing of S-PLUS script programs, but explanations of how the programs work and program output are included in each chapter. S-PLUS is an advanced statistical package with an extensive library of functions that offers flexibility in writing customized statistical routines. The S-PLUS script commands and functions provide the capability of programming object and dialog windows that are commonly used in Windows software applications. The S-PLUS software program also contains pull-down menus for the statistical analysis of data.

ORGANIZATION OF THE TEXT

The early chapters in the textbook offer a rich insight into how probability has shaped statistics in the behavioral sciences. In later chapters, the persons who created various statistics and hypothesis testing are highlighted. A final chapter brings together current thinking on significance testing versus practical importance of research findings.

The chapters are grouped into six parts. Part I includes chapters on statistical theory, random sampling, and basic descriptive statistics (frequency distributions, stem and leaf plots, central tendency, and dispersion). Basic concepts related to calculating and interpreting these measures are covered in the chapter exercises. Unique aspects of Part I are the generating of random numbers, presentation of population distributions, sample size effects, Tchebycheff Inequality Theorem, and determining the probability area under a population distribution. These chapters provide an understanding of how the theoretical normal distribution is developed and used in statistics.

Part II includes chapters that cover the basic ideas behind probability. The content covers probability based on independent outcomes, joint outcomes, combinations, and permutations. The importance of the addition and multiplication laws of probability in statistics is further explained. The importance of probability in understanding basic statistical concepts is further enhanced in the chapter exercises, especially the difference between exact probabilities and theoretical probabilities. The S-PLUS script programs are helpful in examining the various outcomes discussed in the chapters.

Part III includes chapters that extend an understanding of how probability and frequency distributions result in sampling distributions. The concept behind how sampling distributions are used in probability statistics is presented. The binomial distribution, normal distribution, t-distribution, chi-square distribution, and F-distribution are presented in the chapter exercises.

Unique to this part is the discussion of how Monte Carlo methods can be used to create the sampling distribution of a statistic, e.g., z, t, chi-square, and F statistics.

Part IV includes the importance of understanding and interpreting results based on the sampling distribution of a statistic, which will be helpful in understanding chapter exercises in Part V. An important chapter on the Central Limit Theorem provides an understanding of how random samples from any population distribution will result in a normal sampling distribution of a statistic especially as sample size increases. This forms the basis for later discussion on confidence intervals, hypothesis testing, Type I error and Type II error. A key concept emphasized is the inference made from the sample statistic to the population parameter and the consequence of making that decision.

Part V contains the essential chapters on hypothesis testing in research. The basic statistics covered are the z-test, chi-square, t-test, analysis of variance, correlation, and regression. Each chapter begins with an elaboration of the origin of the statistical procedure and the person(s) who created them. Examples demonstrate the various types of research questions, how the statistic is used, and interpretation of results. The chapter content and exercises provide the necessary skills for students to better understand how these statistics are used to answer research questions. The logic and steps taken to conduct statistical hypothesis testing using the scientific method is emphasized.

Part VI introduces the importance of replicating research results. In the absence of being able to reproduce the findings in a research study (replicating the study with another random sample of data), cross-validation, jackknife, and bootstrap methods are used to estimate the replicability of findings. Cross-validation involves the random splitting of a sample, applying the statistical test on both sub-samples, and comparing results. Jackknife involves estimating the sample statistic several times based on dropping a different data value each time. The bootstrap procedure uses resampling (sampling with replacement) to estimate the amount of bias in a sample statistic as an estimate of a population parameter. A chapter also presents meta-analysis techniques, which quantitatively combine and synthesize the results of several related research studies. This provides an understanding of the role converting various statistics to a common scale for comparative purposes plays in meta-analysis. A final chapter compares statistical significance testing and the practical importance of research findings. Although hypothesis testing is stressed in Part V, the last chapter in Part VI provides an understanding that significance testing, i.e., $p < .05$, is not necessarily sufficient evidence of the practical importance of research results. It highlights the importance of reporting the sample statistic, significance level, confidence interval, and effect size. Reporting of these values extends the students' thinking beyond significance testing.

S-PLUS PROGRAMS

Each chapter contains at least one S-PLUS program that produces computer output for the chapter exercises. A CD is available with the book and contains S-PLUS script programs that enhance the basic understanding and concepts in the chapters. The S-PLUS programs on the CD have an extension ".ssc", which refers to a script file in S-PLUS. A chapter number, e.g., chap01.ssc, precedes each script program. After mastering the concepts in the book, the S-PLUS software can be used for data analysis and graphics using pull-down menus. The statistical tests and methods for the replicability of findings in Parts V and VI are included in the S-PLUS statistical software.

When using the supplemental exercises for classroom instruction, S-PLUS will need to be installed on either a stand-alone IBM compatible personal computer (with a roll cart and a projection monitor) or on a local area network for use with a computer-equipped classroom. Information concerning the purchase and installation of S-PLUS on a local area network should be referred to your computing center personnel. Student versions of S-PLUS may also be available for purchase at university bookstores.

There are several Internet web sites that offer information, resources, and assistance with S-PLUS. These can be located by entering "S-PLUS" in the search engines accessible from any Internet browser software. The main Internet URL (Uniform Resource Locator) address for S-PLUS is: www.mathsoft.com. The MathSoft Company markets the S-PLUS software. S-PLUS is a high level programming language for statistics and graphics that was developed at Bell Labs. A second URL is, http://lib.stat.cmu.edu/S/, which accesses Carnegie Mellon University's software library of functions and routines written by various authors. The S-PLUS programs were not written to run in R (an open-source version of S/S-PLUS), although R programs could be written to run most of the chapter exercises (with the exception of dialog boxes). More information about R programs and comparisons to S/S-PLUS is available at: http://lib.stat.cmu.edu/R/CRAN.

Randall E. Schumacker
Allen Akers

ACKNOWLEDGEMENTS

The preparation of this text was greatly facilitated by reviews from three anonymous reviewers, several graduate students at the University of North Texas who enrolled in a graduate level course on Statistical Theory and Simulation, and two colleagues in the field of statistics. They all provided much needed feedback on the importance and accuracy of the material in the chapters. The later chapters on the replication of research findings, especially the chapter on significance testing versus practical importance, were enriched from discussions with the students.

We would like to thank the editorial staff at Lawrence Erlbaum Associates, Inc. Publishers for their assistance in getting this book into print. We are especially grateful to Misty Berend for typing the statistical tables. Finally, we are grateful for permission to reproduce the selected statistical tables from Sir Ronald A. Fisher, F.R.S. and Frank Yates, *Statistical Tables for Biological, Agricultural, and Medical Research*, Oliver & Boyd, Ltd., Edinburgh, which were abridged in the John T. Roscoe, *Fundamental Research Statistics for the Behavioral Sciences* (2nd Ed.) book, 1975.

I

INTRODUCTION AND STATISTICAL THEORY

CHAPTER 1

STATISTICAL THEORY

CHAPTER OBJECTIVES

- To see how the computer can be used to generate random samples of data.
- To understand the difference between a population and a sample.
- To observe that different samples may lead to different sample estimates of population parameters.
- To see that most estimates from samples contain some error of estimation.
- To find a relationship between the size of a sample and the accuracy of the estimate.

The field of statistics uses numerical information obtained from samples to draw inferences about populations. A **population** is a well-defined set of individuals, events, or objects. A **sample** is a selection of individuals, events, or objects taken from a well-defined population. A sample is generally taken from a population with each individual, event, or object being independent and having an equally likely chance of selection. The sample average is an example of a random sample estimate of a population value, i.e., population mean. Population characteristics or **parameters** are inferred from sample estimates, which are called statistics. Examples of population parameters are population proportion, population mean, and population correlation. For example, a student wants to estimate the proportion of teachers in the state who are in favor of year-round school. The student might make the estimate on the basis of information received from a random sample of 500 teachers in the population comprised of all teachers in the state. In another example, a biologist wants to estimate the proportion of tree seeds that will germinate. The biologist plants 1,000 tree seeds and uses the germination rate to establish the rate for all seeds. In marketing research, the proportion of 1,000 randomly sampled consumers who buy one product rather than another helps advertising executives determine product appeal.

Because a sample is only a part of the population, how can the sample estimate accurately reflect the population characteristic? There is an expectation that the sample estimate will be close to the population value if the sample is representative of the population. The difference between the sample estimate and the population value is called **sample error**. In a random sample, all objects have an equal chance of being selected from the population. If the sample is reasonably large, this equally likely chance of any individual, event, or object being selected makes it likely that the random sample will represent the population well. Most statistics are based upon this concept of random sampling from a well-defined population. **Sampling error**, or the error in using a sample estimate as a population estimate does occur. In future chapters, you will learn that several random sample estimates can be averaged to better approximate a population value, although sampling error is still present.

In this chapter, you will use S-PLUS computer software and a STATISTICS program to simulate the sampling of data from a population. You are to determine what proportion of a certain large population of people favor stricter penalties. A random number generator will determine the responses of the people in the sample. A random number generator uses an initial start number to begin data selection, and then uses the computer to generate other numbers at random. You will use the results of these simulated random samples to draw conclusions about the population.

You will be asked to run the S-PLUS STATISTICS program five times. The program can be run more times if you like. Each time you run the program, the true population proportion will be different. Consequently, each time you will be simulating a sample data set from a different population. The four different random samples will be chosen during each computer run. The random samples have various sample sizes: 5, 20, 135, and 1,280. Using these results, you will be able to observe the effect of sample size on the accuracy of estimation. The Gallop Poll, for example, uses a random sample of 1,500 people nationwide to estimate the presidential election outcome within +/- 2% error of estimation. This chapter will help you understand random sampling and how the sampling error of estimation is determined, i.e., difference between the sample statistic and the population parameter.

SUMMARY

In this chapter, you should learn that:

- A random sample is part of a population.
- Random samples are used to draw inferences about population parameters or characteristics.
- Different random samples lead to different sample estimates.
- The estimate from a sample is usually not equal to the population value.
- If a large sample is taken, the standard error is smaller.

How the program STATISTICS works

The STATISTICS program uses a pseudo-random number generator in S-PLUS to select a random number between 0 and 1 for the true proportion. Next, random samples of only 0 or 1 are drawn from the finite population (not values between 0 and 1). The probability of a 0 is (1 − the population proportion) and the probability of a 1 is the same as the population proportion. Random samples of various sizes are taken and the sample proportion and estimation errors are calculated.

The size of the samples varies by the list of sample sizes in the variable *SampleSizes*. The "<−" operator is an assignment operator that places the vector of values (10,100,500,1000,1500) into the variable *SampleSizes*. The **c** before the parentheses means to concatenate these values into a single vector. *NumSamples* is assigned the **length** of the *SampleSizes* vector, which is equivalent to the number of individual sample sizes. *PopProp* is the true proportion in the population and is obtained by taking one random number from a uniform population that is between the values of 0 and 1. The **runif** command means to take a value from a **r**andom **unif**orm population and the number values (1,0,1) correspond to the number of values to be obtained (1), the bottom of the range of values (0), and the top of the range of values (1). There are several other commands within S-PLUS that allow for sampling from other distributions, such as normal (**rnorm**), binomial (**rbinom**), and exponential (**rexp**).

The most complex parts of the program pertain to creating and using matrices, which will be covered in later chapters. The line which begins with *TrialData* **<- matrix** is setting the size of the matrix and associating labels with the values that will be written to it. The **for** statement begins the processing loop. The **for** command assigns to the variable **SampleSize** successive values listed in the **SampleSizes** vector. The parentheses are used to mark the beginning and end of the loop encapsulated by this **for** command. The first line within the processing loop creates a vector of values for the first sample and assigns it to the temporary variable *SampleData*. The **sample** command is a way to sample from a finite population, in this case either 0 or 1, but it can also be very useful for taking a subsample of larger samples. The 0:1 denotes the range of *integer* values between 0:1, which only includes 0 and 1, but the same notation could be used to create a vector of integer values from 1 to 10 (1:10). The **prob** keyword sets the probability of getting each value, with 0 having a probability of 1 minus the population proportion (1-*PopProp*) and 1 having a probability of the population proportion. The **size=***SampleSize* assures that this sample is the same size as the one corresponding to the loop iteration, and **replace=T** means to replace values that have been chosen from the population, so this is sampling WITH replacement. If taking a subsample of a larger population, you can request sampling WITHOUT replacement (**replace=F**).

The next line sums all the zeros and ones from the sample to get the total number of people who were in favor, and then divides that value by the sample size to get the sample proportion. The next to the last line within the processing loop assigns values to one vector within the matrix built earlier in the program for outputting the data. The *i* **<-** *i* **+** 1 line increments the counter used to keep track of the place within the matrix. The last line of the program produces a printout of the matrix. The values in the *SampleSizes* vector can be changed to simulate small or large sample sizes.

STATISTICS Program Output

	Size	No. in Favor	Sample Prop.	True Prop.	Est. Error
Sample 1	10	6	0.600	0.677	0.077
Sample 2	100	59	0.590	0.677	0.087
Sample 3	500	331	0.662	0.677	0.015
Sample 4	1000	670	0.670	0.677	0.007
Sample 5	1500	1037	0.691	0.677	-0.014

	Size	No. in Favor	Sample Prop.	True Prop.	Est. Error
Sample 1	20	1	0.050	0.098	0.048
Sample 2	200	18	0.090	0.098	0.008
Sample 3	1000	110	0.110	0.098	-0.012
Sample 4	2000	194	0.097	0.098	0.001
Sample 5	3000	303	0.101	0.098	-0.003

CHAPTER 1 EXERCISES

1. Run STATISTICS once to obtain the results of people who are in favor of stricter penalties for criminals using the four sample sizes below. Enter the results here.

SAMPLE	SAMPLE SIZE	NO. IN FAVOR	SAMPLE PROPORTION
A	5	_____	_____
B	20	_____	_____
C	135	_____	_____
D	1280	_____	_____

a.   Verify that the sample proportions are correct by using long division or a calculator. To find the sample proportion from the number in favor and the sample size, use the formula:

SAMPLE PROPORTION = (NO. IN FAVOR) ÷ (SAMPLE SIZE)

SAMPLE	COMPUTATION
A	_____
B	_____
C	_____
D	_____

b.   Is the estimate of the population proportion the same for each of the samples? Yes__ No __

c.   Why do you think the sample proportions change?
_____

d.   What is the true population proportion? _____

2. The sample proportion (EST) is an estimate of the true population proportion (P). There are errors in the sample estimates.

a.   Calculate the error for each sample. Some of the errors may be positive or negative (Record the +/- sign with the error). Note: ERROR = EST – P.

SAMPLE	SAMPLE SIZE	SAMPLE PROPORTION TRUE	SAMPLE	ERROR
A	5	_____	_____	_____
B	20	_____	_____	_____
C	135	_____	_____	_____
D	1,280	_____	_____	_____

b.   Which of the four samples gave the best estimate? _____

3.   Run the STATISTICS program 4 more times. Each time, compute the errors in the estimates (P will be different for each program run).

	RUN 1					RUN 2		
SAMPLE	SIZE	TRUE	ERROR		SAMPLE	SIZE	TRUE	ERROR
A	5	_____	_____		A	5	_____	_____
B	20	_____	_____		B	20	_____	_____
C	135	_____	_____		C	135	_____	_____
D	1,280	_____	_____		D	1,280	_____	_____
	TRUE P _____					TRUE P _____		

	RUN 3					RUN 4		
SAMPLE	SIZE	TRUE	ERROR		SAMPLE	SIZE	TRUE	ERROR
A	5	_____	_____		A	5	_____	_____
B	20	_____	_____		B	20	_____	_____
C	135	_____	_____		C	135	_____	_____
D	1,280	_____	_____		D	1,280	_____	_____
	TRUE P _____					TRUE P _____		

a.   For the four program runs, what was the largest and smallest amount of error for each sample size? (Disregard the plus or minus sign.)

SAMPLE SIZE		LARGEST ERROR	SMALLEST ERROR
A	5	_____	_____
B	20	_____	_____
C	135	_____	_____
D	1,280	_____	_____

b.   Was the sample proportion from a smaller sample ever a better estimate of the population proportion than the sample proportion from a larger sample? Yes_____ No _____.

c.   If yes, for which samples (A,B,C, or D) were the errors smaller?
SMALLER SAMPLE _____   LEAST ERROR _____
LARGER SAMPLE _____   LEAST ERROR _____

d.   Why is it possible for a smaller sample to occasionally give a better estimate than a larger sample?   _____

4.   Use the previous exercises to draw a conclusion about the effect of sample size on the estimate of the population proportion.

_____

_____

5.   A newspaper survey indicates that 62% of the people in a certain state favor a bill to allow retail stores to be open on Sunday. Given the examples you just completed, what additional information would help you interpret this report?

_____

_____

TRUE OR FALSE QUESTIONS

T   F   a. A sample is part of a population.

T   F   b. The sample proportion always equals the population proportion.

T   F   c. The larger the sample size the more likely it is that a sample

                    proportion will be close to the population proportion.

T   F   d. Each time a different random sample is taken from the same

                    population the sample proportion could be different.

T   F   e. The sample proportion from a large sample is always a better estimate

                    of the population proportion.

CHAPTER 2

GENERATING RANDOM NUMBERS

CHAPTER OBJECTIVES

- To understand how the computer generates random numbers.
- To understand how samples of random numbers are used in statistics.
- To investigate characteristics of a sequence of random numbers.
- To test the random number generator used by the computer.

Random numbers are used in statistics to investigate the characteristics of different population distributions. We will only be studying the characteristics of the normal distribution. This is because many of the variables that we measure are normally distributed. The statistics we use to test hypotheses about population characteristics based on random samples are created based on certain assumptions and characteristics of the normal distribution. Other population distributions exist (wiebull, hypergeometric, poisson, and elliptical), but we will not be studying their characteristics and associated statistics in the chapter exercises.

Early tables of random numbers helped gamblers to understand their odds of winning. In some instances, exact probabilities or odds of certain outcomes were generated from cards and dice. Today, high-speed computers using computer software with a numerical procedure (algorithm) can produce tables of random numbers. The first mainframe computer, a UNIVAC, produced a set of one million random numbers, which was published in a book by the Rand McNally Corporation. Personal desktop computers today run software that can generate random numbers.

Although many computers have software (mathematical algorithms) to generate random numbers, the software algorithms are not all the same and do not produce the same set of random numbers. Basically, a set of computer-generated numbers is not truly random, so they are called **"pseudo random numbers."** They are called "pseudo random numbers" because the numbers tend to repeat themselves after awhile (repeatedness), correlate with other numbers generated (correlatedness), and don't produce a normal distribution (normality). Consequently, when using a **random number generator**, it is important to report the type of computer used, type of random number generator software (algorithm), start value (start number), repeatedness (when numbers repeat themselves in the algorithm), correlatedness (when numbers begin to correlate in a sequence), and normality (whether or not a normal distribution was produced).

A true random set of numbers has no pattern, and if graphed, would appear as scattered data points across the graph. Because true random numbers have no pattern, the next number generated would not be predicted and would appear with approximately the same frequency as any other number. The concept is simple, but often requires visual confirmation (graph) or other statistical test of randomness and/or normality. Software programs often include statistical tests for testing the randomness and normality of computer-generated random sample data.

In this chapter you will execute the random number generator in the S-PLUS program. Because all random number generators are not the same, acceptable properties for these random numbers should include:

1.   Approximate, equal proportions of odd and even numbers should occur.
2.   Each number between 0 and 9 is generated approximately one-tenth of the time.
3.   For the five consecutive sets of generated number combinations, the percentages should be approximately equal to the theoretical probabilities.

SUMMARY

In this chapter, you should learn that:

- A sequence of random numbers is not truly random (unique).
- A sequence of random numbers is typically unpredictable, but a long sequence of random numbers will tend to repeat, correlate, and not appear normal.
- Our expectation is that about half of the generated numbers are odd and half are even.
- The frequency of occurrence for any random integer between 0 and 9 is approximately one-tenth of the time.
- A set of randomly generated numbers can be tested for randomness and normality.

How the RANDOM program works

The RANDOM program tests the randomness of the pseudo-random number generator used in S-PLUS. The majority of the program code classifies combinations of numbers and formats the output. The creation of sample data and the calculation of the relative frequencies of odd and even digits, and each individual digit, are all contained within the first few lines of the program. Random numbers are sampled from the integer values 0 through 9; the relative frequency of the odd numbers is determined using the modulus (or remainder function) in combination with the **sum** function and dividing by the sample size. The relative frequency of the even numbers is determined in the same manner, only using all values that were not determined to be odd (*SampleSize* – **sum**(*SampleData%%*2)). The relative frequency of each digit is determined by the familiar **factor** and **table** combination, and then all raw data are put into groups of five numbers.

The main processing loop of the program is used primarily to classify the groups of numbers based on various combinations of repeat values. It iterates from 1 to the number of rows in the *GroupedData* matrix, which is the first dimension (**dim**) of that matrix. The first line within the matrix concatenates the values within the current row with no space separation between them (**sep=""**). Next, a double use of the **table** and **factor** function combination yields the various amounts of repeat values within the sample group. The loop begins from the inside and works out. First, the number of times that each number (0 to 9) comes up within the group is tallied, then the outer pair of **factor** and **table** functions count how many of each number of repeats (three of a kind, four of a kind, etc.) are in the group. The next few lines of code use the information contained within the vector just created to classify the different combinations of repeats into unique event values. The event values are fairly arbitrary in this program, unlike earlier programs that used the binary coding scheme, and could really be anything as long as they were matched up with the appropriate labels when they were output. Finally, the last line within the processing loop adds the raw group of numbers to an output vector.

The vectors are factored and tabled to determine how many of each unique event occurred within the sample. The next line builds an output matrix from the relative frequencies that were determined at the beginning of the program, along with their theoretical probabilities, which have been typed directly into the program instead of being calculated. After this, dimension names are assigned for a matrix, a matrix of the event relative frequencies is built, and dimension names are subsequently assigned to that matrix. Finally, the output begins with the groups of numbers from the sample being printed with the **cat** function using the keyword **fill** to assure that lines greater than 80 characters will be wrapped to the next line. Then the two output matrices are printed using the **print.char.matrix** function with a fixed number of decimal places. The **scientific** keyword was used in the second case because there was a problem with some values being represented in scientific notation due to the fact that the default is to print anything with its lead digit more than four places from the decimal in scientific notation. This change increased output to six places.

The RANDOM program allows you to adjust the sample size until you find one that closely approximates the theoretical probabilities. An experienced S-PLUS programmer could easily create an outer loop that would permit the use of automatic iterations for increasingly larger sample sizes. One could also determine the sum of squared errors within each area for a test of randomness (relative frequency of even/odd, relative frequency of each digit, and relative frequency of combinations). These results could then be output in a table with the corresponding sample size to determine which sample size yields a reasonably close estimate to the theoretical probabilities. Additionally, a line graph could be created to view the relationship between the sum of squared error and different sample sizes. The S-PLUS programming required to accomplish these tasks, however, is beyond the scope and activity for the examples in this chapter.

RANDOM Program Output

Number groups:

86526 76376 99385 00396 54480 28574 05502 20873 10308 69425 69363 05530

	Relative Frequency	Probability
Odd	0.45	0.50
Even	0.55	0.50
0	0.17	0.10
1	0.02	0.10
2	0.08	0.10
3	0.13	0.10
4	0.07	0.10
5	0.15	0.10
6	0.13	0.10
7	0.07	0.10
8	0.10	0.10
9	0.08	0.10

	Relative Frequency	Probability
No duplicates	0.2500	0.3024
One pair	0.4167	0.5040
One triple	0.0000	0.0720
Two pairs	0.3333	0.1080
Pair & triple	0.0000	0.0090
Four alike	0.0000	0.0045
All alike	0.0000	0.0001

CHAPTER 2 EXERCISES

1.   Run RANDOM for N = 60. Record the twelve groups of five numbers (5 * 12 = 60 numbers) in the blanks below.

Numbers: _____   _____   _____   _____

                _____   _____   _____   _____

                _____   _____   _____   _____

Write the results below.

	RELATIVE FREQUENCY	PROBABILITY
ODD		
EVEN		
0		
1		
2		
3		
4		
5		
6		
7		
8		
9		

a.   Check that the relative frequencies are correct for the 60 numbers.

b.   What is the largest absolute difference between the relative frequencies and the probabilities? _____

c.   How is the relative frequency for ODD related to the relative frequencies for the ten digits (0 - 9)?_____

2.   Complete the following table from the run of RANDOM for N = 60.

	RELATIVE FREQUENCY	PROBABILITY
NONE		
ONE PAIR		
ONE TRIPLE		
TWO PAIRS		
PAIR & TRIPLE		
FOUR ALIKE		
ALL ALIKE		

a.   Look at the twelve groups of five numbers recorded in Exercise 1.

Have the duplicates been counted correctly and the relative frequencies

computed correctly?

RELATIVE FREQUENCY = FREQUENCY/(NUMBER OF GROUPS OF 5)

b.   How is the probability of ALL ALIKE calculated?

_____

_____

c.   Find the sum of the relative frequencies. _____

Why does the sum have this value? _____

_____

3.   Run RANDOM for N = 200.

a.   What is the maximum absolute value of the differences between the relative

frequencies and their respective probabilities?_____

b.   What is the maximum absolute difference between the relative frequencies of the

duplicates and their respective probabilities? _____

4.   Run RANDOM for N = 500.

a.   What is the maximum absolute value of the differences between the relative

frequencies and their respective probabilities? _____

b.   What is the maximum absolute difference between the relative frequencies of the

duplicates and their respective probabilities? _____

5.   On the basis of the runs for N = 200 and N = 500, are you satisfied with the performance
      of the random number generator? _____.   Why, or why not?

      _____

      _____

      _____

TRUE OR FALSE QUESTIONS

T   F   a.   It is easy to recognize a set of random numbers.

T   F   b.   In any set of truly random numbers, exactly half are even.

T   F   c.   If five of a kind appears consecutively once in a sequence of 10,000
                   numbers, this is evidence that the numbers may not be random.

T   F   d.   In a group of five random numbers, it is more probable that a pair will be
                   found, than finding all of the numbers to be different.

T   F   e.   About seven times out of one hundred in a group of five random digits, a
                   triple will appear.

CHAPTER 3

FREQUENCY DISTRIBUTIONS

CHAPTER OBJECTIVES

- To observe the shapes of histograms and corresponding ogives
- To develop an understanding of histograms and ogives
- To demonstrate the relationship between the shape of a histogram and its corresponding ogive.

A **histogram** is a graph of a frequency distribution of numerical data for different categories of events, individuals, or objects. A **frequency distribution** indicates the individual number of events, individuals, or objects in the separate categories. Most people easily understand histograms because they resemble bar graphs often seen in newspapers and magazines. An **ogive** is a graph of a cumulative frequency distribution of numerical data from the histogram. A **cumulative frequency distribution** indicates the successive addition of the number of events, individuals, or objects in the different categories of the histogram, which always sums to 100. An ogive graph displays numerical data in an S-shaped curve with increasing numbers or percentages that eventually reach 100%. Because cumulative frequency distributions are rarely used in newspapers and magazines, most people never see them. Frequency data from a histogram, however, can easily be displayed in a cumulative frequency ogive.

This chapter will provide you with an understanding of the histogram and its corresponding ogive. You will gain this experience quickly without the work involved in data entry and hand computation. You will be able to view the histogram and cumulative frequency distributions for different sample data sets. The S-PLUS program can be used to display the histogram frequency distributions and ogive cumulative frequency distributions.

To simplify the graphical display and provide similar comparisons between the types of histograms, all histograms in the S-PLUS program will have ten categories. The data for each category are not listed; rather the categories are numbered 1 to 10. You will be asked to enter the frequency for each of the ten categories and the frequencies must be integers greater than zero. The S-PLUS program will print a table listing the frequencies you specified, the relative frequencies, and the less-than-or-equal cumulative relative frequencies. The S-PLUS program prints a histogram and a corresponding ogive, which is output in a separate window (GSD2).

SUMMARY

In this chapter, you should learn that:

- Histograms and ogives have different shapes and vary depending on frequency.
- An ogive always increases from 0% to 100% for cumulative frequencies.
- The shape of a histogram determines the shape of its related ogive.
- A uniform histogram is flat; its ogive is a straight line sloping upward.
- An increasing histogram has higher frequencies for successive categories; its ogive is concave and looks like part of a parabola.
- A decreasing histogram has lower frequencies for successive categories; its ogive is convex and looks like part of a parabola.
- A uni-modal histogram contains a single mound; its ogive is S-shaped.
- A bi-modal histogram contains two mounds; its ogive can be either reverse S-shaped or double S-shaped depending upon the data distribution.
- A right-skewed histogram has a mound on the left and a long tail on the right; its ogive is S-shaped with a large concave portion.
- A left-skewed histogram has a mound on the right and a long tail on the left; its ogive is S-shaped with a large convex portion.

How the program FREQUENCY works

The part of the program that can be changed is a list of values relating to a score distribution observed in a given classroom. The length of this list does not matter; it is never specifically referenced in the program. The *Class* object is given a value for a vector of numbers using the **c** function that was introduced in Chapter 1. Each number within the vector is divided by the sum of all values within the vector. In most programming languages this would involve creating a processing loop similar to the one in the RANDOM program that would add up all the values and then go back and divide each value by the total. In S-PLUS, vectors can be easily created and used. For the FREQUENCY program, the first processing loop is replaced by the simple **sum**(*Class*), which gets a total for all of the values, and this result is then divided into each of the values within the vector by simply typing *Class*/**sum**(*Class*). No additional step is necessary. This feature in S-PLUS makes the language relatively short and easy to follow.

The next program line follows the same logic, only the cumulative sum (**cumsum**) of the vector is determined at each point and these values are divided by the overall sum of the values to give a vector of values labeled *CumRelFreq*. Scaling of the histogram height is performed next so that the histogram bars are not too small compared to the vertical scaling of the graph. The "if then else" clause is used to provide vertical scaling that will be either one tenth greater than the highest relative frequency, or 1 if the value is .95 or above. The **round** function is implemented to insure that the maximum value is set to an even tenth (**digits=1**). The **barplot** function is used to draw the histogram of the relative frequencies with the **RelFreq** vector as the specified target.   The **plot** function is used to draw the ogive of the cumulative relative frequencies with **CumRelFreq** as the target.

The last part of the FREQUENCY program builds a matrix of the class score distribution along with the associated relative frequencies and cumulative relative frequencies.   The line beginning *TableData* <- **matrix** prepares the matrix and initializes all values within it to 0 and makes the dimensions of the matrix to be **length**(*Class*) rows and 3 columns.   The **dimnames** keyword sets the labels for the dimensions and will be used in later chapters with other vectors. The **for** loop iterates from 1 to the number of values within *Class* and assigns each row within the *TableData* matrix to the respective *Class* vector value, relative frequency, and cumulative relative frequency, rounding each frequency to three decimal places.   You will see some error in thc cumulative numbers due to the rounding of the cumulative values. The final line of the program simply prints out the *TableData* matrix.

You can change the values within the *Class* vector to obtain different shaped histograms and corresponding ogives.   The original vector of 10 values breaks the score distribution into 10 intervals, but this can be changed to create histograms with greater resolution.   You could comment out both lines of " **if** " and "**else**" statements that scale the histogram by prefixing them with " **#** " signs to see the effect of not scaling it properly to fit the plot; replace these statements with the ***PlotHeight*** <- **1** statement by removing the # sign in front of it.   Some rounding error does occur in the program when summing the relative frequencies to obtain the cumulative relative frequencies.

FREQUENCY Program Output

	Freq.	Relative Freq.	Cum. Rel. Freq.
Class 1	50	0.182	0.182
Class 2	45	0.164	0.345
Class 3	40	0.145	0.491
Class 4	35	0.127	0.618
Class 5	30	0.109	0.727
Class 6	25	0.091	0.818
Class 7	20	0.073	0.891
Class 8	15	0.055	0.945
Class 9	10	0.036	0.982
Class 10	5	0.018	1.000

Relative Frequency Histogram

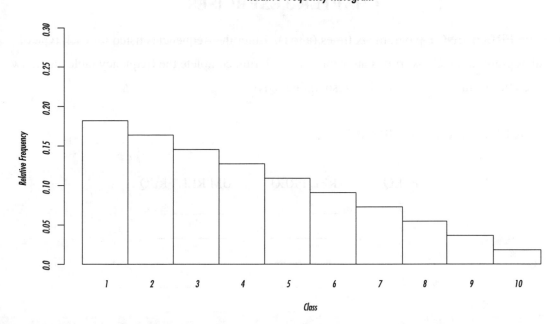

Cumulative Relative Frequency Ogive

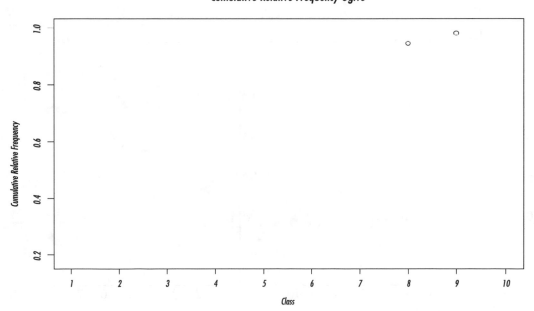

CHAPTER 3 EXERCISES

1. Run FREQUENCY program six times (a to f). Enter the frequencies listed for each type of histogram in the Class array statement. For each run, complete the frequency table and draw sketches of the histogram and corresponding ogive.

a. A UNIFORM HISTOGRAM

CLASS	FREQ	REL FREQ	CUM REL FREQ
1	5	_____	_____
2	5	_____	_____
3	5	_____	_____
4	5	_____	_____
5	5	_____	_____
6	5	_____	_____
7	5	_____	_____
8	5	_____	_____
9	5	_____	_____
10	5	_____	_____

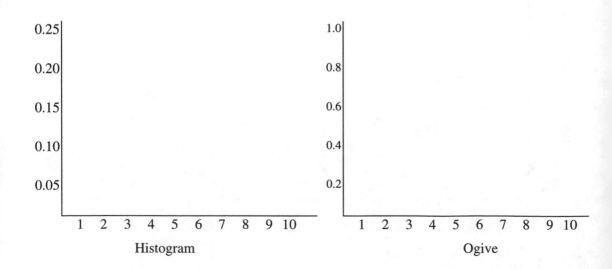

Histogram   Ogive

b. AN INCREASING HISTOGRAM

CLASS	FREQ	REL FREQ	CUM REL FREQ
1	10	_____	_____
2	12	_____	_____
3	14	_____	_____
4	16	_____	_____
5	18	_____	_____
6	20	_____	_____
7	22	_____	_____
8	24	_____	_____
9	26	_____	_____
10	28	_____	_____

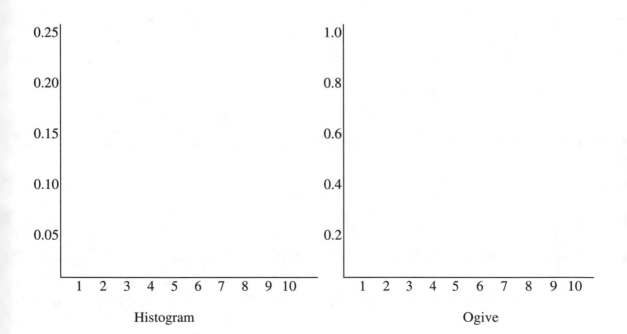

Histogram   Ogive

c. A DECREASING HISTOGRAM

CLASS	FREQ	REL FREQ	CUM REL FREQ
1	50	_____	_____
2	45	_____	_____
3	40	_____	_____
4	35	_____	_____
5	30	_____	_____
6	25	_____	_____
7	20	_____	_____
8	15	_____	_____
9	10	_____	_____
10	5	_____	_____

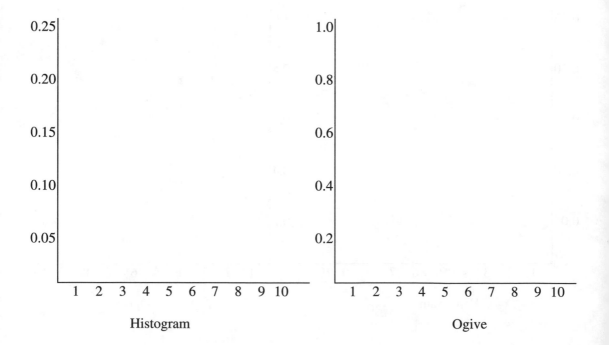

Histogram   Ogive

d.   A UNIMODAL HISTOGRAM

CLASS	FREQ	REL FREQ	CUM REL FREQ
1	2	_____	_____
2	3	_____	_____
3	4	_____	_____
4	5	_____	_____
5	6	_____	_____
6	6	_____	_____
7	5	_____	_____
8	4	_____	_____
9	3	_____	_____
10	2	_____	_____

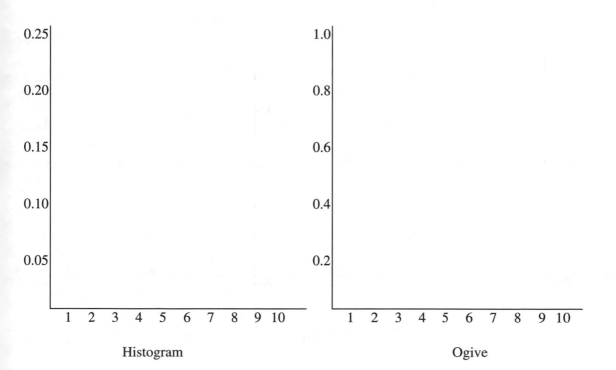

Histogram   Ogive

e.   A BIMODAL HISTOGRAM

CLASS	FREQ	REL FREQ	CUM REL FREQ
1	6	_____	_____
2	5	_____	_____
3	4	_____	_____
4	3	_____	_____
5	2	_____	_____
6	2	_____	_____
7	3	_____	_____
8	4	_____	_____
9	5	_____	_____
10	6	_____	_____

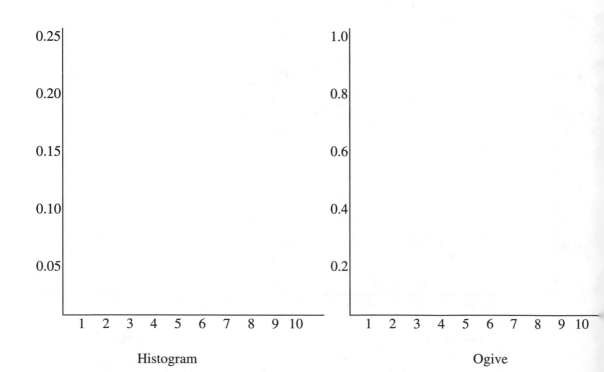

Histogram   Ogive

f.   A RIGHT-SKEWED HISTOGRAM

CLASS	FREQ	REL FREQ	CUM REL FREQ
1	5	_____	_____
2	10	_____	_____
3	25	_____	_____
4	20	_____	_____
5	15	_____	_____
6	10	_____	_____
7	5	_____	_____
8	4	_____	_____
9	3	_____	_____
10	2	_____	_____

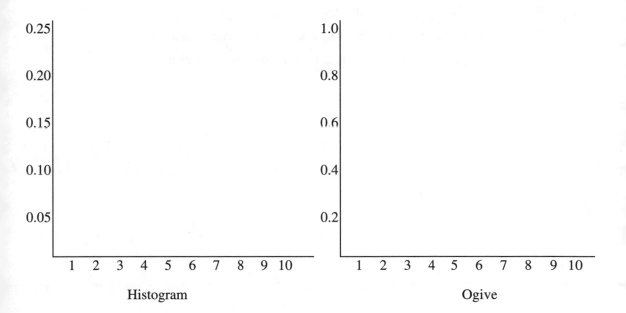

Histogram   Ogive

2. Describe the ogives for each of the following histograms.

	HISTOGRAM	OGIVE
a.	Uniform	_____
b.	Increasing	_____
c.	Decreasing	_____
d.	Unimodal	_____
e.	Bimodal	_____
f.	Skewed right	_____

TRUE OR FALSE QUESTIONS

T   F   a.   The cumulative relative frequencies in a less-than-or-equal ogive are
              never decreasing.

T   F   b.   Some ogives are straight lines.

T   F   c.   An S-shaped ogive indicates a uniform histogram.

T   F   d.   The sum of the relative frequencies in a histogram is always one.

T   F   e.   A parabolic ogive can indicate an increasing histogram.

CHAPTER 4

STEM AND LEAF PLOTS

CHAPTER OBJECTIVES

- To understand how stem-and-leaf plots summarize data.
- To investigate whether the number of groups on a stem has any effect on the shape of the stem-and-leaf plot.
- To be able to find the median value in a stem-and-leaf plot.
- To discover that stem-and-leaf plots are a type of histogram.

Graphical displays are often used to summarize data and usually help to uncover special characteristics of the data set. Histograms and **stem-and-leaf** plots are examples of graphical displays of data. The stem-and-leaf plots are particularly helpful in visualizing the **median** or middle value in data, the **range** or spread of data (distance between the lowest and highest data values), and **quartiles** (the first quartile is a score that separates the bottom 25% of the data in a frequency distribution from the other data and the third quartile is a score that separates the top 25% of the data in a frequency distribution from the other data). The **inter-quartile range** is the distance between the first and third quartile scores. It measures the range of scores in the middle 50% of the frequency distribution.

In graphing data, a decision must be made about how the data are grouped on the x-axis. A few large groups may obscure information and too many small groups may make summarization meaningless. This chapter addresses the problem of the number of groups in the context of stem-and-leaf plots (similar results are also true for histograms).

Consider the following data set of weights (in pounds) for UPS parcel post packages:

1.2	3.6	2.7	1.6	2.4
3.5	3.1	1.9	2.9	2.4

One stem-and-leaf plot for this data set is the following:

```
        1 | 269        +---------------+
        2 | 4479       | Stem:   ones  |
        3 | 156        : Leaves: tenths :
Weights of Packages    +---------------+
       (lbs.)
```

The numbers to the left of the vertical line form the **stem**. In the stem, the numbers represent the digit in the ones place. The numbers to the right of the line are the **leaves**. They represent the digit in the tenths place. Thus "1 | 269" represents the numbers 1.2, 1.6, and 1.9. There are only three groups in this stem-and-leaf plot, i.e., only one for each digit in the stem.

A finer subdivision could have been used in the stem-and-leaf plot. For example,

```
1 | 2
1 | 69
2 | 44
2 | 79
3 | 1
3 | 56
```

Stem: ones
Leaves: tenths

Here the first occurrence of 1 in the stem is used for data values from 1.0 to 1.4, and the second occurrence of 1 is used for 1.5 to 1.9. A similar approach is used for the other digits in the stem. There are six groups in this plot.   Other units can be used for the stem and the leaves. A stem-and-leaf plot of adult heights in inches could have a stem in tens and leaves in ones. A plot of family incomes might have a stem in ten thousands and leaves in thousands.

In the STEM-LEAF program the data sets will be student grades, which range between 0 and 100 inclusive. Two demonstration data sets of 50 student grades each are included in the S-PLUS program. You can enter other data sets. The S-PLUS program will print two versions of a stem-and-leaf plot for each set of student grades. One plot has 11 groups and the other plot has 21 groups. You will be asked to examine these two plots and decide which one is better. By using different data sets of student grades, you should be able to determine which one is the best.

SUMMARY

In this chapter, you should learn that:

- Stem-and-leaf plots are a convenient way to summarize data.
- The number of stems can greatly affect the shape of the stem-and-leaf plot.
- The choice of a stem can make the stem-and-leaf plot either unimodal or bimodal.
- For some data sets, a change in the stem causes very little change in the shape of the stem-and-leaf plot.
- A stem-and-leaf plot is a type of histogram.

How the STEM-LEAF program works

The STEM-LEAF program assigns two large vectors of scores to *Grades1* and *Grades2*. The scores are designed in a manner to demonstrate the importance of proper node assignment in stem-and-leaf plots and should *not* be modified. After the vectors are assigned, one of the GUI (graphical user interface) functions is used to create a dialog box that should be familiar to most people who use Windows software. The dialog box is given a title with four buttons on it. Next, a variable is defined that will be used to control the main processing loop and another dialog box is created that will be used to query the user as to whether they wish to run the program again. After running the last set of data, you should click on "no" to end the program.

After these definitions have taken place, the main processing loop begins. This program introduces the **while** loop, which will continue to run until the condition within the parentheses equates to false. Since *doContinue* was set to "Yes", it is assured that the loop will process at least once. The first line within the loop assigns *GradeButton* with the value of the button selected on the *GradesDialog* dialog box (which is displayed using **dialogbox.display**). The following **if..else** statements select the vector of grades to be used by assigning them to *GradeSample* and select the *LeafSpread* for the stem-and-leaf plot that will be created. The **invisible** function assures that the values of the large grade vectors will not be displayed again as they are assigned to *GradeSample*.

The output and spacing is put between the script echoed to the output window and the output of the program by use of the **cat** command with "\n\n" as the argument. The **cat** command simply prints characters to the standard output and the "\n" special sequence equates to a new line. The number of scores, median, first and third quartiles are printed. The next line outputs the stem-and-leaf plot.

The stem-and-leaf plot is a simple command. The **stem** command is given the *GradeSample* vector as its target and the space between the leaves is set to *LeafSpread*. Another **cat** command creates more space after the stem-and-leaf plot and then the program displays the dialog box that was created earlier to check whether the user wants to run it again. If the user chooses the "No" button then *doContinue* will no longer equate to "Yes" and looping stops, so the program will end.

STEM-LEAF Program Output

SET 1A

```
N = 50    Median = 71
Quartiles = 50, 88

Decimal point is 1 place to the right
of the colon

    0 : z
    1 : 5
    2 : 37
    3 : 0157
    4 : 1457
    5 : 0589
    6 : 1144689
    7 : 01122344
    8 : 55578888
    9 : 0122244689
   10 : 0
```

SET 2A

```
N = 50    Median = 70.5
Quartiles = 56, 87

Decimal point is 1 place to the right
of the colon

    3 : 0168
    4 : 2457
    5 : 03346889
    6 : 12345679
    7 : 01245677
    8 : 00335789
    9 : 12345779
   10 : 00
```

SET 1B

```
N = 50    Median = 71
Quartiles = 50, 88

Decimal point is 1 place to the right
of the colon

    0 : z
    0 :
    1 :
    1 : 5
    2 : 3
    2 : 7
    3 : 01
    3 : 57
    4 : 14
    4 : 57
    5 : 0
    5 : 589
    6 : 1144
    6 : 689
    7 : 01122344
    7 :
    8 :
    8 : 55578888
    9 : 0122244
    9 : 689
   10 : 0
```

SET 2B

```
N = 50    Median = 70.5
Quartiles = 56, 87

Decimal point is 1 place to the right
of the colon

    3 : 01
    3 : 68
    4 : 24
    4 : 57
    5 : 0334
    5 : 6889
    6 : 1234
    6 : 5679
    7 : 0124
    7 : 5677
    8 : 0033
    8 : 5789
    9 : 1234
    9 : 5779
   10 : 00
```

CHAPTER 4 EXERCISES

1. Run STEM-LEAF program for SET 1A and copy the stem-and-leaf plot here.

    PLOT   SET 1A

    ```
     0 |
     1 |
     2 |
     3 |
     4 |
     5 |
     6 |
     7 |
     8 |
     9 |
    10 |
    ```

    ```
    +----------------+
    | Stem:    tens  |
    | Leaves:  ones  |
    +----------------+
    ```


    a. In what way does the stem-and-leaf plot resemble a histogram?

    _____

    _____

    b. Describe the shape. Is it symmetric, right skewed, left skewed, unimodal, or
        bimodal?

    _____

    c. The median is the middle score when an odd number of student grades are arranged
        in order. The median is the average of the two middle scores when an even number
        of student grades is arranged in order. What is the median student grade?

    _____

    d. What is the range of scores (distance between lowest and highest score)?

    _____

    e. The inter-quartile range is the difference between the first and third quartile. What
        is the inter-quartile range?

    _____

2.   Run STEM-LEAF program for SET 1B and copy the stem-leaf plot here.

                        PLOT   SET 1B

                        0 |
                        0 | +----------------+
                        1 | : Stem: tens :
                        1 | : Leaves: ones :
                        2 | +----------------+
                        2 |
                        3 |
                        3 |
                        4 |
                        4 |
                        5 |
                        5 |
                        6 |
                        6 |
                        7 |
                        7 |
                        8 |
                        8 |
                        9 |
                        9 |
                        10 |
                        10 |

        a. Describe the shape of the student grades in this plot.

            _____

        b. What is the median grade? _____

        c. What is the range?   _____

        d. What is the inter-quartile range? _____

3.   Are there any characteristic differences in the two plots of SET 1A and SET 1B?

        _____

        _____

        _____

4.   Run the STEM-LEAF program for SET 2A and SET 2B and enter the plots below.

PLOT SET 2A   PLOT SET 2B

```
 0 |                                               0 |
 1 |                                               0 |
 2 |                                               1 |
 3 |                                               1 |
 4 |                                               2 |
 5 |                                               2 |
 6 |                                               3 |
 7 |                                               3 |
 8 |                                               4 |
 9 |                                               4 |
10 |                                               5 |
                                                   5 |
                                                   6 |
                                                   6 |
                                                   7 |
                                                   7 |
                                                   8 |
                                                   8 |
                                                   9 |
                                                   9 |
                                                  10 |
                                                  10 |
```

a.   Is one of the stems more informative for the set of grades? _____

     Why, or why not?_____

b.   Compare the results. What does this illustrate about the effect of the number of

     stems (groups) in a stem-and-leaf plot?

     _____

TRUE OR FALSE QUESTIONS

T   F   a.   The fewer the number of stems (groups) in a stem-and-leaf plot, the more

               informative the plot will be.

T   F   b.   The number of stems in the plot does not affect the median value.

T   F   c.   Skewness is usually apparent even if the number of stems is changed.

T   F   d.   If a stem-and leaf plot is unimodal for one data set grouping, it will be

               unimodal when a finer subdivision of groups is used.

T   F   e.   If a stem-and-leaf plot is rotated 90 degrees counterclockwise, the plot

                is similar to a histogram.

CHAPTER 5

POPULATION DISTRIBUTIONS

CHAPTER OBJECTIVES

- To understand that large samples of data from a normal population yield a unimodal frequency distribution.
- To observe the variability in the data values obtained by random sampling.
- To understand the usefulness of a histogram for summarizing data.
- To understand that a bimodal sample could indicate two different populations.
- To observe that the distance between the centers of two populations is related to the shape of the histogram of a sample selected from the combined populations.

The heights of adult men form a normal frequency distribution, i.e., a symmetrical distribution with one mode (**unimodal**). A similar population is formed by the heights of adult women. The **mode** is the score that occurs most often in a frequency distribution of data. However, because on the average women are shorter than men, the mean of the population of women's heights is less than the mean height of men. The **mean** is the score that indicates the average of all the scores in a frequency distribution. Imagine that a random sample of adults is chosen and the height of each person is determined. The sample consists of both men and women. In what way will the sample reflect the fact that it was drawn from a combination of two different populations?

In this chapter, you will learn about the shape of a histogram from a sample when the sample is drawn from a combination of two populations. The two populations in this chapter will be unimodal and symmetrical, i.e., normally distributed. To keep the chapter examples simple, the first population will always have a mean of 4. The second population mean can be changed. These mean values are also the modes of the data distributions.

The first time you run the S-PLUS COMBINATION program, the second population will have a mean of 9. If you run the program again, you can select a different mean value for the second population. By changing the distance between the two population means, you can observe the effect of this distance on the shape of the histogram from a sample drawn from two combined populations. Each time you run the program, 500 randomly selected observations will be sampled, 250 from each of the populations. The S-PLUS program will print out a relative frequency table and a histogram for the sample.

SUMMARY

In this chapter, you should learn that:

- A histogram shows the frequency distribution of sample values.
- For large samples taken randomly from a normal population, the shape of the histogram is approximately normal.
- If a sample is taken from a combination of two populations, for which the means are far apart, the histogram of the sample will be **bimodal** (two modes).
- If the means of the two populations are close together, then the sample will be **unimodal** (one mode). In this case, the two populations are considered to be a single population.

How the program COMBINATION works

The COMBINATION program combines the ease of random sampling with the ease of graphing using the S-PLUS language. The program creates two normally distributed random samples centered at different means, with one mean fixed at 4 and the other mean different. The sample sizes can also be changed. The first population data are created from a normal distribution (**rnorm**) with a size of *SampleSize*[1], a mean of 4, and a standard deviation of 1. The values within this vector are rounded to two decimal places. The **round** function is placed within the **invisible** function so that the vector will not be printed while rounding. The second population data are created in the same manner with the mean at the value of the *CenterTwo* variable, a size of *SampleSize*[2], and is also rounded to two decimal places. The two populations are combined into a single population using the **c** function and are treated as a single vector.

In order to create the relative frequency breakdown for various intervals within the combined population, it is necessary to use the **cut** function combined with the **factor** and **table** functions. The **cut** function breaks data into categories at given breakpoints, in this case at intervals of 0.5 from 0 to the largest value within the bimodal distribution of *CombinedPopulation*. The **factor** function takes the results of the **cut** function and assures that unused intervals are still included in the final results by choosing **levels** from 1 to twice the largest value within *CombinedPopulation* (this is because the intervals are only 0.5). These factors are then summarized by the **table** function with the number of points in each interval placed into the vector *FreqPop*. The next two lines create the labels for the intervals held in the *FreqPop* vector, with the first line being the value of the start of each interval and the second line being the value of the end of each interval. The **nsmall** keyword assures that at least one decimal place is preserved, even for whole numbers, to make the output easier to view.

The *FreqPop* vector is placed next into a **matrix** object to make it easier to display the results. The *FreqPop* vector is the input value, there are **length**(*FreqPop*) rows, and only 1 column. The dimension names are set to the interval start and interval end labels for the rows and " Rel Freq" for the single column. The **paste** function is handy when combining strings and vectors of values into a vector of labels. The next line with *FreqPopTable* prints out the matrix. An alternative approach would be to use **print**(*FreqPopTable*), but since there were no other parameters in the **print** function needed for this display, it wasn't necessary.

Most of the S-PLUS program code creates and displays the matrix of relative frequencies. The **hist** function creates a histogram of any vector of values with relatively few keywords which is displayed in a separate output window (GSD2). *CombinedPopulation* is the target of the histogram, and the **lab** keyword with the **c** function specifies 10 units on the x-axis. Default values (,) are specified for the y-axis and label size. The **main** keyword specifies the title to put at the top of the histogram.

The location of the mean for the second population can be changed to view at what point the difference between the population means results in a bimodal distribution. You can also change the size of each sample to see the effect of unequal sample sizes on the shape of the histogram. It is easier to notice differences in the two distributions using a histogram.

COMBINATION Program Output

		Rel. Freq.
0.0 -	0.5	0
0.5 -	1.0	0
1.0 -	1.5	0
1.5 -	2.0	4
2.0 -	2.5	11
2.5 -	3.0	24
3.0 -	3.5	42
3.5 -	4.0	45
4.0 -	4.5	46
4.5 -	5.0	34
5.0 -	5.5	17
5.5 -	6.0	16
6.0 -	6.5	12
6.5 -	7.0	8
7.0 -	7.5	12
7.5 -	8.0	18
8.0 -	8.5	38
8.5 -	9.0	57
9.0 -	9.5	47
9.5 -	10.0	35
10.0 -	10.5	20
10.5 -	11.0	8
11.0 -	11.5	2
11.5 -	12.0	2
12.0 -	12.5	2
12.5 -	13.0	0

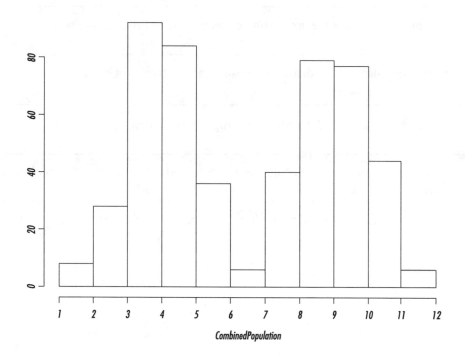

CHAPTER 5 EXERCISES

1. Run the COMBINATION program. A frequency table is printed for the combined
    populations. The first population will always be centered at 4. The second population
    will initially be centered at 9. The histogram is printed in a separate output window.

    a.   What interval contains the approximate mean value in Population One?

            _____

    b.   What interval contains the approximate mean value in Population Two?

            _____

    c.   Describe the shape of the distribution using the relative frequencies.

            _____

    d.   Describe the shape of the distribution using the histogram.

            _____

    e.   Are relative frequencies or histograms better in understanding the distribution of
            data? _____

    f.   Draw a smooth curve on the following axis to represent the histogram.

                    _____

                    Population One Mean   Population Two Mean

2. Run the COMBINATION program again. A frequency table is printed for the combined populations. The first population will always be centered at 4. Set the second population mean at 12. A histogram is printed in a separate output window.

    a. What interval contains the approximate mean value in Population One?

       _____

    b. What interval contains the approximate mean value in Population Two?

       _____

    c. Describe the shape of the distribution using the relative frequencies.

    _____

    d. Describe the shape of the distribution using the histogram.

    _____

    e. Are relative frequencies or histograms better in understanding the distribution of data?

    _____

    f. Draw a smooth curve on the following axis to represent the histogram.

                         _____

             Population One Mean   Population Two Mean

3. Run the COMBINATION program to find the smallest distance between the two means in
    which a bimodal distribution is still apparent (the second mean doesn't need to be a whole
    number, i.e., 8.5 and 5.75). If the means of the two populations are close together, then it is
    appropriate to consider that the two populations are similar.

    a.   What is the smallest distance between the means for which a bimodal distribution is

            still apparent? _____.

    b.   Statistical analyses are generally valid only for data that are randomly sampled from a
            symmetrical unimodal population distribution. What can you do to verify that a
            certain sample of data was randomly selected from a symmetrical unimodal (normal)
            population?

            _____

            _____

TRUE OR FALSE QUESTIONS

T   F   a. The greater the distance between the means of two populations, the more
                 pronounced the bimodal shape of the histogram.
T   F   b. If the means of two populations are close, then the histogram from the
                 combined populations will have a single peak (unimodal) in the middle.
T   F   c. If a sample is taken from a combination of two populations which have means
                 that are far apart, then the sample histogram will be bimodal.
T   F   d. As the means of two different populations get closer, the bimodal shape of the
                 histogram is unchanged.
T   F   e. Large random samples from normal distributions have unimodal shaped
                 histograms.

CHAPTER 6

MEASURES OF CENTRAL TENDENCY

CHAPTER OBJECTIVES

- To understand that the mean and median are measures of central tendency.
- To observe the effect on the mean and median of adding a constant to each value in a data set.
- To observe the effect on the mean and median of multiplying each value in a data set by a constant.
- To observe the effect on the mean and median of adding extreme values in a data set.
- To describe and explain in general terms the effects of these changes on the mean and median.
- To reproduce the original mean and median from the modified mean and median when addition and multiplication have changed the data.

In the previous chapter, unimodal and bimodal score distributions were demonstrated. In addition to the mode, the mean and median are measures of central tendency. **Central tendency** is where most scores occur in the middle of a symmetrical distribution and then spread out. The mode, mean, and median values would all be the same score in a normal distribution.

This chapter examines the effect upon means and medians when data values are transformed and/or extreme data values are added to a data set. The **mean** score is the arithmetic average of numbers in a data set. The mean is computed by taking the sum of the numbers and dividing by the total. The **median** score is the middle score found by arranging a set of numbers from the smallest to the largest (or from the largest to the smallest). If the data set contains an odd number of values, the median is the middle value in the ordered data set. If there is an even number of data values, the median is the average of the two middle values in the ordered data set. The median value is the score that divides the distribution into two equal halves.

Sample data are sometimes modified or transformed to permit comparisons and aid in the interpretation of sample estimates. For example, if the length of cars in inches was changed to meters, one could multiply 0.0254 times the car length to yield meters. What effect does this multiplication have on the mean value representing length of cars? What if an instructor decides to adjust a set of test grades for an exceptionally long test by adding ten points to each student's score? What effect does this addition have on the mean score? If the price of the most expensive house in a neighborhood increases, what happens to the median value of the houses in that neighborhood? What happens to the average value of houses in that neighborhood?

In the S-PLUS program, you will enter an initial data set. The initial data set will have six values and the values must be entered in order from smallest to largest. This initial data will then be transformed in three different ways: (1) add a constant to each data value, (2) multiply each data value by a constant, or (3) replace the largest data value by a smaller data value. The S-PLUS program will print the initial data set with its mean and median followed by the modified data set with its mean and median. The effect of these data modifications on the mean and median can then be observed.

SUMMARY

In this chapter, you should learn that:

- If a constant is added to all the values in a data set:
  1) The mean of the modified data is the mean of the initial data set plus the constant.
  2) The median of the modified data set is the median of the initial data set plus the constant.
- If all of the values in a data set are multiplied by a constant:
  1) The mean of the modified data set is the mean of the initial data set times the constant.
  2) The median of the modified data set is the median of the initial data set times the constant.
- If the largest value in a data set is replaced by a smaller value, then the mean of the modified data set is smaller than the mean of the initial data set, but the median is unchanged. Extreme values affect the mean, but do not affect the median.
- If the mean of a data set is subtracted from each of the data values, then the mean of the modified data set is 0.
- The mean and median of the initial data set can be recovered from the mean and median of the modified data set by adding the negative of the added constant or by dividing by the number that was used as a multiplier.

How the program MEAN-MEDIAN works

The MEAN-MEDIAN program uses dialog boxes in order to minimize repetitive tasks. The program includes a vector of values for the initial data set. The adjustment value used in the program is initialized to 0 with the *doContinue* variable used to control the primary processing loop, which is set to "Yes." The continue dialog box is designed with several other dialog boxes created to retrieve information from the user. One notable addition is the **editfield.control** object that is created to allow the user to enter a number into the dialog box. This is created separately and given an initial value of *adjustValue* (set initially to 0, but will store the value set by the user once the primary loop begins). It is added to the *adjustDialog* dialog box by using the **controls** keyword. The other dialog boxes are basically the same.

After the creation of the dialog box objects, the main processing loop begins. The first dialog box asks the user whether to use the modified data or initial data set. *It is important to select "Initial" the first time the program is run because the object ModifiedData is not actually created yet and this would cause an error.* When you choose "Modified" then *InitialData* is given the value of *ModifiedData* to run the analyses. The initial data values are printed out before any transformations are performed along with the descriptive statistics of **mean** and **median**, which are easily obtained with a single command. The program prompts for the type of function to perform on the data and the value by which to modify it. The *adjustEditfield* object and *adjustDialog* object are redefined here. This is necessary so that the value of the edit field is updated during the loop execution. The previous definitions are not necessary, but included so that all dialog definitions could be seen together. The value from the dialog box is used to update the variable *adjustValue* after being forced to be a single precision (**as.single**) floating point number. This number will therefore have several decimal places of precision.

The several **if** statements evaluate the function to be performed and treat the data accordingly. Most statements have been explained in previous chapters, but one is worth further explanation because it handles data values within a vector. In the section that replaces the last value in the data set, the function **length**(*ModifiedData*) gives the number of values within the vector *ModifiedData*. The *ModifiedData*[ ] notation is how you refer to values within a vector or matrix (a multi-dimensional vector). The line starting with *ModifiedData*[ ] is used to change the last value of the *ModifiedData* vector to a data value of *adjustValue*. Each of the **if** statements ends with a printout of what action was performed for ease of reading just in case the program is run several times before viewing the output. The MEAN-MEDIAN program lists the raw data and descriptive statistics for the new data and then prompts the user to repeat the program again. Since the program is mostly dialog box driven, few statements can be modified.

MEAN-MEDIAN Program Output


```
Initial Data = 2,4,5,9,15,19        Mean = 9        Median = 7

Added 5 to the original data
Modified Data = 7,9,10,14,20,24     Mean = 14       Median = 12


Initial Data = 2,4,5,9,15,19        Mean = 9        Median = 7

Multiplied the original data by 5
Modified Data = 10,20,25,45,75,95   Mean = 45       Median = 35


Initial Data = 2,4,5,9,15,19        Mean = 9        Median = 7

Replaced last value with 5
Modified Data = 2,4,5,9,15,5        Mean = 6.67     Median = 5
```

CHAPTER 6 EXERCISES

1. To run MEAN-MEDIAN program, the initial data set (2, 4, 5, 9, 15, 19) is specified. *Remember to click on "Initial" the first time you run the program. Also, click on "Initial" to return to the initial data set before performing another transformation on the data values.* Use the following transformations and record the results.

INITIAL DATA	MEAN	MEDIAN
ADD		
3	_____	_____
-2	_____	_____
10	_____	_____
5	_____	_____
MULTIPLY BY		
2	_____	_____
-10	_____	_____
.5	_____	_____
REPLACE LAST VALUE WITH		
50	_____	_____
100	_____	_____
500	_____	_____

2. Complete the following statements:

   a. If a constant number is added to each of the data values in a set, then the mean of the modified data is equal to the initial mean _____

   and the median of the modified data set is equal to the initial median _____

   _____.

b. If each data value in a set is multiplied by a constant number, then the mean of the modified data is equal to the initial mean _____

and the median of the modified data is equal to the initial median _____

_____.

c. If the largest value in a data set is replaced by a smaller value, the mean of the modified data is _____

_____

and the median of the modified data set is _____

_____.

3. Run MEAN-MEDIAN and enter the data set: 2, 4, 6, 9, 12, 15.

a. Modify the data by adding + 5 to each value. Record the results.

INITIAL DATA _____

    MEAN _____ MEDIAN _____

MODIFIED DATA (+5)_____

    MEAN _____ MEDIAN _____

b. Run MEAN-MEDIAN with the data set: 7, 9, 11, 14, 17, 20.
Modify the data by subtracting –5 from each data value. Record the results.

INITIAL DATA _____

    MEAN _____ MEDIAN _____

MODIFIED DATA (-5)_____

    MEAN _____ MEDIAN _____

c.　Show how to obtain the mean of the initial data set from the mean of the modified data set.

_____

_____

d.　Show how to obtain the median of the initial data set from the median of the modified data set.

_____

_____

4.　Run MEAN-MEDIAN using the data set: 2, 4, 6, 9, 12, 15.

　　a.　Modify the data by multiplying each value by + 4. Record the results.

　　　　INITIAL DATA _____

　　　　　　　MEAN _____ MEDIAN _____

　　　　MODIFIED DATA (4x)_____

　　　　　　　MEAN _____ MEDIAN _____

　　b.　Run MEAN-MEDIAN using the data set: 8, 16, 24, 36, 48, 60. Modify the data set by multiplying each value by 0.25 (dividing by 4). Record the results.

　　　　INITIAL DATA _____

　　　　　　　MEAN _____ MEDIAN _____

　　　　MODIFIED DATA (.25x) _____

　　　　　　　MEAN _____ MEDIAN _____

c.　Show how to obtain the mean of the initial data set from the mean of the modified data set. _____

　　　　_____

5. The average and median daily temperature for six days in a northern city was 76° F. Daily temperature readings can be changed to a Celsius scale by the formula: $C = (F - 32)(5/9)$; that is, a value of −32 must be added to each data value, and then the results must be multiplied by 5/9.

   a. If the six daily temperatures were 73°, 78°, 81°, 74°, 71°, and 79° on the Fahrenheit scale, use MEAN-MEDIAN program to change to the Celsius scale. (Don't forget to order the data as you enter it, add a −32, and then multiply the values using a decimal format: 5/9 = 0.5556).

   b. What is the average temperature of the city in Celsius? _____

   c. What is the median temperature in Celsius? _____

TRUE OR FALSE QUESTIONS

T   F   a. Changing the largest value in a data set to a value four times as large does not effect the median.

T   F   b. If the mean of a data set is subtracted from every value of the data set, the mean of the modified data is equal to the mean of the initial data set.

T   F   c. Multiplying each value in a data set by ½ causes the median of the modified data to be twice as large as the median of the initial data.

T   F   d. A data set is modified by adding a constant to each value; the mean of the initial data set can be found by subtracting the constant from the mean of the modified data set.

T   F   e. A data set is modified by multiplying all values by 5. The median is now 33.5. The median of the initial data set can be found by multiplying the new median by 0.2

CHAPTER 7

MEASURES OF DISPERSION

CHAPTER OBJECTIVES

- To observe the effect on the range, variance, and standard deviation when adding a constant to each value in a data set.
- To observe the effect on the range, variance, and standard deviation when multiplying a constant times each value in a data set.
- To observe the effect on the range, variance, and standard deviation when adding an extreme value to a data set.
- To describe and explain in general terms the effects of these changes on the range, variance, and standard deviation.
- To reproduce the original range, variance, standard deviation from the modified range, variance, and standard deviation when data has been changed by multiplication.

This chapter continues our understanding of concepts learned in Chapter 6. An initial data set is entered and modified in one of three ways: (1) adding a constant to each data value, (2) multiplying each data value by a constant, or (3) replacing the last value by a different number. The purpose of this chapter, however, is to observe the effect of these modifications on three measures of dispersion: range, variance, and standard deviation. The sample **range** is the difference between the largest and smallest data value. The sample **variance** is the average squared deviation of the data values from their sample mean. The sample **standard deviation** is the square root of the sample variance. The formula for the sample variance is:

$$\text{Variance} = \frac{\sum (\text{data value} - \text{mean data value})^2}{\text{number of data values}} = \frac{SS}{n}$$

The numerator (top of equation) indicates that the mean of all the data values is subtracted from each data value, squared, and summed. The summing of the squared values is denoted by the symbol, Σ. This is referred to as the sum of squared deviations from the mean or simply **sum of squared deviations** (SS). The sum of squared deviations (SS) divided by the number of data values is referred to as the variance.

The standard deviation is the square root of the variance. The formula for the standard deviation is:

$$\text{Standard Deviation} = \sqrt{\frac{SS}{n}}$$

The standard deviation provides a measure in standard units of how far the data values fall from the sample mean. For example, in a **normal distribution**, 68% of the data values fall approximately one standard deviation (1 SD) on either side of the mean, 95% of the data values fall approximately two standard deviations (2 SD) on either side of the mean, and 99% of the data values fall approximately three standard deviations (3 SD) on either side of the mean.

SUMMARY

In this chapter, you should learn that:

- If a constant is added to all the values in a data set, the variance, standard deviation, and range are unchanged.
- If all of the values in a data set are multiplied by a constant:
- The variance of the modified data set is the variance of the initial data set times the constant squared.
- The standard deviation of the modified data set is the standard deviation of the initial data set times the constant.
- The range of the modified data set is the range of the initial data set times the constant.
- If the last value in a data set is replaced by a smaller value, then the variance, standard deviation, and the range are all decreased.
- If the last value in a data set is replaced by a larger value, then the variance, standard deviation, and the range are all increased.
- If the standard deviation of a data set is divided into each of the data values, then the standard deviation of the modified data set is 1.
- The variance of the initial data set can be obtained from the variance of the modified data set by dividing the variance by the constant squared that was used as the multiplier.
- The standard deviation and range of the initial data set can be obtained from the standard deviation and range of the modified data set by dividing them by the constant that was used as the multiplier.

How the program MODIFICATION works

The MODIFICATION program is similar to the MEAN-MEDIAN program. The only changes are that the *adjustEditfield* and *adjustDialog* objects are removed and the descriptive statistics have changed from central tendency statistics (mean and median) to data dispersion statistics (range, variance and standard deviation). The **var** function returns the variance of the vector of data values and the **sqrt (var)** function computes the standard deviation. The **range** function within S-PLUS doesn't give the range value, rather, it lists the minimum and maximum data values not the difference between the two, so **max**(*InitialData*)-**min**(*InitialData*) is used to compute the range. These first six chapters have provided a basic introduction to S-PLUS programming, statistical concepts, and simulation. The next chapter will introduce matrix input and operations.

MODIFICATION Program Output

```
Initial Data= 2,4,5,9,15,19        Variance = 45.2   Std Dev = 6.72  Range = 17

Added 5 to the original data
Modified Data= 7,9,10,14,20,24     Variance = 45.2   Std Dev = 6.72  Range = 17

Initial Data= 2,4,5,9,15,19        Variance = 45.2   Std Dev = 6.72  Range = 17

Multiplied the original data by 5
Modified Data= 10,20,25,45,75,95 Variance = 1130     Std Dev = 33.62 Range = 85

Initial Data= 2,4,5,9,15,19        Variance = 45.2   Std Dev = 6.72  Range = 17

Replaced last value with 5
Modified Data= 2,4,5,9,15,5        Variance = 21.87  Std Dev = 4.68  Range = 13
```

CHAPTER 7 EXERCISES

1. Run the MODIFICATION program with the data set 2, 4, 5, 9, 15, 19. Remember to click on "Initial" the first time to run the program. Use the modifications below and record the results.

INITIAL DATA	VARIANCE	S.D.	RANGE
ADD			
3	_____	_____	_____
-2	_____	_____	_____
10	_____	_____	_____
5	_____	_____	_____
MULTIPLY BY			
2	_____	_____	_____
-10	_____	_____	_____
.5	_____	_____	_____
REPLACE LAST VALUE WITH			
50	_____	_____	_____
100	_____	_____	_____
500	_____	_____	_____

2. Complete the following statements:

    a. If a constant is added to each data value, then the variance of the modified data is equal to _____ , the standard deviation of the modified data set is equal to _____, and the range of the modified data set is equal to _____.

b.   If each data value is multiplied by a constant, then the variance of the
     modified data is equal to the initial variance _____, the standard
     deviation of the modified data is equal to the initial standard deviation
     _____, and the range of the modified data set is equal to the initial
     range _____.

c.   If the last value in a data set is replaced by a larger value, the variance of the
     modified data is _____, the standard deviation
     of the modified data is _____, and the range of the modified data set is
     _____.

3. Run MODIFICATION again using your initial data set and modify it by dividing each
    data value by the standard deviation (multiply by the reciprocal). What is the standard
    deviation of the data? _____.
    Try it again with a new initial data set. Explain why this happens:

    _____

    _____

    _____

4. Run MODIFICATION and enter the data set 2, 4, 6, 9, 12, 15.

    a.   Modify the data by adding +5 to each value. Record the results.

            INITIAL DATA _____
               VARIANCE_____ST. DEV._____ RANGE_____

            MODIFIED DATA_____
               VARIANCE_____ST. DEV._____ RANGE_____

    b.   Run MODIFICATION and enter the data set 7, 9, 11, 14, 17, 20.
            Modify the data by adding −5 to each value. Record the results.

        INITIAL DATA _____

            VARIANCE_____ST. DEV._____ RANGE_____

        MODIFIED DATA _____

            VARIANCE_____ST. DEV._____ RANGE_____

    c.   Show how to obtain the variance of the modified data set from the variance
            of the initial data set.

            _____

    d.   Show how to obtain the standard deviation of the initial data set from the
            standard deviation of the modified data set.

            _____

    e.   Show how to obtain the range of the initial data set values from the range of
            the modified data set values.

            _____

5. The variance of the daily temperatures for six days in a northern city was 14° F, the standard
    deviation was 3.8° F, and the range was 10° F. The daily temperature readings can be
    changed to a Celsius scale by using the formula C = (F-32) (5/9); that is, -32 must be added
    to each data value and the results multiplied by 5/9 (0.5556).

    a.   What is the variance of the temperature for this city in Celsius? _____

    b.   What is the standard deviation of the temperature in degrees Celsius? _____

    c.   What is the range of the temperature in degrees Celsius? _____

6. If the six daily temperatures were 73 °, 78°, 81°, 74°, 71°, and 79° on the Fahrenheit scale, use MODIFICATION to change them to the Celsius scale. (Don't forget to order the data as you enter it and express values in decimal form: 5/9=0.5556).

    a. What is the variance of the temperature for this city in Celsius? _____

    b. What is the standard deviation of the temperature in degrees Celsius? _____

    c. What is the range of the temperature in degrees Celsius? _____

TRUE OR FALSE QUESTIONS

T   F   a. Changing the last value in a data set to a value four times as large always multiplies the range by four.

T   F   b. Adding five to every data value does not affect the standard deviation.

T   F   c. Multiplying each value in a data set by 1/3 causes the variance of the modified data to be 1/6 of the original variance.

T   F   d. If a data set is modified by adding a constant to each value; the range of the initial data set can be found by subtracting the constant from the range of the modified data set.

T   F   e. If a data set is modified by multiplying all values by 5 and the standard deviation is now 33.5; the standard deviation of the original data set can be found by multiplying the new standard deviation by 0.2.

CHAPTER 8

SAMPLE SIZE EFFECTS

CHAPTER OBJECTIVES

- To observe the effect on the range from increasing the number of observations in a sample.
- To determine whether sample size has a predictable effect on the standard deviation.
- To investigate the relationship between the range and the standard deviation.

This chapter builds on our understanding of the sample range and the sample standard deviation. The sample **range** is the difference between the highest and lowest score in a data distribution. The sample **standard deviation** is the square root of the sample variance. When the size of the sample increases, the range of data values will generally increase. The standard deviation with increasing sample sizes should divide the frequency distribution of data into six parts. You should be able to observe the effect of sample size on these measures of data dispersion when completing the chapter exercises.

The S-PLUS program will create a uniform population of integers from 1 to 1,000 based on sampling with replacement. **Sampling with replacement** assumes that data points are returned to the population from which they were drawn. **Sampling without replacement** assumes that data points are *not* returned to the population from which they were drawn. The probability of selection is affected depending upon which sampling technique is used. Various sample sizes will need to be listed in the *Samplesizes* vector. Random sampling will be repeated with new observations for each sample size listed in the vector. A summary table will be printed with the results to allow you to draw conclusions about the effect of sample size on the range and standard deviation. The ratio of the range to the standard deviation will be printed so you can look for a relationship between these two measures of dispersion.

The S-PLUS program can be repeated as many times as needed since the sampling is random. Each time the program is run, the results, however, will be different. This will allow you to further test your understanding and conclusions about how various sample sizes affect the range and standard deviation. The final chapter exercise computes the error one would make when using a sample estimate of the standard deviation as the population value. This exercise is used to answer the question, "Does the sample standard deviation become a more accurate estimate of the population standard deviation as the sample size increases?"

SUMMARY

In this chapter, you should learn that:

- As the sample size increases, the sample range usually increases because observations are chosen from the extreme data values in a population.
- As observations are added to a sample, the range of the sample cannot decrease.
- As observations are added to a sample, the standard deviation fluctuates in an unpredictable manner.
- A rough approximation of the standard deviation is the range divided by four, however, for a uniform population, this will produce an underestimate. Range divided by six better approximates the standard deviation of the normal distribution.

How the SAMPLE program works

The SAMPLE program (Chap8a.ssc) is short and simple, but it does make use of a matrix, so the subject of matrices and vectors will be covered. The program begins with a vector of *SampleSizes*. A vector is a single column of numbers with several rows (nrows x 1). A matrix is then created or initialized. A matrix has several columns and rows (nrows x ncolumns). The number of rows and columns is called the dimension of a matrix. The line beginning with *outputMatrix* **<- matrix** is the definition of the matrix. It is initially filled with zeros and has **length**(*SampleSizes*) rows and 3 columns. The **dimnames** keyword sets the labels for the dimensions of the matrix, with the row labels coming first and the column labels coming second within a **list** object. The row labels are going to be the different values in the *SampleSizes* vector, while the column labels are going to consist of a concatenation (**c** object) of the strings "Sample Range," " Sample StDev," and " Samp Range/Samp StDev." An error will result if the **dimnames** do not contain the same number of values as the rows or columns they are naming. The **dimnames** keyword of the **matrix** object does not reuse the labels if there are not enough to describe the entire set of row and column values.

Once the matrix has been defined and initialized (filled with zero values), the main processing loop begins. An iteration counter is used as the basis of the **for** loop to facilitate placement of values within the matrix. The first line of code within the loop creates the first sample of random integers between 1 and 1,000 from a uniform distribution. The next three lines fill the columns of the matrix at the present row (i) with the range, standard deviation, and range divided by the standard deviation, respectively. The matrix notation [i,1] represents the ith row and the 1st column. If you want to replace an entire row of values, type *outputMatrix*[i,] <-, followed by the assignment of the vector. Leaving a dimension blank means that you are allowing all values along that dimension to be filled with values, if enough are present in the vector being assigned to it. The content of the matrix is printed after the end of the loop.

There are many ways to define and use vectors, and thus to obtain random samples from populations. An **ALTERNATIVE SAMPLE** program (Chap8b.ssc) is included to show that other programming approaches can be used to achieve the same results. The summary values from the two programs will be different due to adding additional random samples to existing data.   Examine this ALTERNATIVE SAMPLE program and try to figure out what the commands are doing. A few hints: (1) assigning a value **NULL** creates an object so that it can be referenced later, but it is given no value; (2) the **rbind** function adds a row to an object.

Sample Program Output (Chap8a.ssc)

N	Range	Standard Dev.	Range/SD
10	893	327.83	2.72
50	937	286.18	3.27
100	979	319.72	3.06
200	991	286.30	3.46
500	997	281.51	3.54
1000	997	288.87	3.45

Alternative Sample Program Output (Chap8b.ssc)

N	Range	Standard Dev.	Range/SD
10	700	253.78	2.76
50	884	257.94	3.43
100	987	290.70	3.40
200	974	283.15	3.44
500	998	282.02	3.54
1000	994	290.87	3.42

CHAPTER 8 EXERCISES

1. Enter the following sample sizes in the *Samplesize* vector and run the SAMPLE program. Record the results below.

	RANGE	STANDARD DEV.	RANGE/SD
20			
40			
60			
80			
100			
120			
140			
160			
180			
200			
220			
240			
260			
280			
300			

2. Provide short answers to the following questions.

   a. As observations are added to the sample, what happens to the sample range?

   _____

   b. What accounts for the relationship between the sample size and the sample range?

   _____

   c. Why is the sample range a less than perfect measure of the spread of the population?

   _____

   d. As observations are added to the sample, what is the relationship between the sample size and the sample standard deviation? _____

   _____

3. Run the SAMPLE program again with the same sample sizes in the *Samplesize* vector.
Record the results below.

	RANGE	STANDARD DEV.	RANGE/SD
20			
40			
60			
80			
100			
120			
140			
160			
180			
200			
220			
240			
260			
280			
300			

a. Did anything different happen the second time? _____
If so, what was different? _____
_____

b. What is your final conclusion about the relationship between sample size and sample
standard deviation? _____

4. The last column above indicates the standard deviations for samples of data from a uniform
distribution. The range of scores divided by 4 is a rough estimate of the standard deviation
of a uniform distribution. Are the standard deviations less than 4 (underestimated) as
expected? Yes _____ No ___

5. What is a good estimate for the standard deviation of a normal population? _____

6. If the sample standard deviation is used as an estimate of the population standard deviation, compute the error of the estimate for each sample size in Exercise 1.

    Note: ERROR = ESTIMATE – 288.67. The population standard deviation was 288.67.

    Record the error of estimate for each sample size with its +/- signs in the following table.

SAMPLE SIZE	ERROR
20	_____
40	_____
60	_____
80	_____
100	_____
120	_____
140	_____
160	_____
180	_____
200	_____
220	_____
240	_____
260	_____
280	_____
300	_____

a. Does the sample standard deviation become a more accurate estimate of the population standard deviation as the sample size increases? _____

TRUE OR FALSE QUESTIONS

T   F   a. The sample range usually decreases as the sample size increases.

T   F   b. The sample standard deviation decreases as the sample size increases.

T   F   c. A rough approximation of the range is four times the variance.

T   F   d. The range of a small sample is usually less than the range of a larger sample from the same population.

T   F   e. The standard deviation of a uniform population is underestimated if one-fourth of the range is used for the estimate.

CHAPTER 9

TCHEBYSHEFF INEQUALITY THEOREM

CHAPTER OBJECTIVES

- To better understand standard deviation as a measure of dispersion.
- To understand the Tchebysheff Inequality Theorem.
- To discover that the Tchebysheff Inequality Theorem is true when applied to samples from different populations.
- To discover that the Tchebysheff lower bound for the percentage of data within an interval is often lower than the true percentage.
- To calculate the amount of error in the estimate of a population mean from the sample mean.
- To calculate the amount of error in the estimate of the population standard deviation from the sample standard deviation.

The sample **standard deviation** is a measure of the dispersion of the sample data around the sample mean. A small standard deviation indicates less dispersion of sample data. A larger standard deviation indicates more dispersion of sample data. This understanding is also true for the **range**, which is the difference between the largest and smallest data value. However, the standard deviation provides more information about the data than the range. The standard deviation permits the formation of intervals that indicate the proportion of the data within those intervals. For example, 68% of the data fall within +/- one standard deviation from the mean, 95% of the data fall within +/- two standard deviations of the mean, and 99% fall within +/- three standard deviations of the mean, in a **normal distribution**. If 100 students took a mathematics test with a mean of 75 and a standard deviation of 5, then 68% of the scores would fall between a score of 70 and 80, assuming a normal distribution. In contrast, given the highest and lowest test scores, 90 and 50 respectively, the range of 40 only indicates that there is a 40-point difference between the highest and lowest test score, i.e., 90 - 50 = 40.

We generally assume our data is normally distributed; however in some cases, the data distribution takes on a different shape. When this occurs, the **Tchebysheff Inequality Theorem** is helpful in determining the percentage of data between the intervals. For example, if the mean mathematics test score was 85, and the standard deviation was 5, then the Tchebysheff Inequality Theorem could be used to make a statement about the proportion of test scores that fall in various intervals around the mean, e.g., between the score interval 75 and 95, *regardless of the shape of the distribution.*

The **Tchebysheff Inequality Theorem** was developed by a Russian mathematician as a proof that given a number k, greater than or equal to 1, and a set of n data points, at least $(1-1/k^2)$ of the measurements will lie within k standard deviations of their mean. Tchebysheff's theorem applies to *any* distribution of scores and could refer to either sample data or the population. To apply the Tchebysheff Inequality Theorem using a population distribution, an interval is constructed which measures $k\sigma$ on either side of the mean, μ. When k = 1, however, $1-1/(1)^2 = 0$, which indicates that 0% of the data points lie in the constructed interval, $\mu - \sigma$ to $\mu + \sigma$, which is not helpful nor useful in explaining data dispersion. However, for values of k greater than 1, the theorem appears to be informative:

k	$1-1/k^2$ (Percent)	Interval
1	0 (0 %)	μ +/- 1σ
2	3 / 4 (75 %)	μ +/- 2σ
3	8 / 9 (89 %)	μ +/- 3σ

An example will help to better illustrate the fraction of n data points that lie in a constructed interval using the Tchebysheff theorem. Given a set of test scores with a mean of 80 and a standard deviation of 5, the Tchebysheff theorem would indicate a constructed interval with lower and upper score limits computed as follows:

$$Lower\ limit\ =\ mean - k * standard\ deviation$$
$$Upper\ limit\ =\ mean + k * standard\ deviation$$

For k = 1, the lower limit would be $80 - 1 * 5 = 75$ and the upper limit would be $80 + 1 * 5 = 85$. Obviously, for k = 1, no data points are implied between the score interval, 75 to 85, which makes no sense. For k = 2, the lower limit would be 70 and the upper limit would be 90. The Tchebysheff Inequality Theorem implies that *at least* $[1 - 1 / k^2]$ of the data values are within the score interval. Thus, for the constructed interval k = 2, 70 to 90, at least $[1 - 1 / (2)^2] = 1 - 1/4 = 1 - .25 = $ *at least* 75% of the data points are between 70 and 90, *regardless of the shape of the data distribution.* The Tchebysheff Inequality Theorem is very conservative, applying to *any* distribution of scores, and in most situations the number of data points exceeds that implied by $1-1/k^2$.

The Tchebysheff Inequality Theorem is generally applied to populations and intervals formed around the population mean using k population standard deviations, where k ranges from 1 to 4. In practice, however, one rarely knows the population parameters (population means and standard deviations). In some instances, the population parameters are known or at least can be estimated. For example, a nationally normed test booklet would contain the population mean and standard deviation, typically called "test norms." Researchers often use tests to measure traits and characteristics of subjects and publish test sample means and standard deviations. In this instance, an average of the results from several published studies would yield a reasonable estimate of the population parameters. In finite populations where every observation is known and recorded, the population parameters are readily obtainable using computer statistical packages to analyze the data. In a few instances, dividing the range of scores by six provides a reasonable estimate of the population standard deviation as an indicator of data dispersion. Since the sample mean and standard deviation are estimates of the population parameters, the Tchebysheff Inequality Theorem can be used with sample data.

In this chapter, you will be able to test whether or not the Tchebysheff Inequality Theorem is useful for describing data dispersion and compare it to the normal distribution percentages where approximately $1\sigma = 68\%$, $2\sigma = 95\%$, and $3\sigma = 99\%$. In the S-PLUS TCHEBYSHEFF program, samples will be selected from four different populations: uniform, normal, exponential, or bimodal. The four different distributions are functions within the S-PLUS language; however, they can be created in other programming software by computing a value for X (i), which is a data vector, using the following equations and functions (RND = round a number; COS = cosine of a number; SQR = square root of a number; LOG = logarithm of a number):

Uniform: X (i) = 1 + 9*RND
Normal: X (i) = COS (6.2832*RND) * SQR(-2*LOG (RND))
Exponential: X (i) = –LOG (RND)
Bimodal: X (i) = (2 + SQR (4 – (8* (1 – RND))))/2
                If RND ≥ .5
                X (i) = (2 – SQR (4 – (8*RND)))/2

The program will require specifying the population and the sample size. The TCHEBYSHEFF program will select a random sample, compute the sample mean and standard deviation, and determine the percentage of the observations within 1.5, 2, 2.5, and 3 standard deviations of the mean. The lower bound for the percentage of data within the interval given by the Tchebysheff Inequality Theorem will also be printed to check whether the theorem is true for the sample data.

SUMMARY

In this chapter, you should learn that:

- The standard deviation can be used to obtain information about the proportion of the sample data that are within certain intervals of a normally distributed population.
- The Tchebysheff Inequality Theorem provides a lower bound for the proportion of sample data within intervals around the mean of any distribution.
- The Tchebysheff Inequality Theorem is true for all samples regardless of the shape of the population distribution from which they were drawn.
- The Tchebysheff lower bound is often a conservative estimate of the true proportion in the population.
- The population mean and standard deviation are estimated more accurately from large samples than from small samples.

How the TCHEBYSHEFF program works

The TCHEBYSHEFF program builds on syntax from the S-PLUS programs in the previous chapters. It also gives examples for taking random samples from different shaped distributions. First, the *Kvals* vector is built to hold the k values used with the Tchebysheff intervals. This is a dialog box, so there is a *continueDialog* box , and then a dialog box used to choose the type of distribution. Within the **while** loop, the matrix to be filled is defined. Next, a random sample is taken from the appropriate distribution based on the response of the user to the *distDialog* box. The "Uniform" selection chooses a random sample of *SampleSize* from a uniform distribution that falls between the values of 1 and 10. "Normal" creates a random sample from a normal distribution with a mean of 0 and standard deviation of 1. "Exponential" creates a random sample from an exponential distribution with a mean of 1. Finally, "Bimodal" creates a random sample from a bimodal distribution (made up of an equal number of points chosen from two adjacent normal distributions). Whichever sample type is taken, the standard deviation and mean are obtained, and then the matrix is filled with values representing the Tchebysheff intervals, the percent of observations in the sample falling within the interval, and the value of the Tchebysheff Lower Bound.

The rest of the program simply outputs the information. The **cat** command prints out the type of distribution along with the descriptive statistics that were calculated. The new function, **print.char.matrix** , is used to display the output matrix. This function creates an orderly display with fixable column widths and customizable separators between columns and rows. The **abbreviate.dimnames** keyword set to F means that dimension names should be spelled out in full, **min.colwidth** sets the minimum column width, and **page.width** sets the minimum page width. Both the column and page width are expressed in terms of the number of characters. The last line of the program displays a dialog box asking whether the user wants to run it again.

The *Kvals* vectors for this program can be changed to give different Tchebysheff intervals, and *SampleSize* can also be adjusted. In addition, review the **cut** function to see how it could be used to obtain the percentage of observations within the Tchebysheff intervals. The population parameters for the distributions can be adjusted and the results observed in the descriptive statistics that are printed (remember, larger sample sizes provide better estimates of population parameters).

TCHEBYSHEFF Program Output

Uniform   N = 50   Sample Mean 4.82   Sample Std Dev 2.43

	Interval	% Obs in Interval	Tcheby. Lower Bound
K = 1.50	1.18 to 8.47	90	56
K = 2.00	-0.04 to 9.69	98	75
K = 2.50	-1.26 to 10.90	100	84
K = 3.00	-2.47 to 12.12	100	89

Normal   N = 50   Sample Mean 0.11   Sample Std Dev 0.92

	Interval	% Obs in Interval	Tcheby. Lower Bound
K = 1.50	-1.28 to 1.49	88	56
K = 2.00	-1.74 to 1.96	96	75
K = 2.50	-2.20 to 2.42	98	84
K = 3.00	-2.67 to 2.88	100	89

Exponential   N = 50   Sample Mean 1.18   Sample Std Dev 1.27

	Interval	% Obs in Interval	Tcheby. Lower Bound
K = 1.50	-0.73 to 3.09	92	56
K = 2.00	-1.36 to 3.72	96	75
K = 2.50	-2.00 to 4.36	98	84
K = 3.00	-2.64 to 5.00	98	89

Bimodal   N = 50   Sample Mean 1.06   Sample Std Dev 0.65

	Interval	% Obs in Interval	Tcheby. Lower Bound
K = 1.50	0.09 to 2.04	84	56
K = 2.00	-0.23 to 2.36	98	75
K = 2.50	-0.56 to 2.68	100	84
K = 3.00	-0.88 to 3.01	100	89

CHAPTER 9 EXERCISES

1. Run TCHEBYSHEFF for the vector of *Kvals* and sample size specified in the program.

UNIFORM   N = 50   Sample Mean _____ Sample St. Dev. _____

K	INTERVAL	% OBS. IN INT.	TCHEBY. LOWER BOUND
1.5	_____	_____	_____
2.0	_____	_____	_____
2.5	_____	_____	_____
3.0	_____	_____	_____

NORMAL   N = 50   Sample Mean _____ Sample St. Dev. _____

K	INTERVAL	% OBS. IN INT.	TCHEBY. LOWER BOUND
1.5	_____	_____	_____
2.0	_____	_____	_____
2.5	_____	_____	_____
3.0	_____	_____	_____

EXPONENTIAL N = 50   Sample Mean _____ Sample St. Dev. _____

K	INTERVAL	% OBS. IN INT.	TCHEBY. LOWER BOUND
1.5	_____	_____	_____
2.0	_____	_____	_____
2.5	_____	_____	_____
3.0	_____	_____	_____

BIMODAL   N = 50   Sample Mean _____ Sample St. Dev. _____

K	INTERVAL	% OBS. IN INT.	TCHEBY. LOWER BOUND
1.5	_____	_____	_____
2.0	_____	_____	_____
2.5	_____	_____	_____
3.0	_____	_____	_____

2. Are the Tchebysheff lower bound values always correct in the table?

_____

3. The Tchebysheff lower bound is very conservative; it is often a lower bound far below the actual percentage of data in the interval. For which population is the Tchebysheff lower bound the least conservative? Run TCHEBYSHEFF several times with different sample sizes to verify your conclusion.

_____

_____

4. The actual population means and standard deviations of the four populations are:

	POP. MEAN	POP. ST. DEV.
UNIFORM	5.5	2.60
NORMAL	0	1
EXPONENTIAL	1	1
BIMODAL	1	0.707

The sample means and standard deviations computed in TCHEBYSHEFF can be used as estimates of these population parameter values.

a. Run TCHEBYSHEFF to complete the following table. Recall that
ERROR = SAMPLE ESTIMATE – POPULATION VALUE.

SAMPLE SIZE	SAMPLE MEAN	POP. MEAN	ERROR	SAMPLE ST. DEV.	POP ST. DEV.	ERROR
UNIFORM						
20	_____	_____	_____	_____	_____	_____
50	_____	_____	_____	_____	_____	_____
100	_____	_____	_____	_____	_____	_____
NORMAL						
20	_____	_____	_____	_____	_____	_____
50	_____	_____	_____	_____	_____	_____
100	_____	_____	_____	_____	_____	_____

EXPONENTIAL

20   _____ _____ _____ _____ _____ _____

50   _____ _____ _____ _____ _____ _____

100   _____ _____ _____ _____ _____ _____

BIMODAL

20   _____ _____ _____ _____ _____ _____

50   _____ _____ _____ _____ _____ _____

100   _____ _____ _____ _____ _____ _____

b. Is there a relationship between the sample size and the absolute value of the error in the estimates of the mean? _____

_____

c. Is there a relationship between the sample size and the absolute value of the error in the estimates of the standard deviation? _____

_____

TRUE OR FALSE QUESTIONS

T   F   a. The Tchebysheff Inequality Theorem gives the approximate percentage of observations within certain intervals of the population.

T   F   b. If $k = 1$, the Tchebysheff Inequality Theorem states that at least 0% of the data are within one standard deviation of the mean.

T   F   c. The Tchebysheff Inequality Theorem is always true and does not depend on the shape of the population.

T   F   d. The error in the estimate of the standard deviation is usually larger for larger samples.

T   F   e. The Tchebysheff Inequality Theorem states that in a sample, at least 93.75 % of the data are within four standard deviations of the mean.

CHAPTER 10

NORMAL BELL-SHAPED CURVE

CHAPTER OBJECTIVES

- Develop an understanding of the Normal Bell-Shaped Curve for large samples from normal populations.
- To investigate the Normal Bell-Shaped Curve for small samples from normal populations.
- To investigate the use of the Normal Bell-Shaped Curve for samples from populations that are not approximately normal.

In a normal population, referred to as normal **bell-shaped curve**, the proportion of data within intervals around the mean is known. The proportion of sample data within k standard deviations around the mean for $k = 1, 2,$ and 3 are as follows:

INTERVAL		DATA PERCENT
LOWER LIMIT	UPPER LIMIT	IN THE INTERVAL
$\mu - 1\sigma$	$\mu + 1\sigma$	68 %
$\mu - 2\sigma$	$\mu + 2\sigma$	95 %
$\mu - 3\sigma$	$\mu + 3\sigma$	99 %

If a large random sample is selected from a normal population, these lower and upper intervals will approximate the percent of data within the intervals of a normal bell-shaped curve. The proportions of sample data should be good approximations if the population is approximately normal, symmetrical, and unimodal. If the population is non-normal, the bell-shaped curve may not provide results close to these proportions of sample data.

In this chapter, the S-PLUS BELL-SHAPED CURVE program will create large sample data sets chosen at random from the same four populations used in Chapter 9: uniform, normal, exponential, and bimodal. The BELL-SHAPED CURVE program will determine the proportion of the sample within the specified intervals. The tabled output should allow you to check the accuracy of the Normal Bell-Shaped Curve for large samples from a normal population and the other populations. The proportions within the specified intervals for smaller samples can also be checked.

The BELL-SHAPED CURVE program is similar to the TCHEBYSHEFF program in Chapter 9. The only difference is in the use of a **cut** function to determine the different score intervals. The different population distribution functions in the S-PLUS language permit the random sampling of data from different population distributions. The different population values can be adjusted and the population parameters for the different distributions are:

	MEAN	STANDARD DEVIATION
UNIFORM	5.5	2.60
NORMAL	0	1
EXPONENTIAL	1	1
BIMODAL	1	0.707

SUMMARY

In this chapter, you should learn that:

- The Normal Bell-Shaped Curve gives an approximation of the proportion of a sample that is within one, two, and three standard deviations of the population mean if the sample is large and is chosen at random from a normal population.
- The percentages of data within one, two, and three standard deviations of the mean for a normal population are respectively 68%, 95%, and 99%.
- The Normal Bell-Shaped Curve does not give good approximations for samples chosen from uniform, exponential, or bimodal populations.
- The Normal Bell-Shaped Curve does not give good approximations for small samples.

How the BELL-SHAPED CURVE program works

The BELL-SHAPED CURVE program is similar to the TCHEBYSHEFF program in Chapter 9. The only difference is the calculation of the score intervals. The line from the TCHEBYSHEFF program is commented out using the # symbol. The intervals are created using the percentages which are specified by *Pvals <- c(68,95,99)*; which corresponds to 1, 2, or 3 standard deviations from the population mean, respectively. The sample size is initially set at *SampleSize <- 50*.

Dialog boxes are used to select the type of population distribution (uniform, normal, exponential, and bimodal). Subsequent commands determine how many points are in a given interval using the **cut** function for the different types of distributions. The program takes the absolute difference between the sample mean and each point within the distribution and uses a Boolean (true or false) <= operator to determine whether the point is plus or minus that many standard deviations of the mean. In S-PLUS, Boolean operations that result in true are equal to 1 and those that result in false are equal to 0. Given this, the sum of the values for the Boolean test of each point falling within the given range results in a number equal to the total number of points within the interval. The use of Boolean operators in this manner is very helpful, but should be used with caution. The program then divides the number of values within the interval by the total number of points, multiplies by 100, and rounds to an even percent. The use of a Boolean operator is the only real difference between the TCHEBYSHEFF program and the BELL-SHAPED CURVE program, so it does permit a percentage of data points for $k = 1$.

BELL-SHAPED CURVE Program Output

```
Uniform    N = 50   Sample Mean = 5.87   Sample Std Dev = 2.63
```

	Interval	% Observed	% Predicted
K = 1.00	3.24 to 8.50	58	68
K = 2.00	0.62 to 11.13	100	95
K = 3.00	-2.01 to 13.75	100	99

```
Normal    N = 50   Sample Mean = -0.05   Sample Std Dev = 1.09
```

	Interval	% Observed	% Predicted
K = 1.00	-1.14 to 1.03	62	68
K = 2.00	-2.22 to 2.12	98	95
K = 3.00	-3.31 to 3.21	100	99

```
Exponential    N = 50   Sample Mean = 1.16   Sample Std Dev = 1.13
```

	Interval	% Observed	% Predicted
K = 1.00	0.03 to 2.29	84	68
K = 2.00	-1.11 to 3.43	90	95
K = 3.00	-2.24 to 4.56	100	99

```
Bimodal    N = 50   Sample Mean = 0.93   Sample Std Dev = 0.72
```

	Interval	% Observed	% Predicted
K = 1.00	0.22 to 1.65	66	68
K = 2.00	-0.50 to 2.37	96	95
K = 3.00	-1.22 to 3.09	100	99

CHAPTER 10 EXERCISES

1.   Run BELL-SHAPED CURVE for a sample size of 250, and complete the following
      tables. Note: ERROR = % OBSERVED – % PREDICTED.

UNIFORM: N =   Sample Mean =   Sample Std Dev =

k	INTERVAL	% OBSERVED	% PREDICTED	ERROR
1	_____	_____	68	_____
2	_____	_____	95	_____
3	_____	_____	99	_____

NORMAL: N =   Sample Mean =   Sample Std Dev =

k	INTERVAL	% OBSERVED	% PREDICTED	ERROR
1	_____	_____	68	_____
2	_____	_____	95	_____
3	_____	_____	99	_____

EXPONENTIAL: N =   Sample Mean =   Sample Std Dev =

k	INTERVAL	% OBSERVED	% PREDICTED	ERROR
1	_____	_____	68	_____
2	_____	_____	95	_____
3	_____	_____	99	_____

BIMODAL: N =   Sample Mean =   Sample Std Dev =

k	INTERVAL	% OBSERVED	% PREDICTED	ERROR
1	_____	_____	68	_____
2	_____	_____	95	_____
3	_____	_____	99	_____

a. Compute the lower and the upper limits of the interval for the uniform population with $k = 3$, using the following formula:

LOWER LIMIT = MEAN – K*STANDARD DEVIATION = _____

UPPER LIMIT = MEAN + K*STANDARD DEVIATION = _____

b. Which population produced a sample that is approximated best by the Normal Bell-Shaped Curve? _____

c. Run BELL-SHAPED CURVE program again for sample size 500 to test your conclusions. Comment on the results.

_____

2. Run BELL-SHAPED CURVE program again for a sample size of 1,000 and complete the tables.

UNIFORM: N =   Sample Mean =   Sample Std Dev =

k	INTERVAL	% OBSERVED	% PREDICTED	ERROR
1	_____	_____	68	_____
2	_____	_____	95	_____
3	_____	_____	99	_____

NORMAL: N =   Sample Mean =   Sample Std Dev =

k	INTERVAL	% OBSERVED	% PREDICTED	ERROR
1	_____	_____	68	_____
2	_____	_____	95	_____
3	_____	_____	99	_____

EXPONENTIAL: N =   Sample Mean =   Sample Std Dev =

k	INTERVAL	% OBSERVED	% PREDICTED	ERROR
1	_____	_____	68	_____
2	_____	_____	95	_____
3	_____	_____	99	_____

BIMODAL: N =   Sample Mean =   Sample Std Dev =

k	INTERVAL	% OBSERVED	% PREDICTED	ERROR
1	_____	_____	68	_____
2	_____	_____	95	_____
3	_____	_____	99	_____

    a. Compare the results for the samples of size 1,000 with the results for samples of size 250. For which sample size (250 or 1,000) were the approximations best for the normal population? _____

    b. Was there more error in the nonnormal populations (uniform, exponential, or bimodal)? Yes _____ No _____

3.   The uniform, exponential, and the bimodal populations all have shapes that are very different from the normal population.

    a. In what way is the uniform population different from the normal population?

    _____

    b. In what way is the exponential population different from the normal population?

    _____

    c. In what way is the bimodal population different from the normal population?

    _____

    d. Which population type had the most error?

    _____

4.   Run BELL-SHAPED CURVE program for a sample size of n = 20 for all four
        populations.

        a.   Enter the percent of data for each value of k in the table.

k	UNIFORM	NORMAL	EXPONENTIAL	BIMODAL
1	‾‾‾‾‾‾‾	‾‾‾‾‾‾‾	‾‾‾‾‾‾‾‾‾‾	‾‾‾‾‾‾‾
2	‾‾‾‾‾‾‾	‾‾‾‾‾‾‾	‾‾‾‾‾‾‾‾‾‾	‾‾‾‾‾‾‾
3	‾‾‾‾‾‾‾	‾‾‾‾‾‾‾	‾‾‾‾‾‾‾‾‾‾	‾‾‾‾‾‾‾

        b.   Comment on the accuracy of the Normal Bell-Shaped Curve for small samples.
             Hint: Is the Normal Bell-Shaped Curve still better than the others?

        _____

TRUE OR FALSE QUESTIONS

T   F   a. The Normal Bell-Shaped Curve gives a lower limit for the percentage of the
              data set within certain intervals.
T   F   b. The Normal Bell-Shaped Curve is based on what is known about a normal
              population and assumes that the sample is large and unimodal.
T   F   c. The Normal Bell-Shaped Curve gives accurate estimates for an exponential
              population.
T   F   d. The Normal Bell-Shaped Curve gives good estimates for small data sets.
T   F   e. Although the Normal Bell-Shaped Curve gives a more precise statement than
              the TCHEBYSHEFF lower bound, the Normal Bell-Shaped Curve has the
              disadvantage that it does not apply to populations of all possible shapes.

II

PROBABILITY AND PROBABILITY DISTRIBUTIONS

CHAPTER 11

PROBABILITY

CHAPTER OBJECTIVES

- To understand probability.
- To observe the distribution of relative frequencies of scores.
- To know what assumption is made when using the relative frequency definition of probability.
- To compare the distributions of relative frequencies of an event having probability close to 0.1 or 0.9 with the relative frequencies of an event having probability close to 0.5.

The previous chapters have covered statistical theory, generating random numbers, frequency distributions, data display in stem and leaf plots, population characteristics, measures of central tendency and dispersion, sample size effects, Tchebysheff theorem, and the normal bell-shaped curve. These chapters laid the foundation for understanding statistical concepts using S-PLUS. Basically, a random sample of data from a population can be graphically displayed and described by measures of central tendency and dispersion. This chapter, and the others that follow, describe the role probability plays in statistics. Basically, probability operates under seven fundamental rules that are covered in Chapters 11 - 16.

One's ability to determine the probability of an event is based upon whether the event occurs in a finite or infinite population. In a **finite population**, the number of objects or events is known. An exact **probability** or fraction can be determined. For example, given a population of 1,000 cars with 500 Ford, 200 Chevrolet, 200 Chrysler, and 100 Oldsmobile, the probability of selecting a Ford is one-half or 50% (500/1,000). The probability of selecting a Chevrolet is one-fifth or 20% (200/1,000), the probability of selecting a Chrysler is one-fifth or 20% (200/1,000), and the probability of selecting an Oldsmobile is one-tenth or 10% (100/1,000). The individual probabilities add up to 100%.

In an **infinite population**, the numbers of objects or events are so numerous that exact probabilities are difficult to determine. One approach to determine the probability of an event occurring in an infinite population is to use the relative frequency definition of probability. Using this approach, trials are repeated a large number of times, N. The number of times the event occurs is counted, and the probability of the event is approximated by $P(A) \approx n(A)/N$ in which $n(A)$ is the number of times event A occurred out of N trials.

For example, the probability of obtaining heads when a coin is tossed could be determined by tossing the coin 500 times, counting the number of heads, n (heads) = 241, and computing $P(\text{heads}) \approx 241/500 = 0.482$. The probability of getting heads in the population is therefore approximately 48%. The probability of *not* getting heads is 52%, since the two events must sum to 100%. We know from experience that the probability of obtaining heads when a coin is tossed should be approximately 50% or one-half, given an unbiased coin (a coin that is not weighted or not a trick coin).

An important point needs to be emphasized. In order for an approximation to be reasonable (representative), the relative frequency of the event (e.g., heads) must begin to stabilize and approach some fixed number as the number of trials increases. If this does not occur, then very different approximations would be assigned to the same event as the number of trials increases. Typically, more trials (coin tosses) are required to potentially achieve the 50% probability of obtaining heads. Experience in the real world has shown that the relative frequency of obtaining heads when coins are tossed stabilizes or better approximates the expected probability of 50%, as the number of trials increases.

This approximation phenomenon (stabilization or representativeness) occurs in the relative frequencies of other events too. There is no actual proof of this because of the nature of an infinite population, but experience does support it. Using the relative frequency definition, the approximation, which the relative frequencies provide, is regarded as our best estimate of the actual probability of the event.

In this chapter, you will have an opportunity to observe the stabilization of the relative frequencies. You will be able to choose the probability of the event and the S-PLUS program will simulate the number of trials. As the number of trials increase, the new results are pooled with the earlier ones, and the relative frequency of the event is computed and plotted on a graph. The first program example starts with a sample size of 100 and increases the sample size in increments of 100 up to 1,000.

SUMMARY

In this chapter, you should learn that:

- In the real world we observe that as the number of trials increases the relative frequency of an event approaches a fixed value.
- The probability of an event can be defined as the fixed value approximated by the relative frequencies of the event as the number of trials increase.
- The relative frequency definition of probability assumes that the relative frequencies stabilize as the number of trials increase.
- Although the relative frequencies get closer to a fixed value as the number of trials increase, it is possible for a certain number of trials to produce a relative frequency that is not closer to the approximated fixed value.
- An event with a probability close to 0.1 or 0.9 will have relative frequencies that stabilize faster than an event with probability close to .50.

How the PROBABILITY program works

The PROBABILITY program simulates flipping a coin a different number of times for different samples, and observing the different frequencies across sample sizes. The population probability is also adjusted so that the interaction between sample size and probability may be observed. The population probability is set in the variable *Probability* and the *SampleSizes* are created using the **seq** function, instead of specifying each value within a **c** function as before (which would be 50 numbers in this case). The **seq** function creates a vector of values from 50 to 2,500 with intervals of 50. Next, the *SampleFreqs* object is set to **NULL** so that it may be constructed into a vector by appending values using the **c** function. A **for** loop iterates through all values within the *SampleSizes* vector, assigning each value in turn to the *SampleSize* variable. The *SampleFreqs* vector is then increased by appending the sum of the samples of size *SampleSize* taken from the population of 0 and 1. This results in 0 having a probability of (1-*Probability*) and 1 having a probability of *Probability*, which is divided by *SampleSize* to get the relative frequency. The *SampleFreqs* vector now contains the relative frequencies of heads in each sample size. These relative frequencies are plotted with a line graph using the generic **plot** function. *SampleSize* is used for the data on the x-axis and *SampleFreqs* for the data on the y-axis. **Type**="l" (a lower case L) is for line graph and the **ylim** keyword sets the upper and lower limits of values for the y-axis.

Using the full range of possible values for the y-axis (0 to 1) resulted in difficulty distinguishing differences in the graphs because of the small variation of the values compared to the overall scale. Since values rarely fall .10 above or .10 below the population probability, the y-axis limits were set to *Probability* - .10 and *Probability* + .10. The x-axis label, y-axis label, and main title are all set by use of keywords.

The values from the graph are constructed into a matrix for output. The matrix starts out as a **NULL** object that is built using **rbind** (row bind). A row of values is added to the matrix for each iteration of the **for** loop, appending the relative frequency of the given sample, the population probability, and the error of estimation for each sample (relative frequency – population probability). After the matrix is constructed and the **for** loop is ended, the **dimnames** function is used to assign dimension names to the constructed matrix. The **paste** function is again utilized to create a vector of labels for the rows of the matrix resulting in "sample size = 50", "sample size = 100", etc. The **print.char.matrix** function is used to actually output the matrix in order to make the rows and columns clearly delineated.

Various population probabilities should be output to see the effect on both the appearance of the graph and the errors of estimation. The **seq** function can be changed in order to obtain different sized samples. The **c** function can be used instead of **seq** to create a vector of values for *SampleSizes*. Creating a vector using the **c** function doesn't affect the rest of the program. In S-PLUS script programs, a vector can be created in different ways.

PROBABILITY Program Output

```
                         Sample %   Population %    Error
--------------------+------------+------------+------------+
sample size = 100   |0.58        |0.500       |0.08        |
--------------------+------------+------------+------------+
sample size = 200   |0.48        |0.500       |-0.02       |
--------------------+------------+------------+------------+
sample size = 300   |0.543       |0.500       |0.043       |
--------------------+------------+------------+------------+
sample size = 400   |0.462       |0.500       |-0.037      |
--------------------+------------+------------+------------+
sample size = 500   |0.518       |0.500       |0.018       |
--------------------+------------+------------+------------+
sample size = 600   |0.515       |0.500       |0.015       |
--------------------+------------+------------+------------+
sample size = 700   |0.506       |0.500       |0.006       |
--------------------+------------+------------+------------+
sample size = 800   |0.532       |0.500       |0.032       |
--------------------+------------+------------+------------+
sample size = 900   |0.492       |0.500       |-0.008      |
--------------------+------------+------------+------------+
sample size = 1000  |0.478       |0.500       |-0.022      |
--------------------+------------+------------+------------+
```

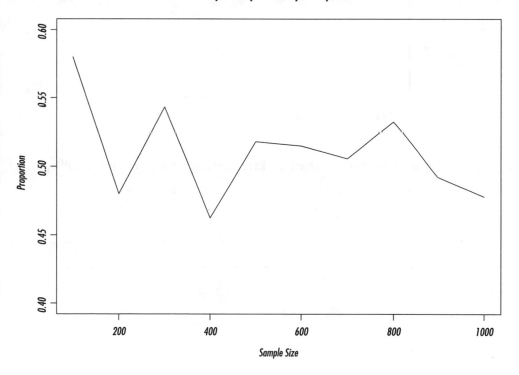

Sample Proportion by Sample Size

CHAPTER 11 EXERCISES

1.   Run PROBABILITY for sample sizes of 50 in increments of 50 up to 1,000, i.e.,
      SampleSizes <- seq(50,1000,50). This is a simulation of flipping an unbiased, balanced
      coin and recording the relative frequency of obtaining heads, which has an expected
      probability of p = .50.

      a.   Complete the graph of relative frequencies for sample sizes of n = 50, in
            increments of 50, up to 1,000, for *p* = .50.

            Proportion

            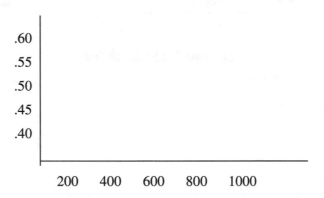

      b.   Complete the table below. Does the Error (difference between the sample percent
            and the population percent of .50) ever become less than 0.01?
            If so, for what sample sizes?

            _____

            _____

Table of Sample and Population Percents for Coin Toss

	Sample %	Population %	Error
sample size = 50		0.500	
sample size = 100		0.500	
sample size = 150		0.500	
sample size = 200		0.500	
sample size = 250		0.500	
sample size = 300		0.500	
sample size = 350		0.500	
sample size = 400		0.500	
sample size = 450		0.500	
sample size = 500		0.500	
sample size = 550		0.500	
sample size = 600		0.500	
sample size = 650		0.500	
sample size = 700		0.500	
sample size = 750		0.500	
sample size = 800		0.500	
sample size = 850		0.500	
sample size = 900		0.500	
sample size = 950		0.500	
sample size = 1000		0.500	

2.   Run PROBABILITY for sample sizes of 50 in increments of 50 up to 1,000, i.e.,
        SampleSizes <- seq(50,1000,50). This time change the population percent to 25%, i.e.,
        Probability <- .25. You are simulating the flipping of a biased, unbalanced coin.

a.   Complete the graph of relative frequencies for sample sizes of n = 50, in increments of
        50, up to 1,000, for p = .25.

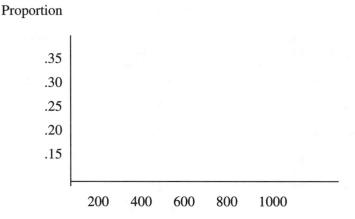

Proportion

b.   Complete the table below. Does the absolute difference between the sample percent and
        the population percent of .250 ever become less than 0.01?
        If so, for what sample sizes?

        _____

        _____

Table of Sample and Population Percents for Coin Toss

	Sample %	Population %	Error
sample size = 50		0.250	
sample size = 100		0.250	
sample size = 150		0.250	
sample size = 200		0.250	
sample size = 250		0.250	
sample size = 300		0.250	
sample size = 350		0.250	
sample size = 400		0.250	
sample size = 450		0.250	
sample size = 500		0.250	
sample size = 550		0.250	
sample size = 600		0.250	
sample size = 650		0.250	
sample size = 700		0.250	
sample size = 750		0.250	
sample size = 800		0.250	
sample size = 850		0.250	
sample size = 900		0.250	
sample size = 950		0.250	
sample size = 1000		0.250	

c.   In what way is this graph for $p = .25$ different from the first graph for $p = .50$?

_____

_____

3.   Run PROBABILITY again for sample sizes of 50, in increments of 50, up to 1,000, but
      this time for $p = .10$ and $p = .90$. Draw the graphs below.

$p = .10$

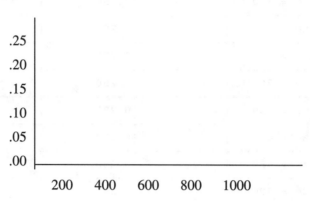

$p = .90$

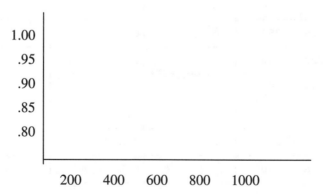

a. In what way are these graphs different from the graphs for a probability of .50?

      _____

      _____

      _____

b. What is the implication of this difference when you approximate a very small or a very large probability?

_____

_____

_____

c. Run PROBABILITY for $p = .20, .30, .40, .60, .70,$ and $.80$. Describe the graphs in comparison with those for probabilities of $.10, .90,$ and $.50$.

_____

_____

_____

TRUE OR FALSE QUESTIONS

T   F   a.   As additional trials are conducted, the relative frequency of heads is always closer to 0.5 than for any previous smaller sample size.

T   F   b.   As sample size increases, the relative frequency of an event approaches a fixed value.

T   F   c.   The relative frequency of an event with probability of .65 stabilizes faster than an event with probability of .10.

T   F   d.   In understanding probability, it is assumed that the relative frequencies approach a fixed number as the sample size increases because this corresponds to our experience of the real world.

T   F   e.   The relative frequency of an event in one hundred trials is the probability of the event.

CHAPTER 12

JOINT PROBABILITY

CHAPTER OBJECTIVES

- To determine whether the theoretical probability for the joint occurrence of two independent events is reflected in the relative frequency of their joint occurrence.
- To understand the multiplication law of probability for two independent events.
- To determine whether the theoretical probability for the union of two events is reflected in the relative frequency of the occurrence of either event.
- To understand the addition law of probability for two mutually exclusive events.

If an unbiased coin is flipped two times, the possible outcomes form a sample space, S. The sample space S = {HH, HT, TH, TT}, in which H stands for a head and T for a tail, with the pair of letters indicating the order of the outcomes. Therefore, with two separate flips of a coin, four possible outcomes can occur: two heads, first a head then a tail, first a tail then a head, or two tails. The sample space that contains the number of heads in the two flips is S = {0, 1, 2}. If an unbiased coin is flipped twice, a large number of times, the outcomes can be used to compute the frequencies. The frequencies can be used to approximate the joint probabilities of the outcomes in the sample space.

Probabilities can also be assigned to the outcomes by using a theoretical approach. Since a head and a tail are equally likely to occur on a single flip of an unbiased coin, the theoretical approach uses a definition of probability that is applicable to equally likely events. The probability of a head, P(H), is 1/2 because a head is one of the two equally likely outcomes. The probability of a tail, P(T), is 1/2, since a tail represents the other equally likely outcome. Since the two flips of the coin are independent, the multiplication law of probability for independent events can be used to find the joint probability for the pairs in the sample space. For example, the probability of flipping an unbiased coin and getting heads both times is: P(HH) = (1/2)*(1/2) = 1/4. The probability of getting a head and then a tail would be: P(HT) = (1/2) * (1/2) = 1/4 with the other pairs in the sample space determined in the same manner.

If the coin is *biased,* meaning that P(H) is some value other than .50, for example .60, then P(T) = 1 − P(H) = 1 − .60 = .40. The independence of the coin flips can be used to find the **joint probability** for the pair. For example, P(HT) = P(H)*P(T) = (.60) *(.40) = .24.

If the sample space being used is S = {0, 1, 2}, with the integers representing the number of heads, then the frequency of 0 is the frequency of TT; the frequency of 1 is the frequency of HT plus the frequency of TH; and the frequency of 2 is the frequency of HH. The theoretical probabilities for S can also be obtained by using the addition law of probability for mutually exclusive events. For example, P(1) = P(HT) + P(TH).

In this chapter, the S-PLUS JOINTP program specifies the probability of tossing a head P(H), and the number of repetitions of the two coin flips. The JOINTP program will simulate tossing the coin, compute the frequencies and the probabilities. You should be able to determine that the frequencies approximate the probabilities. This supports the conclusion that the theoretical laws used to compute the probabilities give results that agree with what actually happens in the program. Each time the JOINTP program is run, the frequencies will be different because random flips of the coin are simulated.

SUMMARY

In this chapter, you should learn that:

- The multiplication law of probability for independent events reflects the properties of frequencies.
- The addition law of probability for two mutually exclusive events reflects the properties of frequencies.
- If two events A and B are independent, then P (A and B) = P (A)*P (B).
- If two events A and B are mutually exclusive, then P (A and B) = P (A) + P (B).

How the JOINTP program works

The JOINTP program simulates tossing two (or more) coins N number of times. The program begins by initializing the probability of obtaining a head, the number of coins to be tossed, and the number of times to toss each coin. A vector of heads (1) or tails (0) values is created, and then grouped into a **matrix** with the number of columns equal to the number of coins (column 1 = coin 1, etc.) and the number of rows equal to the number of times each coin is tossed. Next, a vector is initialized and then filled using a **for** loop with the sum of the number of heads in each round of tosses. A complex nested function allows for any number of coins to be tossed.

Vectors for the event labels (HH, HT, TH, TT), the event probabilities, and the number of heads present in each event are initialized with the appropriate values. The outer loop represents the range of possible events given the number of coins. The number of possible events is $2^{numCoins}$, which is read 2 to the power of $numCoins$. The loop range is set to 0 for $2^{numCoins}-1$. A temporary holding variable is set to the current value of the outer loop counter, $i,$ and then the inner loop begins, which represents each coin tossed in a given round taken in reverse order.

In order to make each event unique, a binary coding system is used whereby the event's value (i) is broken down into binary values for each toss of a coin in the group. An event value of zero for two coins would mean tails-tails (or 0-0). An event value of one, for two coin tosses, would mean heads-tails (or 1-0). The first coin tossed has a value of either 0 or 1. The second coin tossed a value of either 0 or 2. The third coin tossed (if there were a third coin) would have a value of 0 or 4. The *nth* toss would have a value of 0 or $2^{(n-1)}$, i.e., $2^{numCoins}-1$. In this manner, all the unique events (from 0 to $2^{numCoins}-1$) are broken down into whether the first and/or second (and/or third and/or fourth, etc) coins are heads or tails for that event. Labels are created with ordered letters representing what the binary coding represents internally. The label "HH" for an event of head-head is more readily understood than an event code of 3.

The number of total heads for each event is recorded. The vector containing the heads count is factored for all possible values (from 0 to *numCoins*) and then counted by means of a **table** function to determine the total number of events resulting in 0 heads, 1 head, 2 heads, and so forth, depending upon the number of coin tosses. The total number of events is then used in calculating the probabilities in the **for** loop.

The **for** loop calculates the probabilities for each number of heads by the order of the event. If the probability of getting a head is .60, then the probability of getting two tails (or no heads) on the first toss is (1)(.40)(.40) = .16. This implies that there is only one way to get two tails (1), times the probability of tails (.40), times the probability of tails (.40). The probability of getting one head and one tail is (2)(.60)(.40) = .48. There are two different ways (head-tail or tail-head) you could get the pair of heads and tails (2), times probability of heads (.60), times probability of tails (.40). The loop variable, i, represents the number of heads and $numEvents[i+1]$ represents the number of events in the event space for that number of heads. The probability of a head (pH) is taken to the power of the number of heads obtained (i) and any coins that aren't heads must be tails ($numCoins - i$), so the probability of a tail ($1 - pH$) is taken to the power of that value. For an event that involves flipping a coin two times, the loop will go from 0 to 2 and the $numEvents$ vector will contain 1,2,1 (one event with no heads, two events with one head, and one event with two heads). The probability of heads can be set to any value between 0 and 1.

A second loop codes all of the rounds of tosses into a binary coding scheme in order to count the number in each group. The results are now put into matrices in order to print. The **table** and **factor** functions are invaluable in sorting categorical data for summarizing and reporting. The first matrix contains: (1) row labels with the possible number of heads that could be obtained (0 to *numCoins*); (2) the frequency of each round of flips that obtained that number of heads divided by the total number of rounds (giving the frequency), and (3) the theoretical probability of obtaining that many heads. The second matrix contains: (1) row labels with the event labels (HH,TH,HT,TT); (2) the frequency of each event obtained during all rounds, and (3) the theoretical probability of obtaining each event. The last two lines of the program merely prints out the matrices. The JOINTP program is complicated and detailed, but it allows the user to set the probability of heads and choose any number of coins. The number of coins selected should not exceed five and sample sizes larger than 5,000 will require a few more minutes for the program to run.

JOINTP Program Output

Given these values:

```
pH <- .5
numCoins <- 2
N <- 100
```

	Frequency	Probability
0 Heads	0.28	0.25
1 Heads	0.54	0.50
2 Heads	0.18	0.25

	Frequency	Probability
TT	0.28	0.25
HT	0.33	0.25
TH	0.21	0.25
HH	0.18	0.25

Given these values:

```
pH <- .5
numCoins <- 3
N <- 100
```

	Frequency	Probability
0 Heads	0.17	0.125
1 Heads	0.42	0.375
2 Heads	0.35	0.375
3 Heads	0.06	0.125

	Frequency	Probability
TTT	0.17	0.125
HTT	0.19	0.125
THT	0.11	0.125
HHT	0.13	0.125
TTH	0.12	0.125
HTH	0.11	0.125
THH	0.11	0.125
HHH	0.06	0.125

CHAPTER 12 EXERCISES

1. Run JOINTP program with pH = .50 and *numCoins* =2 for the following sample sizes. Complete the table.

FREQUENCY				
EVENT	N=100	N=1,000	N=5,000	PROBABILITY (P)
TT				
HT				
TH				
HH				
HEADS				
0				
1				
2				

a. Compare the frequency of TT, HT, TH, and HH with the probability of these events. Do the frequencies provide a reasonable approximation to the probabilities?

Yes_____ No _____

b. For which sample size does the frequency give the best approximation?

N = 100 _____ N = 1,000 _____ N = 5,000 _____

c. Under HEADS, a value of 1 gives the joint probability for HT and TH.

$P(1) = P(HT) + P(TH)$ by the addition law. Compute $P(1)$ for each sample size.

N = 100 _____ N=1,000 _____ N = 5,000 _____

d. Show that the same is true for the frequency.

$F(1) = F(HT) + F(TH)$ by the addition law. Compute $F(1)$ for each sample size.

N = 100 _____ N = 1,000 _____ N = 5,000 _____

2. From the previous table for N = 100, record the frequency and probability in the table below. Compute the ERROR by subtracting the probability from the frequency.

   Note: ERROR = FREQUENCY – PROBABILITY. Keep the +/- sign for each error.

EVENT	FREQUENCY	PROBABILITY	ERROR
TT			
HT			
TH			
HH			
HEADS			
0			
1			
2			

   a. Is the ERROR under HEADS for a value of 1 related to the errors for HT and TH?

   YES _____   NO _____

   b. What is the sum of the ERRORS for the four events? _____

TRUE OR FALSE QUESTIONS

T   F   a. The addition and multiplication laws of probability are reasonable because these properties are true for frequencies.

T   F   b. If two events are independent, the addition law is used to find their joint probability.

T   F   c. The sum of the probabilities for all of the events in a sample space is 1.

T   F   d. $P(1) = P(HT) + P(TH)$ because HT and TH are independent events.

T   F   e. $F(HT) \approx P(H)*P(T)$ because H and T are independent events.

CHAPTER 13

ADDITION LAW OF PROBABILITY

CHAPTER OBJECTIVES

- To have the computer simulate the rolling of two dice.
- To compare the relative frequencies of the sums of the numbers on the two dice with corresponding theoretical probabilities.
- To understand how the theoretical probabilities for the sums are computed.
- To understand the effect of sample size on the relative frequencies of the sums.
- To use the addition law of probability to find the probability of an even sum.
- To use the law of complements to find the probability of an odd sum.

This chapter will illustrate that **probability** can help determine the odds of events occurring in practice. For example, a deck of cards contains 52 cards. A deck of cards has four suits (Hearts, Diamonds, Spades, and Clubs). Therefore each suit has 13 cards (4 x 13 = 52). The probability of selecting any Heart from a deck of cards would be 13/52 = .25. This would be the same probability for selecting any Diamond, Spade, or Club, assuming selection with replacement of the card each time. Similarly, there are four Kings (one in each suit). The probability of selecting a King out of a deck of cards would be 4/52 = .076923.

The ADDITION program simulates the tossing of two dice. It records the number of times that each of the possible sums of the two dice occurs, and then changes these counts into relative frequencies. The frequency and relative frequency of each sum, and the theoretical probability are printed. Since the computation of the theoretical probabilities depends on the "equally likely" definition of probability, the chapter exercises will illustrate how the definition of probability is reasonable and does reflect practice.

The sample space for the sum of the numbers on the two dice can be conceptualized as follows:

FIRST DIE

		1	2	3	4	5	6
	1	2	3	4	5	6	7
	2	3	4	5	6	7	8
SECOND	3	4	5	6	7	8	9
DIE	4	5	6	7	8	9	10
	5	6	7	8	9	10	11
	6	7	8	9	10	11	12

If the dice are unbiased, all of the 36 outcomes are equally likely. The probability of any sum, S, can be calculated theoretically by the formula: $P(S)$ = (Number of ways S can occur)/36. For example, $P(7) = 6/36 = 1/6$ (a number 7 occurs in the diagonal six times).

In the ADDITION program, the number of times that the two dice are tossed is specified. This will once again permit an observation of the relative frequencies of an event approaching a fixed number as the sample size increases. In this chapter, different events are examined simultaneously, but are independent.

The theory of probability relates to possible outcomes of events occurring in a sample space. The relative frequencies for the different sums in this chapter are not readily apparent. Our earlier approach assumed that all events were equally likely. In this chapter, we discover that the sums have 36 outcomes, which are equally likely outcomes, but certain sums occur more frequently (e.g., sum = 6). The theory of probability helps us to understand the frequency of outcomes and apply this in practice.

SUMMARY

In this chapter, you should learn that:

- The theoretical probabilities for the sums of the numbers on two dice agree well with what happens in practice.
- The theoretical probabilities for the sums can be found by listing all of the outcomes in a two-way table and using the "equally likely" definition of probability; for the sum S, $P(S)$ = (Number of ways S can occur)/36.
- The relative frequencies of the sums get very close to the theoretical probabilities given large sample sizes.
- The probability of an odd sum can be found from the probability of an even sum by using the **law of complements**: $P(ODD) = 1 - P(EVEN)$.

How the ADDITION program works

This program should be straightforward given the explanations in previous chapters. The program starts with the familiar vector of sample sizes and then creates a vector of probabilities that correspond to the chances of obtaining a 2 through 12 from rolling two dice. The *DiceFreq* object is set to **NULL** so that it may be used to build a matrix within the main processing loop. The loop iterates through the values in *SampleSizes* and obtains a random sample of values from 1 to 6 of size *SampleSize* for *Die1* and then repeats the process for *Die2*. The two vectors of simulated rolls are summed together to obtain a vector for the total of both dice. [Note: the same vector could have been obtained by removing the *Die1* and *Die2* variables and just typing *DiceSum* <- **sample**(2:12,**size**=*SampleSize*,**replace**=T), but that hides the fact that we have two independent events and destroys the chance to analyze specific dice combinations.] The relative frequency of each outcome (2 through 12) is appended to the *DiceFreq* matrix for each different sample size as the loop continues through the values of the *SampleSizes* vector. Finally, the *outputMatrix* is built from the *DiceFreq* matrix, **cbind**ed to the *Probs* vector to yield a matrix with relative frequencies for each value outcome of the dice, for each sample size, along with the theoretical probabilities of obtaining each value outcome. The **print.char.matrix** function is used to output the information. Run the ADDITION program using various sample sizes to see how closely you can approximate the theoretical probabilities.

ADDITION Program Output

	N= 100	N= 500	N= 1000	N= 5000	Prob.
2	0.01	0.024	0.024	0.0286	0.0278
3	0.08	0.058	0.05	0.0576	0.0556
4	0.08	0.078	0.08	0.086	0.0833
5	0.04	0.112	0.113	0.1094	0.1111
6	0.18	0.12	0.14	0.1414	0.1389
7	0.2	0.186	0.174	0.1708	0.1667
8	0.12	0.14	0.129	0.1444	0.1389
9	0.1	0.118	0.117	0.1038	0.1111
10	0.11	0.088	0.084	0.077	0.0833
11	0.02	0.05	0.066	0.0528	0.0556
12	0.06	0.026	0.023	0.0282	0.0278

CHAPTER 13 EXERCISES

1.   Run ADDITION for the sample sizes indicated below. Complete the table.

RELATIVE FREQUENCY				
SUM	N=360	N=1,200	N=7,200	PROBABILITY
2				
3				
4				
5				
6				
7				
8				
9				
10				
11				
12				

a.   Check that the probabilities listed correspond to values in the sequence 1/36, 2/36, 3/36, 4/36, 5/36, 6/36, 5/36, 4/36, 3/36, 2/36, and 1/36 (sum = 1 within rounding).

b.   Which sample size provides the best estimate of the probabilities? _____

2.   The addition law for mutually exclusive events states that the sum of frequencies for *even* numbers should be about 50% and the sum of frequencies for *odd* numbers should be about 50 %.

a.   For N = 7,200 above, add the frequency for all even sums (2,4,6,8,10,12) and the frequency for all odd sums (1,3,5,7,9,11). Enter the two frequencies in the table below.

SUM	FREQUENCY	PROBABILITY
EVEN		.50
ODD		.50

b.   Why do you expect these frequencies to be around 50%?

_____

_____

3.   Using the sum of frequencies for all *even* numbers and all *odd* numbers, answer the following questions.

a.   How can the probability of all *odd* numbers be obtained from the probability of all *even* numbers?

_____

_____

b.   What is the name of this probability law?

_____

TRUE OR FALSE QUESTIONS

T   F   a.   Probabilities would be the same if the dice were biased.

T   F   b.   Since there are 12 distinct sums and 6 of them are even, the probability of an even sum is 6/12.

T   F   c.   The stabilizing property of relative frequencies is true for a group of outcomes as well as for a single outcome.

T   F   d.   Large numbers of repetitions will provide good estimates of probabilities.

T   F   e.   Each time the program is run for N = 1200, the relative frequencies will be the same.

CHAPTER 14

MULTIPLICATION LAW OF PROBABILITY

CHAPTER OBJECTIVES

- To understand the multiplication law of probability for independent events.
- To observe that the multiplication law for independent events reflects the properties of relative frequency.
- To observe the effect of sample size on the accuracy of the relative frequency approximation of probability.

One of the basic properties of **probability** is the multiplication law for independent events. For example, if two dice are tossed and the events A, B, and C occur as follows:

> A: An odd number on the first die
> B: An odd number on the second die
> C: An odd number on both dice

then the **multiplication law** for independent events states that: Probability (Event C) = Probability (Event A) x Probability (Event B).

This multiplication law of probability reflects the properties of relative frequency in practice. If two dice are tossed a large number of times, the relative frequencies of events A, B, and C should approximate the probabilities of these events. Also, the product of the relative frequency of A times the relative frequency of B should approximate the relative frequency of C. This can be stated as: Frequency (Event C) ≈ Frequency (Event A) x Frequency (Event B).

The MULTIPLICATION program simulates the tossing of two dice and records the frequency of an odd number on the first die, an odd number on the second die, and an odd number on both of the dice. The frequencies are then changed to relative frequencies, and the results are rounded to three decimal places. The program inputs the number of times the two dice are tossed. The program illustrates a comparison between relative frequency and the multiplication law for the probability of independent events. Since sample size can be changed, the effect of sample size on the relative frequency as it relates to the multiplication law can be observed.

SUMMARY

In this chapter, you should learn that:

- The multiplication law for independent events states that if two events A and B are independent, then Probability (A and B) = Probability (A) x Probability (B)
- The multiplication law for independent events is modeled on the behavior of relative frequency.
- For relative frequency, Frequency (A and B) is approximately Frequency (A) x Frequency (B).
- As sample size increases, Frequency (A and B) tends to be closer to Frequency (A) x Frequency (B).

How the MULTIPLICATON program works

The MULTIPLICATION program is a modification of the ADDITION program in Chapter 13. The program reflects how the probability of both dice ending up odd relates to the probability of either of the dice being odd. It begins with a vector of sample sizes, creates a **NULL** object to become a matrix, builds a processing loop to iterate through the values of *SampleSizes*, and simulates the rolling of two dice. The next two lines calculate the relative frequency of odds in the first die and the relative frequency of odds in the second die. It does this using a modulo operator (%%). The modulo operator performs an integer division and returns only the remainder portion. This means that 13%%5 would equal 3, because 13 divided by 5 equals 2 with remainder 3. Performing a modulo operation with a 2 on each die result would give values of 0 for even numbers and 1 for odd numbers. The odd numbers are counted up using the **sum** function and then divided by the sample size to get the relative frequency of odds in the sample. Next, the modulo 2 result for both dice are added together, so if both were odd then the result would be 2, otherwise it would be 0 or 1. The integer number is divided by 2 (%/%), which only returns a whole number. This would result in 0 for values of 0 or 1, because 2 doesn't go into either of those numbers evenly, but would be 1 for a value of 2. In this way, the rolls in which both dice come up odd are added together and divided by the sample size to give the relative frequency of both being odd in the sample. These three values are **rbind**ed into *outputMatrix* along with the difference of the relative frequency of both being odd and the product of the relative frequencies of each being odd. After the loop is completed, dimension names are assigned to the rows and columns of the matrix and it is printed using the **print.char.matrix** function. Different sample sizes can be input to see the effect sample size has on the relative frequencies and to observe what sample sizes are required to reduce the error to a minimum.

MULTIPLICATION Program Output

Given the following sample sizes: `SampleSizes <- c(100,500,1000)`

	1st Odd	2nd Odd	Both Odd	F1*F2	Error
N= 100	0.59	0.45	0.26	0.266	-0.006
N= 500	0.492	0.488	0.238	0.24	-0.002
N= 1000	0.502	0.534	0.257	0.268	-0.011

Given the following sample sizes: `SampleSizes <- c(1000,2000,3000)`

	1st Odd	2nd Odd	Both Odd	F1*F2	Error
N= 1000	0.509	0.498	0.26	0.253	0.007
N= 2000	0.485	0.498	0.251	0.242	0.009
N= 3000	0.497	0.502	0.247	0.249	-0.002

CHAPTER 14 EXERCISES

1. Run MULTIPLICATION for samples sizes 100, 500, and 1,000.
    Record the results below.

FREQUENCY

SAMPLE SIZE	FIRST ODD	SECOND ODD	BOTH ODD	F1 * F2	ERROR
100					
500					
1,000					

a. What is the theoretical probability that the first die will be odd?   _____

b. What is the probability that the second die will be odd?   _____

c. What is the probability that both dice are odd?   _____

d. What law of probability are you using to find the probability that both are odd?

    _____

e. What effect does sample size have on these approximations?

    _____

    _____

f. Compute the error in this approximation by: ERROR = BOTH ODD - (F1 x F2)

    Do all of the differences have the same sign?   YES _____ NO _____

g. Does sample size have an effect on the amount of error?

                                            YES _____ NO_____

2. Run MULTIPLICATION for samples sizes 1,000, 2,000, and 3,000.

Record the results below.

FREQUENCY

SAMPLE SIZE	FIRST ODD	SECOND ODD	BOTH ODD	F1 * F2	ERROR
1,000					
2,000					
3,000					

a. What is the theoretical probability that the first die will be odd?   _____

b. What is the probability that the second die will be odd?   _____

c. What is the probability that both dice are odd?   _____

d. What effect does sample size have on these approximations?

_____

e. Do all of the differences have the same sign?   YES _____ NO _____

f. Does sample size have an effect on the amount of error?

YES _____ NO_____

TRUE OR FALSE QUESTIONS

T   F   a. If two events are independent, then the probability of both events occurring is the product of their probabilities.

T   F   b. If two events are independent, then the relative frequency of both events occurring is the product of their relative frequencies.

T   F   c. In general, relative frequencies obtained from small samples give the best approximations of probabilities.

T   F   d. If two biased dice were tossed, then the events FIRST ODD and SECOND ODD are not independent.

T   F   e. The events FIRST ODD and BOTH ODD are mutually exclusive events.

CHAPTER 15

CONDITIONAL PROBABILITY

CHAPTER OBJECTIVES

- To understand joint, marginal, and conditional probabilities.
- To determine that conditional probability agrees with the properties of relative frequency for conditional events.
- To determine the relationship between sample size and the accuracy of the relative frequencies as an estimate of conditional probability.

A child has a toy train that requires six "C" batteries to run. The child has accidentally mixed four good batteries with two bad batteries. If we were to randomly select two of the six batteries without replacement, the odds of getting a bad battery are conditionally determined. Let's assume that the first battery chosen was bad (Event A) and the second battery chosen was good (Event B). The two selections of the two batteries are dependent events. The probability of event B has two different values depending upon whether or not event A occurs. If event A occurs, then there are four good batteries among the remaining five batteries, and the probability of event B is 4/5. If a battery is chosen and event A does not occur, then there are only three good batteries remaining among the five batteries, and the probability of B is 3/5.

In probability terms this can be represented by: $P(B|A) = 4/5$ and $P(B|$ not-A$) = 3/5$. These terms are read, "the probability of B given A" and "the probability of B given not-A", respectively. Probabilities of this type are called **conditional probabilities** because the probability of B is conditional upon the occurrence or nonoccurrence of A. Conditional probabilities are related to joint probabilities and marginal probabilities. This relationship can be illustrated by the following example. Consider a sample space that contains all pairs of batteries selected from the six batteries without replacement. The X's in the table below indicate the 30 possible outcomes.

SECOND BATTERY

		DEAD1	DEAD2	GOOD1	GOOD2	GOOD3	GOOD4
	DEAD1		✕	✕	✕	✕	✕
	DEAD2	✕		✕	✕	✕	✕
FIRST	GOOD1	✕	✕		✕	✕	✕
BATTERY	GOOD2	✕	✕	✕		✕	✕
	GOOD3	✕	✕	✕	✕		✕
	GOOD4	✕	✕	✕	✕	✕	

Since these 30 outcomes are equally likely, the **joint probabilities**, P(A and B), can be summarized in the following table.

JOINT PROBABILITIES

SECOND BATTERY

		DEAD	GOOD	MARGINAL PROBABILITY
FIRST	DEAD	2/30	8/30	10/30
BATTERY	GOOD	8/30	12/30	20/30
MARGINAL PROBABILITY		10/30	20/30	30/30 (Total)

The row totals are the **marginal probabilities** for the first battery:

$$P(\text{First is dead}) = 10/30$$
$$P(\text{First is good}) = 20/30.$$

The column totals are the **marginal probabilities** for the second battery:

$$P(\text{Second is dead}) = 10/30$$
$$P(\text{Second is good}) = 20/30.$$

Conditional probabilities are related to these joint probabilities and marginal probabilities by the following formula:

$$P(B|A) = P(B \text{ and } A) / P(A).$$

If event A results in a bad battery and event B results in a good battery, then

$$P(B|A) = P(\text{Second is good} | \text{First is dead})$$
$$= P(\text{Second is good and First is dead}) / P(\text{First is dead})$$
$$= (4/15) / (5/15)$$
$$= 4/5.$$

These conditional probabilities are theoretical probabilities assigned to the events by making use of the definition of probability for **equally likely events** (it is assumed that each of the batteries and each of the pairs are equally likely to be chosen).   If these conditional probabilities are reasonable, they should reflect what happens in practice.   Consequently, given a large number of replications in which two batteries are selected from a group of six batteries (in which two of the batteries are dead), the relative frequencies for the conditional events should approximate the theoretical conditional probabilities.

In this chapter, the CONDITIONAL program will simulate random selection without replacement of two batteries from a group of six in which two of the batteries are dead.   The number of replications can be specified in the program.   As noticed in earlier chapters, the relative frequencies from a small number of replications will not provide good approximations of the probabilities.   A large number of replications should provide relative frequencies that will be very close to the theoretical probabilities.

The CONDITIONAL program will permit you to observe that the theoretical rules of probability for conditional events do in fact reflect practice.   The theoretical probabilities are important in statistics because they provide reasonable rules to adopt for analyzing what happens in the real world.

SUMMARY

In this chapter, you should learn that:

- The conditional probability of B given A is the joint probability of A and B divided by the marginal probability of A, if $P(A) \neq 0$.
- The conditional probability agrees with the behavior of relative frequency for conditional events.
- For large sample sizes, the relative frequency of a conditional event is a good approximation of the conditional probability.

How the CONDITIONAL program works

The CONDITIONAL program determines the probability of conditional events by selecting two batteries from a group of batteries with a certain number of good batteries and a certain number of bad batteries.   The total number of batteries is assigned, followed by the number of bad batteries and the number of times the two selections should be replicated. The number of good batteries is determined by subtraction of the number of bad batteries from the total number of batteries.   The probabilities of the possible event outcomes are then determined and assigned to the variables: *pGG, pBB, pGB,* and *pBG.*

The total number of batteries is defined so that sampling can occur from a finite population.   The **rep** function creates *numGood* (number of 0s) and the **c** function concatenates those with *numBad* (number of 1s) to complete the population of batteries.   The receiving objects *FirstBattery* and *SecondBattery* are set to **NULL** before the main processing loop begins.   The loop takes a sample of two batteries WITHOUT replacement, since these are conditional events.

The two batteries are then added to their respective vectors. They are also added to an *eventList* vector using the same type of binary encoding scheme presented in earlier chapters. The encoding is much simpler since the number of picks is fixed at two.

After the processing loop is finished, output matrices are created. The *eventTable* vector is built from the *eventList* vector factored for all the possible coded event values from 0 to 3. Two vectors of values are then created and put into the matrices for even column spacing in the output. The first vector is moved into a 4 by 4 matrix for display with no **dimnames** set, since the column and row headers were included within the vector. The same thing is done with the second vector, only it is printed out using **print.char.matrix**, since it doesn't have multiple column or row headers. The CONDITIONAL program is flexible enough to permit different numbers of total and bad batteries, as well as different sample sizes.

CONDITIONAL Program Output

Given the following values:

```
numBatteries <- 6
numBad <- 2
SampleSize <- 1000

                Second Battery
                Bad     Good
First   Bad   0.08    0.281
Battery Good  0.244   0.395
```

No. Bad	Rel Freq	Probability
0	0.395	0.4
1	0.525	0.534
2	0.08	0.067

Given the following values:

```
numBatteries <- 6
numBad <- 2
SampleSize <- 5000

                Second Battery
                Bad     Good
First   Bad   0.064   0.279
Battery Good  0.265   0.392
```

No. Bad	Rel Freq	Probability
0	0.392	0.4
1	0.544	0.534
2	0.064	0.067

CHAPTER 15 EXERCISES

1. Run CONDITIONAL for N = 1,000 with 6 total batteries and 2 bad batteries.

   a.   Enter the probabilities of the joint events and the marginal probabilities in the table.

		Second Battery		Marginal
		Bad	Good	Probability
First	Bad			
Battery	Good			

   Marginal   (Total)
   Probability

   b.   Do the marginal probabilities indicate that approximately 1/3 (.33) of the batteries are bad and 2/3 (.67) of the batteries are good?

   YES _____   NO _____

   c.   Do the marginal probabilities sum to 1.0?

   YES _____   NO _____

2. From the CONDITIONAL program with N = 1,000, enter the relative frequencies of 0, 1, and 2 bad batteries.

   a.   Compute the error and record it in the table.

   ERROR = REL FREQ - PROBABILITY

No. BAD	REL FREQ	PROBABILITY	ERROR
0			
1			
2			

b. Some of the errors should be positive and others negative.
    Do the errors sum to zero (0)?   YES _____   NO _____

c. Do the frequencies sum to 1.0?   YES _____   NO _____

d. Do the probabilities sum to 1.0?   YES _____   NO _____

3. Run CONDITIONAL for N = 5,000 with 6 total batteries and 2 bad batteries.

a. Enter the probabilities of the joint events and the marginal probabilities in the
    table.

		Second Battery		Marginal
		Bad	Good	Probability
First	Bad			
Battery	Good			
Marginal Probability				(Total)

b. Do the marginal probabilities indicate that approximately 1/3 (.33) of the

    batteries are bad and 2/3 (.67) of the batteries are good?

    YES _____   NO _____

c. Do the marginal probabilities sum to 1.0?

    YES _____   NO _____

4. From the CONDITIONAL program with N = 5,000, enter the relative frequencies of 0, 1, and 2 bad batteries.

   a. Compute the error and record it in the table.
       ERROR = REL FREQ - PROBABILITY

No. BAD	REL FREQ	PROBABILITY	ERROR
0			
1			
2			

   b. Some of the errors should be positive and others negative.
       Do the errors sum to zero (0)?   YES _____ NO _____
   c. Do the frequencies sum to 1.0?   YES _____ NO _____
   d. Do the probabilities sum to 1.0? YES _____ NO _____

TRUE OR FALSE QUESTIONS

T   F   a.   If two batteries are selected with replacement from a group
                 of six batteries, in which two of the batteries are bad, the FIRST BAD and
                 the SECOND GOOD are dependent events.

T   F   b. $P(A \text{ and } B) = P(A) \times P(B|A)$

T   F   c.   If the probability of event A is not affected by whether or not
                 event B occurs, then A and B are independent events.

T   F   d. $P(A)$, the marginal probability for event A, is equal to the sum of the joint
                 probabilities of A and all other events that can occur with A.

T   F   e.   If two events A and B are independent, then $P(B|A) = P(B)$.

CHAPTER 16

COMBINATIONS AND PERMUTATIONS

CHAPTER OBJECTIVES

- To know the seven rules of probability
- To understand factorial notation.
- To understand and compute permutations for ordered events from a group.
- To understand and compute combinations for choosing events from a group.
- To simulate the classic birthday problem.
- To understand how the probabilities are computed for permutations and combinations.
- To investigate how the size of the group will affect probability.

Probability theory helps us to determine characteristics of a population from a random sample. A **random sample** is chosen so that every object, event, or individual in the population has an equal chance of being selected. The probability that the object, event, or individual will be selected is based upon the relative frequency of occurrence of the object, event, or individual in the population. For example, if a population consisted of 1,000 individuals with 700 men and 300 women, then the probability of selecting a male is 700/1,000 or .70. The probability of selecting a woman is 300/1,000 or .30. The important idea is that the selection of the individual is a chance event.

Probability theory operates under seven fundamental rules, which have been covered in Chapters 11 - 15. These seven rules can be succinctly stated as:

1. The probability of a single event occurring in a set of equally likely events is one divided by the number of events, i.e., P (single event) = 1/N. For example, a single marble from a set of 100 marbles has a 1/100 chance of being selected.

2. If there is more than one event in a group, then the probability of selecting an event from the group is equal to the group frequency divided by the number of events, i.e., P (Group | single event) = group frequency/N. For example, a set of 100 marbles contains 20 red, 50 green, 20 yellow, and 10 black. The probability of picking a black marble is 10/100 or 1/10.

3.   The probability of an event ranges between 0 and 1, i.e., there
        are no negative probabilities and no probabilities greater than
        one. Probability ranges between 0 and 1 in equally likely
        chance events, i.e., $0 \leq P$ (event) ≤ 1.

4.   The sum of the probabilities in a population equal one, i.e., the
        sum of all frequencies of occurrence equals 1.0, i.e.,
        Σ (Probabilities) = 1.

5.   The probability of an event occurring plus the probability of an
        event *not* occurring is equal to one. If the probability of
        selecting a black marble is 1/10, then the probability of *not*
        selecting a black marble is 9/10, i.e., $P + Q = 1$ where $P =$
        probability of occurrence and $Q = 1 - P$.

6.   The probability that any one event from a set of mutually
        exclusive events will occur is the sum of the probabilities
        (addition rule of probability). The probability of selecting a
        black marble (10/100) *or* a yellow marble (20/100) is the sum of
        their individual probabilities (30/100 or 3/10), i.e., $P(B$ or $Y) =$
        $P(B) + P(Y)$.

7.   The probability that a combination of independent events will
        occur is the product of their separate probabilities
        (multiplication rule of probability). Assuming sampling with
        replacement, the probability that a yellow marble will be
        selected the first time (2/10) and the probability that a yellow
        marble will be selected the second time (2/10) combine by
        multiplication to produce the probability of getting a yellow
        marble on both selections (2/10 x 2/10 = 4/100 or .04), i.e., $P(Y$
        and $Y) = P(Y) * P(Y)$.

Factorial notation is useful for designating probability when samples are taken *without* replacement. For example, a corporate executive officer (CEO) must rank the top five department managers according to their sales productivity. After ranking the first manager, only four managers are remaining to choose from. After ranking the second manager, only three managers remain, and so forth, until only one manager remains. If the CEO selects managers at random, then the probability of any particular manager order is: $1/5 * 1/4 * 1/3 * 1/2 * 1/1$, or 1/120.

The probability is based upon the total number of possible ways the five managers could be ranked by the CEO. This is based upon the number of managers in the company available to select from, which changes each time. Consequently, the product yields the total number of choices available: $5 * 4 * 3 * 2 * 1 = 120$. This product is referred to as **factoring** and uses **factorial notation** to reflect the product multiplication, i.e., n!. The factorial notation, 3! (read 3-factorial), would imply, $3 * 2 * 1$, or 6, which indicates the number of different ways 3 things could be ordered. Imagine a restaurant that serves hamburgers with the following toppings:

pickle, onion, and tomato. How many different ways could you order these ingredients on top of your hamburger?

Permutations involve selecting objects, events, or individuals from a group and then determining the number of different ways they can be ordered. The number of permutations (different ways you can order something) is designated as **n** objects taken **x** at a time, or:

$$P(n, x) = \frac{n!}{(n-x)!}$$

For example, if a teacher needed to select three students from a group of five and order them according to mathematics ability, the number of *permutations* (or different ways three out of five students could be selected and ranked) would be:

$$P(n, x) = \frac{n!}{(n-x)!} = \frac{5!}{(5-3)!} = \frac{5*4*3*2*1}{2*1} = 60.$$

Probability can also be based upon the number of *combinations* possible when choosing a certain number of objects, events, or individuals from a group. The ordering of observations (permutations) is not important when determining the number of combinations. For example, a teacher must only choose the three best students with mathematics ability from a group of five (no ordering occurs). The number of possible combinations of three students out of a group of five is designated as:

$$P(n, x) = \frac{n!}{x!(n-x)!} \quad \text{or} \quad \frac{5!}{3!(5-3)!} = 10.$$

The number of possible combinations can be illustrated by determining the number of students in a classroom that have their birthday on the same day. This classic example can be used in a class to determine the probability that two students have the same birthday. The probability of two students having a common birthday, given five students in a class, can be estimated as follows (assuming 365 days per year and equally likely chance):

$$P(2 \mid 5) = 1 - \frac{365}{365} * \frac{364}{365} * \frac{363}{365} * \frac{362}{365} * \frac{361}{365} = 0.027$$

The numerator decreases by one because as each student's birthday is selected, there is one less day available.

The probability of at least two students out of five *not* having the same birthday is 1 - P (see probability rule 5). The probability of *no* students having a birthday in common for a class of 5 students, is computed as:

$$P(No\ 2 \mid 5) = \frac{365}{365} * \frac{364}{365} * \frac{363}{365} * \frac{362}{365} * \frac{361}{365} = 0.973$$

Therefore, the probability of at least two students having the same birthday is the complement of *no* students having the same birthday, or P (2|5) = 1 − .973 = .027. The formula clearly indicates that this probability would increase quickly as the number of objects, events, or individuals in the group increases.

In this chapter, the S-PLUS BIRTHDAY program simulates the birthday example for N individuals by using a random number generator and checking for a common birthday. The relative frequency of at least one common birthday is reported. This relative frequency approximates the probability of occurrence in a group of N individuals. The size of the group and the number of replications can be changed.

SUMMARY

In this chapter, you should learn that:

- The seven rules of probability apply to everyday occurrences.
- The number of possible outcomes of independent events is designated as a factorial (n!).
- Permutations refer to the number of possible ways to order things when selected from a group (**n** objects, **x** order).
- Combinations refer to the number of possible sub-groups of a given size from a larger group (**n** objects, **x** size).
- The birthday problem is a classic example of how to determine whether two individuals in a group of size N have the same birthdays.
- The relative frequencies produced by a simulation of the birthday problem are good approximations of the actual probabilities.
- The *accuracy* of the relative frequencies as approximations of the actual probabilities in the birthday problem is not affected by the size of the group of people, rather by increasing the number of repetitions in the program.

How the program BIRTHDAY works

The BIRTHDAY program simulates selecting groups of people of various sizes over a given number of replications in order to compute estimates of probabilities. The sizes of the groups of people are assigned to the vector *numPeople*. The *replicationSize* variable represents the number of times that the selection of random birthdays will occur for each group size. In the initial program settings, the probability of five birthdays in common is chosen, and duplication or non-duplication reported for 250 replications. The *numPeople* vector then indicates that 10 birthdays will be chosen at a time for the 250 replications. This is repeated for 20 and 50 birthdays. The sampling and replications can be time-consuming for a computer, so it would be wise *not* to select 10,000 replications for a *numPeople* vector of from 1 to 100, unless you are willing to wait.

The *repeatVector* object is simply a vector containing the number of times there was a common birthday for a given group size. The outer processing loop iterates through the values of group sizes and the inner processing loop defines each replication for the given group size. Within this inner loop, a random sample is taken from the range of values from 1 to 365 with replacement and a sample size of *numPeople[i]*. The vector created is run through the **table** function to group the sample points that fell on the same day, and if the **max** of that table is greater than 1, then it means there was at least one birthday in common. If this occurs, then the corresponding value in the vector for the number of replications containing repeated values is increased by one. Because this takes place within the inner-processing loop, it continues for all replications of all group sizes.

Once the simulation in the loops is concluded, the counts within the *repeatVector* are changed into relative frequencies by dividing the *repeatVector* by the replication size. This creates a new vector of values that contains the relative frequencies of replications with birthday duplications. Theoretical probabilities are computed using a small processing loop that iterates through the group sizes and creates a vector of probabilities of duplication for each group size. The single line of code within the loop represents the mathematical notation, 1 − (365/365)*(364/365)*(363/365)…((366-group size)/365.

A **list** object is created to hold the dimension labels for the output matrix. The output matrix is built by concatenating the relative frequency vector, the theoretical probability vector, and the difference between the relative frequency vector and the theoretical probability vector, giving an error vector. The **dimnames** keyword is given the value of the **list** object that was created making the line easier to read. The matrix is output using **print.char.matrix.** Values are reported within three decimal places using the **nsmall** keyword of the **format** function.

After running the initial BIRTHDAY program, change the *numPeople* vector to have a group size from 10 to 60 with intervals of 10. Use the **seq** function to perform this. Next, run the program with different numbers of replications and compare the error columns. You can change the program to automate this process of changing replication size and re-running the program.

BIRTHDAY Program Output

Given these values:

```
numPeople <- c(5,10,20,50)
replicationSize <- 250
```

	Rel. Freq.	Common Birthday	Error
N= 5	0.016	0.027	-0.011
N= 10	0.112	0.117	-0.005
N= 20	0.424	0.411	0.013
N= 50	0.952	0.970	-0.018

Given these values:

```
numPeople <- c(5,10,20,50)
replicationSize <- 500
```

	Rel. Freq.	Common Birthday	Error
N= 5	0.030	0.027	0.003
N= 10	0.112	0.117	-0.005
N= 20	0.402	0.411	-0.009
N= 50	0.974	0.970	0.004

CHAPTER 16 EXERCISES

1.   Run BIRTHDAY for the following sample sizes and complete the table.

GROUP SIZE	REL. FREQ.	COMMON BIRTHDAY	ERROR
5	_____	_____	_____
10	_____	_____	_____
15	_____	_____	_____
20	_____	_____	_____

a.   As the size of the group increases, does the probability of a common birthday increase?

YES _____ NO _____

b.   As the size of the group increases, do the relative frequencies more closely approximate the common birthday probabilities? Hint: Does error decrease?

YES _____ NO _____

2.   Run BIRTHDAY again for the same sample sizes. Complete the table.

GROUP SIZE	REL. FREQ.	COMMON BIRTHDAY	ERROR
5	_____	_____	_____
10	_____	_____	_____
15	_____	_____	_____
20	_____	_____	_____

a.   Are the common birthday probabilities the same?

YES _____ NO _____

b.   Are the relative frequencies close to the common birthday probabilities?

YES _____ NO _____

3.   Run BIRTHDAY again using sample sizes listed below with 500
        replications. Complete the table.

GROUP SIZE	REL. FREQ.	COMMON BIRTHDAY	ERROR
10	_____	_____	_____
20	_____	_____	_____
30	_____	_____	_____
40	_____	_____	_____
50	_____	_____	_____

a.   As the size of the group increases, does the probability of a common birthday

        increase?

        YES _____ NO _____

b.   As the size of the group increases, do the relative frequencies more closely

        approximate the common birthday probabilities? Hint: Does error decrease?

        YES _____ NO _____

TRUE OR FALSE QUESTIONS

T   F   a.   As the size of the group increases, the probability decreases
                        that two people have the same birthday.

T   F   b.   The probability of *no* common birthday is the complement of
                        the probability of having a common birthday.

T   F   c.   If a group consists of only two people, the probability that
                        they have the same birthday is 1/365.

T   F   d.   In a group of 50 people, there will *always* be at least two
                        people with the same birthday.

T   F   e.   The error in the relative frequency as an approximation of
                        the probability is reduced for large groups of people.

III

MONTE CARLO AND STATISTICAL DISTRIBUTIONS

CHAPTER 17

BINOMIAL DISTRIBUTION

CHAPTER OBJECTIVES

- To understand the type of data that produces a binomial distribution.
- To use the computer to simulate data and display the binomial distribution.
- To compare relative frequencies of binomial data with the theoretical probabilities.
- To compare the mean and variance of expected number of successes with the theoretical probabilities.
- To understand the shape of the binomial distribution given the probability of successes and the number of trials.

The previous chapters, 11 through 16, have helped our understanding of the role probability plays in statistics. The next set of chapters, 17 through 22, provides incite into how probability distributions for different types of statistics are formed. This chapter indicates the relationship between the **binomial distribution** (frequency distribution of dichotomous data) and **normal distribution** (frequency distribution of continuous data). The next chapter presents the Monte Carlo technique, which is used to create statistical distributions. The remaining chapters present several statistical distributions and how they are used in the field of statistics.

Many variables in education, psychology, and business are dichotomous. Examples of dichotomous variables are: boy versus girl; correct versus incorrect answers; delinquent versus non-delinquent; young versus old; part-time versus full-time worker. These variables reflect mutually exclusive and exhaustive categories (i.e., an individual, object, or event can only occur in one or the other category, but not both). Populations that are divided into two exclusive categories are called **dichotomous populations**, which can be represented by the binomial probability distribution. The derivation of the binomial probability is similar to the combination probability derived in Chapter 16.

The **binomial probability distribution** is computed by:

$$P(x \ in \ n) = \binom{n}{x} P^x Q^{n-x}$$

where the following values are used:

n = size of random sample
x = number of events, objects, or individuals in first category
n − x = number of events, objects, or individuals in second category
P = probability of event, object, or individual occurring in the first category
Q = probability of event, object, or individual occurring in the second category, (1−P).

Since the **binomial distribution** is a theoretical probability distribution based upon objects, events, or individuals belonging in one of only two groups, the values for P and Q probabilities associated with group membership must have some basis for selection. An example will illustrate how to use the formula and interpret the resulting binomial distribution.

Students are given five true-false items. The items are scored correct or incorrect with the probability of a correct guess equal to one-half. What is the probability that a student will get four or more true-false items correct? For this example, **n** = 5, P and Q are both .50 (one-half based on guessing the item correct), and **x** ranges from 0 (all wrong) to 5 (all correct) to produce the binomial probability combinations. The calculation of all binomial probability combinations is not necessary to solve the problem, but tabled for illustration and interpretation.

x	n x	P^x	Q^{n-x}	Probability
5	1	$.5^5$	$.5^0$	1/ 32 = .03
4	5	$.5^4$	$.5^1$	5/ 32 = .16
3	10	$.5^3$	$.5^2$	10/ 32 = .31
2	10	$.5^2$	$.5^3$	10/ 32 = .31
1	5	$.5^1$	$.5^4$	5/ 32 = .16
0	1	$.5^0$	$.5^5$	1/ 32 = .03
				32/32 =1.00

Using the addition rule, the probability of a student getting four or more items correct is: .16 + .03 = .19. The answer is based on the sum of the probabilities for getting four items correct plus five items correct.

The combination formula yields an individual "coefficient" for taking **x** events, objects, or individuals from a group size **n**. Notice that these individual coefficients sum to the total number of possible combinations and are symmetrical across the binomial distribution. The binomial distribution is symmetrical because P = Q = .50. When P does not equal Q, the binomial distribution will not be symmetrical. Determining the number of possible combinations and multiplying it times P and then Q will yield the theoretical probability for a certain outcome. The individual outcome probabilities add to 1.0.

A binomial distribution can be used to compare sample probabilities to theoretical probabilities if:

    a.   There are only two outcomes, e.g., success or failure.
    b.   The process is repeated a fixed number of times.
    c.   The replications are independent of each other.
    d.   The probability of success in a group is a fixed value, P.
    e.   The number of successes, x, in group size n, is of interest.

A binomial distribution based on dichotomous data approximates a normal distribution based on continuous data when the sample size is large and P = .50. Consequently, the mean of a binomial distribution is equal to n * P with variance equal to n * P * Q. A standardized score (**z-score**), which forms the basis for the normal distribution, can be computed from dichotomous data as follows:

$$z = \frac{x - nP}{\sqrt{nPQ}}$$

where:

x	= score
nP	= mean
nPQ	= variance.

A frequency distribution of standard scores (z-scores) has a mean of zero and a standard deviation of one. The z-scores typically range in value from −3.0 to + 3.0 in a symmetrical distribution. A graph of the binomial distribution, given P=Q and a large sample size, will be symmetrical and appear normally distributed.

Knowledge of the binomial distribution is helpful in conducting research and useful in practice. In the BINOMIAL program, you will be able to simulate binomial probability outcomes. The number of replications, number of trials, and probability value can be input to observe various binomial probability outcomes. Trying different values should allow you to observe the properties of the binomial distribution. The BINOMIAL program can be replicated any number of times, but extreme values are not necessary to observe the shape of the distribution. The relative frequencies of **x** successes will be used to obtain the approximations of the binomial probabilities. The theoretical probabilities, mean and variance of the relative frequency distribution, and error will be computed and printed.

SUMMARY

In this chapter, you should learn that:

- Binomial distributions are skewed except for those with a probability of success equal to .50. If P > .50, the binomial distribution is skewed left; if P < .50, the binomial distribution is skewed right.
- The mean of a binomial distribution is n * P and the variance is n*P*Q .
- The binomial distribution given by P(x in n) uses the combination formula, multiplication and addition rules of probability.
- The binomial distribution can be used to compare sample probabilities to expected theoretical probabilities.
- For P = .50 and large sample sizes, the binomial distribution approximates the normal distribution.

How the BINOMIAL program works

The BINOMIAL program must specify *numReplications* to indicate the number of replications, *numTrials* to indicate the number of respondents (or sampling points) per replication, and *Probability* to indicate the probability of success (or population proportion). The initial values are set at 5 respondents (sample size or number of trials), 500 replications, and a population proportion of .50.

The program starts by defining these values and then creates a random sample from the binomial distribution of size *numReplications* with *numTrials* sampling points per replication and a probability of success, *Probability*. A vector is created and factored from 0 to the number of sampling points per replication. The vector is then run through the **table** function in order to divide the replications into the number of successful trials (or sampling points in agreement), which range from none to all 5 in the sample. The vector is then divided by *numReplications* in order to express each level as a relative frequency.

The variables *eventProbs*, *expSuccess*, and *expVariance* are initialized prior to a main processing loop. The loop iterates from 0 to the number of trials per replication and calculates the theoretical probability of obtaining each number of successful trials. This is done by means of the **choose** function, which finds the number of unique combinations taking *numTrials, i* at a time (if the keyword **order.matters** were given a value of T then the **choose** function would return a permutation instead of a combination). The combination value is then multiplied by the true probability of success to the power of *i* (the number of successful trials) and then again by one minus the true probability (the probability of failure) to the power of *numTrials* minus *i* (the number of unsuccessful trials). The next line keeps up with the expected number of successes by taking the probability just calculated and multiplying it by the number of successful trials and then keeping that total running for the entire range of possible levels. Then the following line does the same for calculating the total expected variance by keeping a running total of the number of successful trials taken to the power of twice the probability of that number of successes. After the loop is finished, the *expVariance* (expected variance) must be adjusted by taking the total and subtracting the expected number of successes squared.

The rest of the program code outputs the data. The table of factored values from the replications, the theoretical probabilities of each number of successes, and the difference of those two vectors (the error vector) are combined into a matrix. Dimension names are then applied to the matrix using the **dimnames** function. Next, two concatenations of data and text are created and then output using the **cat** function. Finally, the matrix is output with all numbers forced to three decimal points of precision using a combination of the **round** and **format** functions.

BINOMIAL Program Output

Given the following values:

```
numTrials <- 5
numReplications <- 500
Probability <- .50
```

Mean number of successes = 2.516
Mean expected number of successes = 2.5

Sample variance = 1.148
Expected variance = 1.25

	Rel. Freq.	Probability	Error
Successes = 0	0.028	0.031	-0.003
Successes = 1	0.140	0.156	-0.016
Successes = 2	0.318	0.312	0.006
Successes = 3	0.342	0.312	0.030
Successes = 4	0.146	0.156	-0.010
Successes = 5	0.026	0.031	-0.005

Given the following values:

```
numTrials <- 5
numReplications <- 1000
Probability <- .50
```

Mean number of successes = 2.429
Mean expected number of successes = 2.5

Sample variance = 1.294
Expected variance = 1.25

	Rel. Freq.	Probability	Error
Successes = 0	0.043	0.031	0.012
Successes = 1	0.171	0.156	0.015
Successes = 2	0.295	0.312	-0.018
Successes = 3	0.325	0.312	0.013
Successes = 4	0.137	0.156	-0.019
Successes = 5	0.029	0.031	-0.002

CHAPTER 17 EXERCISES

1. Run BINOMIAL for n = 5, **P = .50**, and 500 replications. Enter the results below.

NO. SUCCESSES N	REL FREQ.	PROBABILITY P	ERROR
0			
1			
2			
3			
4			
5			

a. What is the maximum absolute value of the errors?   _____

b. Use the P (x in n) formula for the binomial distribution to prove P (3 in 5) is correct.

    _____

c. What is the mean number of successes in the simulation?   _____

d. What is the mean expected number of successes?   _____

e. What is the sample variance?   _____

f. What is the expected variance?   _____

g. Use the probabilities to calculate the expected mean and variance.

    Mean = _____   Variance = _____

h. Draw a bar graph to indicate both the relative frequencies (dashed line) and the theoretical probabilities (solid line).

    i.   Are the two graphs symmetrical or skewed?   _____

    ii. If the graphs are skewed, in what direction?   _____

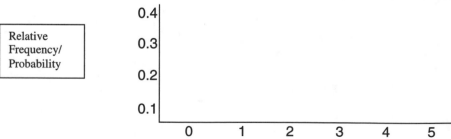

2. Run BINOMIAL for n = 5, **P = .30**, and 500 replications. Enter the results below.

NO. SUCCESSES N	REL FREQ.	PROBABILITY P	ERROR
0			
1			
2			
3			
4			
5			

a. What is the maximum absolute value of the errors?   _____

b. Use the P (x in n) formula for the binomial distribution to prove P (3 in 5) is correct.

   _____

c. What is the mean number of successes in the simulation?   _____

d. What is the mean expected number of successes?   _____

e. What is the sample variance?   _____

f. What is the expected variance?   _____

g. Use the probabilities to calculate the expected mean and variance.

   _____

h. Draw a bar graph on the following axes to indicate the relative frequencies (dashed line) and the theoretical probabilities (solid line).

   i.   Are the graphs symmetrical or skewed?   _____

   ii. If the graphs are skewed, in what direction?   _____

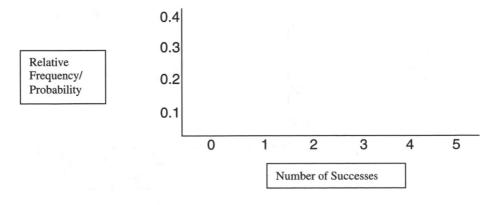

3. Run BINOMIAL for n = 5, **P = .70**, and 500 replications. Enter the results below.

NO. SUCCESSES N	REL FREQ.	PROBABILITY P	ERROR
0			
1			
2			
3			
4			
5			

a. What is the maximum absolute value of the errors?   _____

b. Use the P (x in n) formula for the binomial distribution to prove P (3 in 5) is correct.

_____

c. What is the mean number of successes in the simulation?   _____

d. What is the mean expected number of successes?   _____

e. What is the sample variance?   _____

f. What is the expected variance?   _____

g. Use the probabilities to calculate the expected mean and variance.

_____

_____

h. Draw a bar graph on the following axes to indicate the relative frequencies (dashed
line) and the theoretical probabilities (solid line).

  i.   Are the graphs symmetrical or skewed?   _____

  ii. If the graphs are skewed, in what direction?   _____

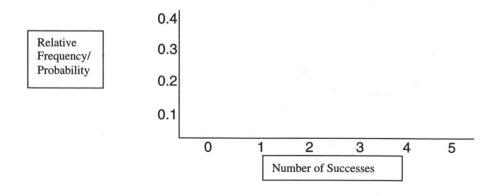

TRUE OR FALSE QUESTIONS

T   F   a. All binomial distributions are symmetrical.

T   F   b. If n = 10 and P = .50, then 50% of the time x = 5.

T   F   c. The binomial distribution approximates the normal distribution when sample size is large and P = .50.

T   F   d. If a binomial process consists of n trials, then the number of successes, x, will range from 0 to n.

T   F   e. A binomial distribution is created based on dichotomous variables.

T   F   f. As sample size increases for P = .50, the mean of the binomial distribution (nP) more closely approximates the population mean.

T   F   g. As the number of replications increase the absolute value of the error decreases.

T   F   h. If P < .50, the binomial distribution is skewed right.

T   F   i. If P > .50, the binomial distribution is skewed left.

CHAPTER 18

MONTE CARLO SIMULATION

CHAPTER OBJECTIVES

- To understand uniform, linear, and exponential probability density functions.
- To graph continuous random variables and determine their probability distribution.
- To use the Monte Carlo Method for approximating probabilities of continuous random variables.
- To compare the Monte Carlo approximations with the true probabilities for continuous probability distributions.

Many research studies in education, psychology, and business involve variables that are measured at the interval or ratio scale of measurement. Interval scaled variables do not have a true zero point. Ratio scaled data, in contrast, has a true zero point. Examples of interval or ratio scaled variables include height, weight, age, blood pressure, temperature, time, distance, number of sales, and amount of product used in production. Variables measured on an interval or ratio scale are typically treated as continuous data. The continuous probability distribution is used to study variables that are treated as continuous rather than dichotomous data. The **Monte Carlo** technique simulates these continuous random variable probability distributions.

A continuous probability distribution is expressed as a density function depicting the functional relationship between two variables. When one variable is determined by the value of another variable, they are a function of each other. This functional relationship can be expressed by a general equation, e.g., $Y = bX$. Some common functions used in statistics are uniform, linear, and exponential depending upon values of Y and X. The continuous probability distribution is mathematically represented in a graph as a curve in a plane with the probabilities represented as the areas under the curve.

In mathematics, calculus is used to find the exact probability area under the curve. In statistics, the probability tables for many common distributions are given in the appendix of the book so that calculus is not necessary. The Monte Carlo technique can also be used to obtain approximate probability areas under the curve. In simple examples, the exact probabilities can be determined to understand how the probabilities are obtained, but in most studies random variables are modeled by complex curves requiring integral calculus.

A uniform (rectangular) function can be represented by the time of day and birth number at a large hospital.   The probability distribution could be represented as in Figure 1.

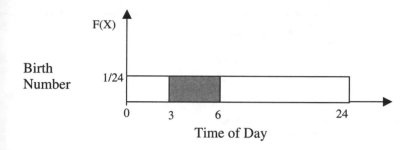

Figure 1. A continuous uniform distribution

A **uniform distribution** has a density of F(X) = 1/(B – A).   The function, F (X) = 1/24, is a straight line called the density function of the random variable X to determine the probability of a single birth in a 24-hour period.   The graph of the random variable X (time of day for a single birth) is a continuous uniform distribution on the interval 0 to 24 hours (A <---> B), where A and B are the two end point values for the time of day. The dark area on the graph represents the probability that a birth will occur within the specific time period between 3am and 6am, or P (3< X <6). This probability area is bounded by the lower and upper limits of the time period (x-axis) and the density (y-axis).   Since the function forms a rectangle, the area can be determined by using the familiar formula for the area of a rectangle, height * width (Area = H * W). In this example, the probability is (1/24) * (6 – 3) = 3/24 = .125.

A **linear function**, Y = bX, represents an angled straight line with a constant rate of change for the density function of the random variable X. For example, the tabled data indicate the number of pages read (Y) as a function of time in minutes (X). The straight-line function is displayed in Figure 2. For every one-minute increase in X, Y increases by 10 pages.

X	Y	ΔY
0	0	0
1	10	10
2	20	10
3	30	10
4	40	10
5	50	10

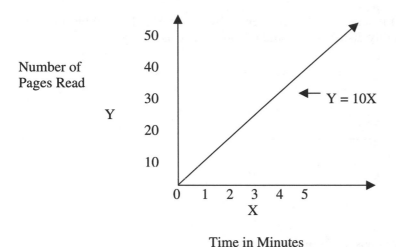

Number of
Pages Read

Time in Minutes

Figure 2. A continuous linear distribution

The rate of change for Y given changes in X can be determined by the formula:

$$\Delta Y = \frac{Y_2 - Y_1}{X_2 - X_1}$$

which indicates the ratio of the difference in adjacent values for Y and X, respectively. The rate of change is constant and indicated by the straight-line graph in Figure 2. The value of *b* in the equation Y=bX denotes this rate of change, which is commonly called the **slope**.

Exponential functions are useful in understanding such things as the carbon dating of pre-historic bones, amplification of music tones, and the length of piano strings in a baby grand piano. An **exponential function**, expressed as $Y = 2^X$, doesn't have a constant rate of change and is graphed as a curved line. The density function of the random variable X, the exponent in the equation, determines the exponential relationship between the two variables. The tabled data below indicate the previous data for the random variable X (time in minutes) as an exponential function of the number of pages read (Y). A curved line in Figure 3 displays this exponential function.

X	Y	ΔY
0	1	--
1	2	2
2	4	4
3	8	8
4	16	16
5	32	32

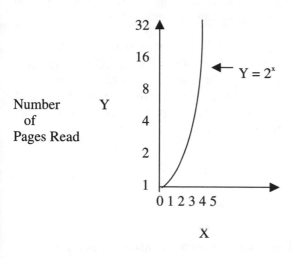

Number   Y
  of
Pages Read

Time in Minutes

Figure 3. A continuous exponential distribution

Another example of an exponential function between two variables is: $Y = 3^x$. If the continuous random variable, X, ranges from 0 to 1 (Time in tenths of an hour), the curved line for a value of $Y = 3$ (Number of Pages Read) is depicted in Figure 4.

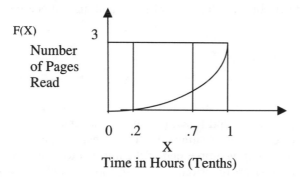

Time in Hours (Tenths)

Figure 4. A continuous exponential distribution

A probability area can be determined for the types of mathematical functions specified in Figure 4. For example, if two values are specified for X, .2 and .7 in Figure 4, and a level of density specified (height of Y, in this case 3), then random points can be chosen in the rectangle for the distance from .2 to .7 and a height of 3. The percentage of random points that fall below the density (horizontal line drawn at height of 3) times the area of the rectangle is an approximation of the probability area below the curve inside the rectangle [P (.2 < X < .7)]. The area of the rectangle (A = H * W) is 1.5. Simulation of random points for the function is accomplished by using the Monte Carlo technique.

In this chapter, you will use the Monte Carlo technique to find the probabilities for uniform, exponential, and linear probability distributions. The MONTE CARLO program will allow you to specify the type of density function and the specific interval for which you want the probability. The program generates 1,000 random points for each approximation. In the case of the uniform distribution, you can easily compare the estimated probability with the true probability since the value is the area of the rectangle.

SUMMARY

In this chapter, you should learn that:

- Uniform, linear, and exponential functions model relationships between two variables.
- Linear and exponential functions have different rates of change.
- Areas under their density curves represent probability for continuous random variables.
- If a continuous random variable, Y, can only have values between A and B, then P (A< Y <B) = 1.
- The probability that a continuous random variable, Y, is equal to a specific value is 0.
- The Monte Carlo Method provides a good approximation of probability for continuous random variables if a large number of random points are used.

How the MONTE CARLO program works

The MONTE CARLO program returns estimates for three different density functions: uniform (rectangular), exponential (parabolic), and linear (y = bx). The first line of the program sets the number of points that will be randomly sampled. The density type is chosen next, followed by the lower end of the interval and the upper end of the interval to be estimated.

The program continues with a **switch** function, which on the basis of the value of the *DensityType* variable decides the routine to perform. For example, if *DensityType* was equal to 2 then the second routine after *DensityType* would be performed, namely *DensityHeight* <– 3. This sets the height of the rectangular region within which the random points are placed. The value can be greater than the highest point in the distribution density, but if the value is too high it will reduce the precision of the estimates. The random points are then selected along the x-axis within the chosen interval and along the y-axis between 0 and *DensityHeight*.

The next few **if** statements determine how many of the randomly selected points fall within the distribution (below the curve) and also calculates the theoretical probability of a value falling within this range of the distribution. The *withinRange* variable is calculated using the sum of Boolean operations, which takes the number of points which fall within the distribution divided by the total number of points, to get a percentage of the points within. The percentage of points within is multiplied by the area of the rectangular region (interval width times height) to obtain the approximate probability area under the curve. The estimated and true probabilities are now calculated and must fall within the allowable range for probabilities (0 to 1). A vector of output data is created next. This is followed by a list of labels. The output vector is moved into a matrix, the labels applied, and the matrix printed.

MONTE CARLO Program Output

Given the following values:

```
NumPoints <- 1000
DensityType <- 3    # 1 = uniform, 2 = exponential, 3 = linear
IntervalMin <- .5
IntervalMax <- 1

Interval    Monte Carlo    True P      Error
 0.5<X<1      0.742         0.75       -0.008
```

Given the following values:

```
NumPoints <- 5000
DensityType <- 3    # 1 = uniform, 2 = exponential, 3 = linear
IntervalMin <- .5
IntervalMax <- 1

Interval    Monte Carlo    True P      Error
 0.5<X<1      0.752         0.75        0.002
```

Given the following values:

```
NumPoints <- 10000
DensityType <- 3    # 1 = uniform, 2 = exponential, 3 = linear
IntervalMin <- .5
IntervalMax <- 1

Interval    Monte Carlo    True P      Error
 0.5<X<1      0.751         0.75        0.001
```

CHAPTER 18 EXERCISES

1.   Run MONTECARLO for the uniform distribution (**DensityType <– 1**) and intervals of X
      (IntervalMin and IntervalMax) listed in the table. Set NumPoints <– 1000. Enter the
      probabilities in the table.

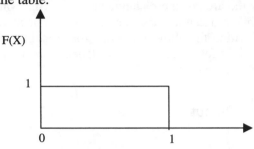

UNIFORM DISTRIBUTION

INTERVAL	MONTE CARLO	TRUE P	ERROR
.00 < X < .50			
.25 < X < .50			
.10 < X < .90			
.60 < X < .70			
.75 < X < 1.00			

   a.   Use the formula for the area of a rectangle to verify the probabilities.

   b.   Verify that the ERROR values are correct using the following formula.
         ERROR = MONTE CARLO – TRUE P

2.   Run MONTE CARLO for the exponential distribution (**DensityType <– 2**) and intervals
      of X (IntervalMin and IntervalMax) listed in the table. Set NumPoints <– 1000. Enter
      the probabilities in the table.

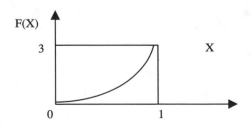

EXPONENTIAL DISTRIBUTION

INTERVAL	MONTE CARLO	TRUE P	ERROR
.00 < X < .50			
.25 < X < .50			
.10 < X < .90			
.60 < X < .70			
.75 < X < 1.00			

a. The exact probabilities (determined by calculus) are listed in the
    TRUE P column of the table, i.e., $P (A < X < B = B^3 - A^3)$.

b. Verify that the ERROR values are correct using the following formula.
    ERROR = MONTE CARLO − TRUE P

3. Run MONTECARLO for the linear distribution (**DensityType <− 3**) and intervals of X
    (IntervalMin and IntervalMax) listed in the table. Set NumPoints < - 1000. Enter the
    probabilities in the table.

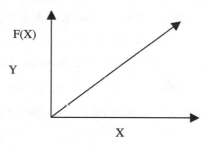

LINEAR DISTRIBUTION

INTERVAL	MONTE CARLO	TRUE P	ERROR
.00 < X < .50			
.25 < X < .50			
.10 < X < .90			
.60 < X < .70			
.75 < X < 1.00			

a. Are the linear and uniform distribution MONTE CARLO probabilities the
    same?

        YES _____ NO _____

b. Are the linear and uniform TRUE P values the same?

        YES _____ NO _____

c. Why are the linear and uniform TRUE P values different?

        _____
        _____
        _____

TRUE OR FALSE QUESTIONS

T   F   a.   Monte Carlo techniques yield exact probabilities.

T   F   b.   If X is a continuous random variable, the probability
                        that X equals a specific value is 0.

T   F   c.   The probability that X is in the interval (0,1) is
                        different for the uniform and the exponential distributions.

T   F   d.   The probability that X is in the interval (.2, .4) is
                        different for the uniform and the exponential distribution.

T   F   e.   If a density is defined for X within (0,1), then P (0< X < .5) is
                        .50 because the length of the interval (.50) is half of the length
                        between (0,1).

T   F   f.   If N indicates the number of random points out of
                        1,000 that fall below the curve, H the density (height), and
                        (A - B) the specified interval for X, then the probability area
                        under the curve in the rectangle is: N*H*(A –B)/1,000.

CHAPTER 19

NORMAL DISTRIBUTION

CHAPTER OBJECTIVES

- To understand characteristics of the normal distribution.
- To graph the normal probability distribution.
- To compare the Monte Carlo estimates of normal probabilities with the theoretical probabilities.
- To understand the origin of the normal bell-shaped curve.
- To determine the approximate probability area in certain intervals in the normal distribution.

In the seventeenth and eighteenth centuries, two mathematicians were asked by gamblers to help them improve their chances of winning at cards and dice. The two mathematicians, who first studied this area of probability, were James Bernoulli and Abraham DeMoivre. **James Bernoulli** developed the formula for combinations and permutations, and their binomial expansions, which lead to the binomial distribution discussed in Chapter 17. **Abraham DeMoivre** coined the phrase *law of errors* from observing events such as archery matches. The basic idea was that negative errors occurred about as often as positive errors. DeMoivre used this understanding to derive an equation for an *error curve*. DeMoivre in 1733 was credited with developing the mathematical equation for the *normal curve*. In the nineteenth century, **Carl Fredrick Gauss** (1777-1855), working in the field of astronomy further developed the concept of a mathematical bell-shaped curve and probability. Today, his picture and mathematical equation for the normal curve appear on the zehn deutsche mark currency of Germany.

The normal distribution or normal curve is a mathematical equation for random chance errors. The frequency distribution of many continuous random variables used in research closely approximates the normal distribution. Consequently, the normal distribution is a useful mathematical model in which to study variable relationships in the physical and social sciences.

The mathematical equation for the normal distribution indicates a normal density that is an exponential function of a quadratic form. The normal curve equation defines an infinite number of curves, depending upon the values of the mean and standard deviation. The **normal curve** equation is defined as:

$$Y = \frac{1}{\sigma\sqrt{2\pi}} e^{-(x-\mu)^2/2\sigma^2}$$

where: Y = height of the curve at a given score
X = score at a given height
μ = mean of the X variable
σ = standard deviation of X variable
π = constant equal to 3.1416 (pi)
e = constant equal to 2.7183 (base of natural logarithm)

When a set of X scores are transformed to have a mean of zero (0) and a standard deviation of one (1), which are called standard scores or z scores, the mathematical equation is reduced to:

$$Y = \frac{1}{\sqrt{2\pi}} e^{-z^2/2}$$

This equation using standard scores is referred to as the *standard normal curve* with z score values that range primarily from − 3 to + 3 and correspond to the ordinates of Y (density or height of the curve). A **z score** is calculated as: (X - mean) / standard deviation (also reported in Chapter 17 for dichotomous data). The tabled values indicate the z score values between − 3 and + 3 corresponding to each y ordinate value. A graph of these values yields a normal distribution or bell-shaped curve.

Table of z score and y ordinate values.

z score	y ordinates
- 3.0	.004
- 2.5	.018
- 2.0	.054
- 1.5	.130
- 1.0	.242
- 0.5	.352
0.0	.399
+0.5	.352
+1.0	.242
+1.5	.130
+2.0	.054
+2.5	.018
+3.0	.004

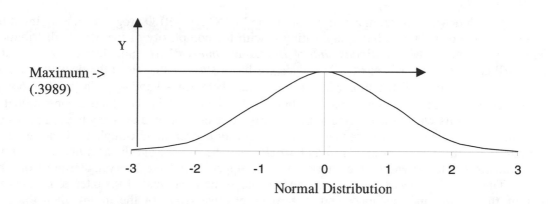

Maximum ->
(.3989)

Normal Distribution

The standard normal distribution has a mean of 0, and a standard deviation of 1. The standard normal distribution is bell-shaped and symmetrical. The probability area under the standard normal curve is 1.0 corresponding to 100% of the area under the curve. The density function is reasonably complex enough that the usual method of finding the probability area between two specified values requires using integral calculus to calculate the probabilities. The standard normal table of z values in the appendix of textbooks has been derived by this method of integral calculus. It is not necessary, however, to use calculus to derive the exact probabilities if estimates using the Monte Carlo technique are closely approximated with little error.

In this chapter, the NORMAL program is run to observe the Monte Carlo approximations of the standard normal probabilities. Initial values are set for 1,000 random numbers between the z score intervals 0 and 3 to correspond to +/- 3 standard deviations around the mean. The *DensityHeight* is fixed at .3989 corresponding to the normal distribution. The normal curve height is calculated as 1/SQRT (2*3.1416)= 0.3989. Changing the *IntervalMax* value to 4 can change the NORMAL program to modify the range of z score values to correspond to +/- 4 standard deviations around the mean.

SUMMARY

In this chapter, you should learn that:

- The normal distribution is an exponential function.
- The normal distribution is a symmetrical curve, with inflection points at −1 and 1.
- The bell-shaped curve approaches but never touches the X-axis.
- The normal distribution has an infinite number of different curves based upon the values of the mean and standard deviation.
- The normal distribution using z scores is called the standard normal curve.
- The probabilities of the bell-shaped curve are based on the normal distribution.
- Standard normal probabilities can be estimated by the Monte Carlo technique.

How the NORMAL program works

The NORMAL program is a variation of the MONTE CARLO program, simplifying it by using only one distribution, but complicating it with the complexity of the normal distribution density function. The *NumPoints*, *IntervalMin*, and *IntervalMax* variables, as well as the *IntervalWidth*, remain unchanged. *DensityHeight* has a single value since the density function corresponds to a single distribution with z score values between − 3 and + 3. The random points are selected in exactly the same manner, but the formula used in the Boolean operation for determining points within the distribution is slightly more complicated than any used in previous programs. The calculation for the theoretical probability is even more complicated and requires creating two extra variables, *MinProb* and *MaxProb*. These represent the area under the curve for values at the lower end of the interval and the upper end of the interval, starting from the mean. These two extra variables are needed because if the lower end of the interval is negative (left of the mean) and the upper end is zero or positive (right of the mean), then the two probabilities are added together to get the total probability. If both are positive then the lower is subtracted from the upper to leave only the area between the two. If both are negative, then the upper (which would be the smaller absolute difference from the mean) is subtracted from the lower. If you graph the probability area between two points under the normal curve on paper, the calculations become clearer.

The Monte Carlo approximation in the NORMAL program is carried out in the same manner as in Chapter 18. Specify an interval (A <--> B) and determine the probability, P (A < Z < B). Each approximation is made on the basis of 1,000 random points with an interval A <--> B corresponding to +/− 3 and a maximum height of 0.3989. The theoretical probabilities are computed and printed. In order to avoid entering a standard normal probability table into the program, an approximation is used. It was given by **Stephen E. Derenzo** in "Approximations for Hand Calculators using Small Integer Coefficients," *Mathematics of Computation*, *31*, 1977, pp. 214-225. For A ≥ 0, the approximation is:

$$P (Z < A) = 1 - \frac{1}{2} \exp \left[\frac{- ((83A + 351)A + 562)A}{703 + 165A} \right]$$

in which 1/2 exp [x] means 1/2 e^{x}. This approximation has an error of no more than 0.001 for sample sizes of 10,000 or more.

NORMAL Program Output

Given the following values:

```
                    NumPoints <- 1000
                    IntervalMin <- 0
                    IntervalMax <- 3
```

Interval	Monte Carlo	True P	Error
0< Z <3	0.528	0.499	0.029

CHAPTER 19 EXERCISES

1. Run the NORMAL program and complete the following table (NumPoints <- 1000).
    Draw small graphs in the last column and shade the area that represents the probability.

Z INTERVAL	MONTE CARLO APPROXIMATIONS	THEORETICAL TRUE PROBABILITY	GRAPH
0< Z < 1			
-1< Z < 1			
0< Z < 2			
-2< Z < 2			
0< Z < 3			
-3< Z < 3			
1.54< Z < 2.67			
-0.45< Z < 1.15			

2.   Run the NORMAL program again with `NumPoints <- 10000` for the Z intervals.

Z INTERVAL	MONTE CARLO APPROXIMATIONS	THEORETICAL TRUE PROBABILITY	GRAPH
$0 < Z < 1$			
$-1 < Z < 1$			
$0 < Z < 2$			
$-2 < Z < 2$			
$0 < Z < 3$			
$-3 < Z < 3$			
$1.54 < Z < 2.67$			
$-0.45 < Z < 1.15$			

a.   Does `NumPoints <- 1000` or `NumPoints <- 10000` give better approximations?

_____

b.   In general will larger sample sizes more closely approximate the normal distribution?

YES _____   NO _____

3.   Compare the IntervalWidth (- 3 < Z < +3) and DensityHeight of .3989 to the
      IntervalWidth (-4 < Z < +4) and DensityHeight of .3989 in the NORMAL program.

Z INTERVAL	MONTE CARLO APPROXIMATIONS	THEORETICAL TRUE PROBABILITY	DENSITY HEIGHT
-3< Z < +3			.3989
-4< Z < +4			.3989

a. Will the approximations be different?
     YES _____   NO _____
b. Will the approximations become more similar as sample size increases?
     YES _____   NO _____

TRUE OR FALSE QUESTIONS

T   F   a. The standard normal distribution is a skewed distribution.

T   F   b. The value of the standard normal density Y at point Z is the
                   probability that the random variable has a value equal to Z.

T   F   c. The standard normal distribution has a mean of 0, and standard deviation of 1.

T   F   d. The probability area under the normal curve can be approximated in
                   the interval − 4 to + 4.

T   F   e. The Monte Carlo approximations of the standard normal probabilities
                   are close to the integral calculus exact theoretical probabilities.

T   F   f. As sample size increases, the probabilities more closely approximate a
                   standard normal distribution.

CHAPTER 20

t Distribution

CHAPTER OBJECTIVES

- To understand the origin and purpose of the t distribution.
- To contrast the t distribution with the standard normal distribution.
- To compare t values with z values for samples of the same size.
- To determine whether the population mean and variance have an effect on the t distribution.
- To observe the shape of the t distribution for increasing sample size.

The early history of statistics involved probability and inference using large samples and the normal distribution. The standard normal curve provided a probability distribution that was bell-shaped for large samples, but was peaked for small samples, which resulted in larger probability areas in the tails of the distribution. At the turn of the century, a chemist named **William S. Gossett**, who was employed at a brewery in Dublin, Ireland, discovered the inadequacy of the normal curve for small samples. Gossett was concerned with the quality control of the brewing process and took small samples to test the beer, but didn't obtain a normal bell-shaped curve when his results were graphed.

William Gossett empirically established sampling distributions for smaller samples of various sizes using body measurements of 3,000 British criminals. He started with an approximate normal distribution, drew large samples and small samples, to compare the resulting sampling distributions. He quickly discovered that probability distributions for small samples differed markedly from the normal distribution. William Gossett wrote a mathematical expression for these small sample distributions, and in 1908 he published the results under the pen name, "Student." The Student's t distribution was a major breakthrough in the field of statistics.

The standard normal distribution is bell-shaped, symmetrical, and has a mean of zero and standard deviation of one. The **t distribution** is uni-modal, symmetrical, and has a mean of zero, but not a standard deviation of one. The standard deviation of the t distribution varies, so when small sample sizes are drawn at random and graphed, the t distribution is more peaked (leptokurtic). The probability areas in the tails of the t distribution are consequently higher than those found in the standard normal distribution. For example, the probability area = .046 in the standard normal distribution at two standard deviations from the mean, but the probability area = .140 in the t distribution at two standard deviations for a sample size of four. This indicates a greater probability of making an error using smaller samples. As sample sizes become larger, the t distribution and standard normal distribution take on the same bell-shaped curve. In fact, the t values and the z-score values become identical around sample sizes of 10,000, which is within .001 error of approximation as indicated in the previous chapter. Researchers today often use the t distribution for both small sample and large sample estimation because it becomes identical to the normal distribution as sample size increases.

140

In many disciplines, such as education, psychology, and business, variable values are normally distributed. Achievement tests, psychological tests, the height or weight of individuals, and the time to complete a task are examples of variables commonly used in these disciplines. In many instances, the population mean and standard deviation for these variables are not known, but rather estimated from sample data. This forms the basis for making an inference about the population parameters (e.g., mean and standard deviation) from the sample statistics (sample mean and standard deviation). Given small random samples, the t distribution would better estimate the probability under the frequency distribution curve. Given large random samples, both the standard normal distribution and t distribution would both yield similar probabilities under the frequency distribution curve.

If the population standard deviation is known, the z score can be computed as:

$$z = \frac{\overline{X} - \mu}{\sigma / \sqrt{n}}$$

Otherwise, the sample standard deviation is used to compute a t value:

$$t = \frac{\overline{X} - \mu}{S / \sqrt{n}}$$

The sample standard deviation, S, as an estimate of the population standard deviation, σ, is typically in error, thus the sample means are not distributed as a standard normal distribution, but rather a t distribution. When sample sizes are larger, the sample standard deviation estimate becomes similar to the population standard deviation. Therefore, the shape of the t distribution is similar to the standard normal distribution. This points out why the estimate of the population standard deviation is critical in the field of statistics. A researchers can estimate the unknown population standard deviation by one of the following methods:

1) use test publisher norms when available (μ, σ)
2) take an average value from several research studies using the same variable
3) take large samples of data for better representation
4) divide the range of sample data by six (see Chapter 9).

In this chapter, you will be able to observe the shape of the t distribution. You will be able to specify the particular normal distribution to be sampled, and specify the sample size. The program will select a random sample of that size; compute the sample mean and sample standard deviation, and then the z and t statistics. This process will be repeated 250 times. The resulting 250 z and t statistics, which arise from these simulations, will be tabulated and printed in frequency tables. By comparing the frequency tables, you will be able to observe the higher probability in the heavier tails of the t distribution. By varying the sample size, you will be able to observe how the shape of the t distribution changes as the sample size increases.

SUMMARY

In this chapter, you should learn that:

- The t distribution is symmetrical, unimodal, and has a mean of zero.
- The t distribution has a greater probability area in its tails than the standard normal distribution due to sample estimation of the population standard deviation.
- The shape of the t distribution is not affected by the mean and variance of the population from which random sampling occurs.
- As the sample size increases, the t distribution becomes similar to the standard normal distribution.

How the t distribution program works

The t distribution program uses a few new functions and keywords, but most of the code has been used in previous S-PLUS programs. The program first defines four variables for the population mean, population standard deviation, sample size, and number of replications (number of samples). The *zData* and *tData* objects are set to **NULL** to build vectors of values. The replication loop then begins and takes a random sample of data from a normally distributed population with a mean of *popMean* and a standard deviation of *popStdDev*. These data are transformed into a z statistic, entered into the *zData* object, and transformed into a t statistic, and entered into the *tData* object. The calculation of z is performed using a formula, but the *t* statistic is obtained using the built-in S-PLUS function **t.test**. The **mu** keyword identifies the population mean and the **$statistic** after the **t.test** function indicates that the program should only extract the t value from the normal output of the **t.test** function.

When the replication loop ends, a sequence of numbers in the range of values for a standardized normal distribution (−4 to +4) is created with intervals of 0.5. The next line creates labels describing the beginning and ending of each interval in the preceding sequence by using the **paste** command. The whole numbers are expanded to include one decimal place for clearer output by using the **format** function. The next two lines cut the *tData* and *zData* vectors, respectively, into the intervals defined by *normSeq*, then count the number of points in each interval and divide by the number of replications to obtain a relative frequency that falls within the interval. These relative frequencies are reported to three decimal places by the combined use of the **round** and **format** functions.

The final output objects are created and displayed. Three vectors are combined as separate columns using **cbind** and put into a matrix with a column for each. This matrix is then given dimension names using the **dimnames** function with blank row labels and column labels of "Interval", "Freq t", and "Freq z." Next, the maximum absolute value for the t distribution (*maxOutlier*) is obtained for scaling the histograms. The t distribution typically has the larger outliers, so both the z and t distribution histograms will be scaled using this value so that they can be easily compared. After obtaining the x-axis scaling, the two histograms are created with their respective distributions (bar breaks at 0.5 intervals ranging from the value −*maxOutlier* to

+*maxOutlier*), appropriate titles, y axes representing probabilities, and limits on the y axis of 0.6 for optimal scaling. The final line of the program prints out the matrix.

The t distribution program can be run several times with various sample sizes to see the effect on the normal (z) distribution and t distribution. You can try various values for the population mean and standard deviation while holding the sample size constant. After viewing these effects, you may want to modify the program by removing the output of the program using the # symbol (the histograms and output matrix) so that the program can be changed to summarize these differences. Leave the lines of code through the definition of *normSeq*, but comment out (#) or remove the lines for the interval labels and the **format** command for assignment in *tVector* and *zVector*. Subtract the *zVector* from the *tVector* and square it to obtain a squared error for each interval, then sum the squared errors. Now enclose the part of the code within a main processing loop that will iterate through a vector of sample sizes from 5 to 30 and obtain a sum of squared error for each sample size. Build a vector of these errors and output them alongside their respective sample sizes to view the effect of increasing sample size on the differences between the normal (z) and t distributions.

t distribution Program Output

Given the following values:

```
popMean <- 50
popStdDev <- 15
sampleSize <- 30
replicationSize <- 250
```

Interval	Freq t	Freq z
(-4.0,-3.5)	0.000	0.000
(-3.5,-3.0)	0.000	0.004
(-3.0,-2.5)	0.004	0.000
(-2.5,-2.0)	0.036	0.024
(-2.0,-1.5)	0.064	0.064
(-1.5,-1.0)	0.116	0.116
(-1.0,-0.5)	0.104	0.116
(-0.5, 0.0)	0.152	0.152
(0.0, 0.5)	0.172	0.172
(0.5, 1.0)	0.168	0.160
(1.0, 1.5)	0.096	0.100
(1.5, 2.0)	0.040	0.072
(2.0, 2.5)	0.036	0.016
(2.5, 3.0)	0.004	0.000
(3.0, 3.5)	0.008	0.004
(3.5, 4.0)	0.000	0.000

z Statistics

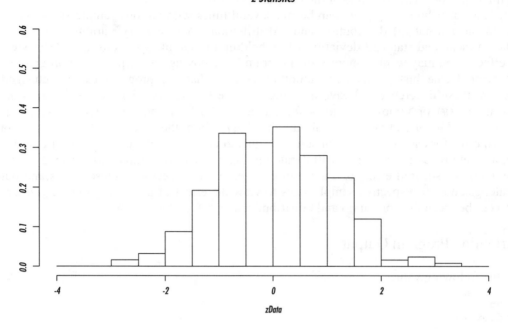

t Statistics

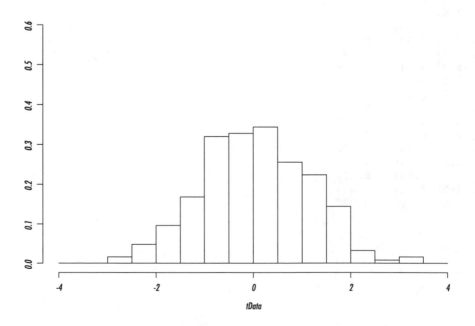

CHAPTER 20 EXERCISES

1. Run t distribution for population mean of 0 and a standard deviation of 1. Use a sample size of 5 and perform 1,000 replications (popMean <- 0, popStdDev <- 1, sampleSize <- 5, replicationSize <- 1000).   Record the results below.

INTERVAL	FREQ t	FREQ z
(-4.0, -3.5)	_____	_____
(-3.5, -3.0)	_____	_____
(-3.0, -2.5)	_____	_____
(-2.5, -2.0)	_____	_____
(-2.0, -1.5)	_____	_____
(-1.5, -1.0)	_____	_____
(-1.0, -0.5)	_____	_____
(-0.5, 0.0)	_____	_____
(0.0, 0.5)	_____	_____
(0.5, 1.0)	_____	_____
(1.0, 1.5)	_____	_____
(1.5, 2.0)	_____	_____
(2.0, 2.5)	_____	_____
(2.5, 3.0)	_____	_____
(3.0, 3.5)	_____	_____
(3.5, 4.0)	_____	_____

a. Does the t statistic distribution have higher frequencies in the tails of the distribution than the z statistic distribution?   YES _____ NO _____

b. Graph the z statistic distribution with a *solid line* and the t statistic distribution with a *dashed line*. Are the two distributions the same?   YES _____ NO _____

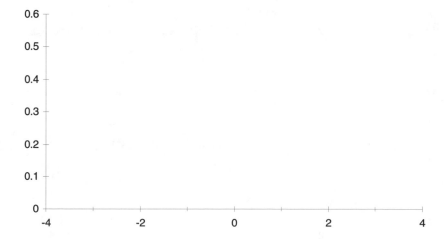

2. Run t distribution again for population mean of 0 and a standard deviation of 1. Use a sample size of 100 and perform 1,000 replications (popMean <- 0, popStdDev <- 1, sampleSize <- 100, replicationSize <- 1000). Record the results below.

INTERVAL	FREQ t	FREQ z
(-4.0, -3.5)	_____	_____
(-3.5, -3.0)	_____	_____
(-3.0, -2.5)	_____	_____
(-2.5, -2.0)	_____	_____
(-2.0, -1.5)	_____	_____
(-1.5, -1.0)	_____	_____
(-1.0, -0.5)	_____	_____
(-0.5, 0.0)	_____	_____
(0.0, 0.5)	_____	_____
(0.5, 1.0)	_____	_____
(1.0, 1.5)	_____	_____
(1.5, 2.0)	_____	_____
(2.0, 2.5)	_____	_____
(2.5, 3.0)	_____	_____
(3.0, 3.5)	_____	_____
(3.5, 4.0)	_____	_____

a. Does the t statistic distribution have higher frequencies in the tails of the distribution than the z statistic distribution?   YES _____ NO _____

b. Graph the z statistic distribution with a *solid line* and the t statistic distribution with a *dashed line*. Are the two distributions the same?   YES _____ NO _____

c. As sample size increased from n = 5 to n = 100, did the t statistic distribution more closely approximate a normal distribution?   YES _____ NO _____

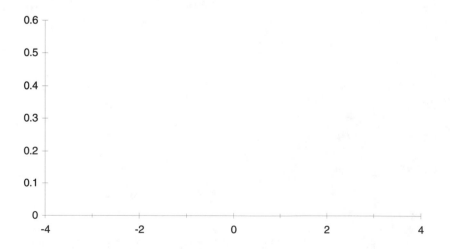

3. Run t distribution again for population mean of 0 and a standard deviation of 15. Use a sample size of 5 and perform 1,000 replications (popMean <- 0, popStdDev <- 15, sampleSize <- 5, replicationSize <- 1000). Record the results below.

INTERVAL	FREQ t	FREQ z
(-4.0, -3.5)	_____	_____
(-3.5, -3.0)	_____	_____
(-3.0, -2.5)	_____	_____
(-2.5, -2.0)	_____	_____
(-2.0, -1.5)	_____	_____
(-1.5, -1.0)	_____	_____
(-1.0, -0.5)	_____	_____
(-0.5, 0.0)	_____	_____
(0.0, 0.5)	_____	_____
(0.5, 1.0)	_____	_____
(1.0, 1.5)	_____	_____
(1.5, 2.0)	_____	_____
(2.0, 2.5)	_____	_____
(2.5, 3.0)	_____	_____
(3.0, 3.5)	_____	_____
(3.5, 4.0)	_____	_____

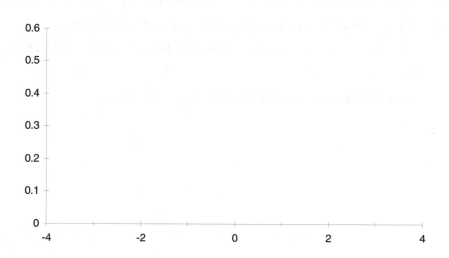

a. Does the t statistic distribution have higher frequencies in the tails of the
    distribution than the z statistic distribution?   YES _____ NO _____
b. Graph the z statistic distribution with a *solid line* and the t statistic distribution with a
    dashed line. Are the two distributions the same?   YES _____ NO _____
c. Is the t statistic distribution affected by the population standard deviation value?
                                                                     YES _____ NO _____
d. Is the t statistic distribution affected by the population mean value?
                                                                     YES _____ NO _____

TRUE OR FALSE QUESTIONS

T   F   a. The shape of the t distribution depends on the standard deviation of the
               population distribution.
T   F   b. The smaller the sample size, the larger the probability area in the tails of the
               t distribution.
T   F   c. The population mean value has *no* effect on the shape of the t distribution.
T   F   d. The t distribution is symmetrical, unimodal, and mean of zero.
T   F   e. For large sample sizes, the t distribution is the same as the standard normal
               distribution.
T   F   f. The z statistic distribution will always be normally distributed.

CHAPTER 21

CHI-SQUARE DISTRIBUTION

CHAPTER OBJECTIVES

- To know the origin of the chi-square distribution.
- To observe that the chi-square distribution is based on the normal distribution.
- To calculate a specific chi-square distribution based on the statistic $\chi^2 = (N - 1)S^2/\sigma$ (where S^2 is the sample variance of size N from a normal distribution with variance σ^2).
- To simulate and graph the chi-square distribution.
- To understand the effect of sample size on the shape of the chi-square distribution.
- To determine if the mean and variance of the normal distribution being sampled has any effect on the chi-square distribution.
- To compare the mode of the simulated chi-square distribution with the mode of the theoretical maximum.
- To compare the range of the simulated chi-square distribution with four times the standard deviation of the theoretical chi-square distribution.

In the previous chapters, the simulations included a large number of random samples of the same size from a normal distribution. We learned that with large sample sizes, t values and z values were similar, as were their frequency distributions. The **chi-square distribution**, like the t-distribution, is a function of sample size. There are an infinite number of chi-square curves based on sample size. In fact, as sample size increases, the chi-square distribution becomes symmetrical and bell-shaped (normal), but with a mean equal to the degrees of freedom (df) and mode equal to df − 2.

The degrees of freedom are related to sample size, because it takes on a value of N − 1. The degree of freedom concept relates to the number of values or parameters free to vary. If a set of five numbers are given, e.g., 5 4 3 2 1, and the sum of the numbers is known, i.e., $\Sigma X = 15$, then knowledge of four numbers implies that the fifth number is not free to vary. For example, four out of five numbers are 10, 15, 25, and 45 with $\Sigma X = 100$. Since the four numbers sum to 95, the fifth number must be 5 in order for the sum of the five numbers to equal 100. This same principle applies to a set of numbers and the mean.

Karl Pearson first derived the chi-square distribution as a frequency distribution of squared *z score* values. The chi-square statistic was computed as:

$$\chi^2 = \sum \left(\frac{X_i - M}{\sigma} \right)^2$$

with df = N − 1. A **z score** was calculated as z = [(X − Mean) / Standard deviation]; where X = a raw score, M = the sample mean, and σ = population standard deviation. The *z score* transformed a raw score into a standard score based on standard deviation units. The population standard deviation (σ) is indicated in the formula, but as noted in earlier chapters, a sample standard deviation estimate was generally used because the population value was not typically known.

Chi-square is related to the variance of a sample. If we squared both the numerator and denominator in the previous formula, we would get:

$$\chi^2 = \frac{\Sigma(X - M)^2 / N - 1}{\sigma^2}$$

The numerator of the formula can be expressed as sample variance because $\Sigma(X - M)^2$ represents the sum of squared deviations, denoted as SS, so the sample variance in the numerator can be written as: $S^2 = SS / N - 1$. With a little math, SS = (N − 1) S^2. Consequently, if samples of size N with variances, S_2, are computed from a normal distribution with variance of σ_2, the χ^2 statistic could be written as:

$$\chi^2 = \frac{(N - 1)S^2}{\sigma^2}$$

with N−1 degrees of freedom.   The chi-square statistic is therefore useful in testing whether a sample variance differs significantly from a population variance because it forms a ratio of sample variance to population variance. Since the chi-square distribution reflects this ratio of variances, all chi-square values are positive and range continuously from zero to positive infinity.

In this chapter, the CHISQUARE program can produce an unlimited number of chi-square distributions, one for each degree of freedom. For small degrees of freedom, the chi-square distribution should be skewed right. As the degrees of freedom increases, i.e., sample size increases, the mode of the chi-square distribution moves to the right. The chi-square values should be positive and range continuously from zero to positive infinity.   The CHISQUARE program permits selection of different sample sizes from a normal distribution. The program will initially select 250 samples of the desired size. Each time, the sample variance and the chi-square statistic will be calculated.   The 250 sample results will simulate the theoretical chi-square distribution. The chi-square statistics will be recorded in a relative frequency table. The table and a histogram will be printed. Since you can vary the underlying normal distribution and the sample size, you will have an opportunity to observe the effect, if any, of these changes on the chi-square distribution.

SUMMARY

In this chapter, you should learn that:

- The chi-square statistic, $\chi^2 = (N - 1)\ S^2\ /\ \sigma^2$, computed by taking random samples from a normal population, produces a different chi-square distribution for each degree of freedom $(N - 1)$.
- The chi-square distribution has a mean equal to the degrees of freedom (df) and a mode equal to df $- 2$.
- The chi-square distribution becomes symmetrical and bell-shaped as sample size increases.
- The variance of the chi-square distribution is two times the degree of freedom $(2 * df)$.

How the CHISQUARE program works

The CHISQUARE program uses most of the program code from the last chapter. No new functions or techniques are introduced. The same variables are initialized and the main processing loop run, however, the chi-square statistic is calculated for each sample instead of the t and z. The *normSeq* vector is the same, but the range of the chi-square values is calculated and placed into the *dataRange* variable. Since the same sequence is used, the same labels associated with that sequence are used. The *cVector* is formed in much the same way, except the **format** function isn't used, so numbers are not changed to characters. Instead, the **format** function is used directly within the assignment of *cVector* for the output matrix. Since there are only two columns in the output matrix, the *outputVector* is removed. The dimension names are simply assigned for the two columns in the output matrix.

The next part of the program determines which group contains the greatest number of values. This is known as the modal class or mode. The **max** function isn't used because it returns the highest value instead of which group had the highest value. The loop and the **if** statement are relatively straightforward to understand. The value *i* iterates from 1 to the number of elements in *cVector*. For every iteration, *i*, the value in *cVector* is compared to the previous high value, so that when the loop finishes, the group number with the highest value is assigned to the *highGroup* variable. A **barplot** is used to graphically display the relative frequencies within each group. The group interval and frequency, along with the title and scaling, are set to the default for the Y-axis and scaled from 1 to 20 on the X-axis, so extra attention should be paid when comparing graphs from different runs. Finally, the output matrix is printed along with the modal group and the range of the chi-square values. Run the CHISQUARE program for various sample sizes between 1 and 30. Compare the tables and the graphs, along with the modal group and the range of the chi-square values. It will be helpful to print out the graphs for different sample sizes to compare them, since they will disappear each time you run the program.

CHISQUARE Program Output

Given the following values:

```
Interval     Rel Freq
```

```
popMean <- 0
popStdDev <- 1
sampleSize <- 6
replicationSize <- 250
```

```
( 0.0, 1.0)  0.060
( 1.0, 2.0)  0.104
( 2.0, 3.0)  0.152
( 3.0, 4.0)  0.160
( 4.0, 5.0)  0.120
( 5.0, 6.0)  0.100
( 6.0, 7.0)  0.080
( 7.0, 8.0)  0.080
( 8.0, 9.0)  0.036
( 9.0,10.0)  0.040
(10.0,11.0)  0.012
(11.0,12.0)  0.028
(12.0,13.0)  0.004
(13.0,14.0)  0.008
(14.0,15.0)  0.000
(15.0,16.0)  0.004
(16.0,17.0)  0.004
(17.0,18.0)  0.004
(18.0,19.0)  0.004
(19.0,20.0)  0.000
```

```
Modal Group = 4      Range of chi-square values = 18.6
```

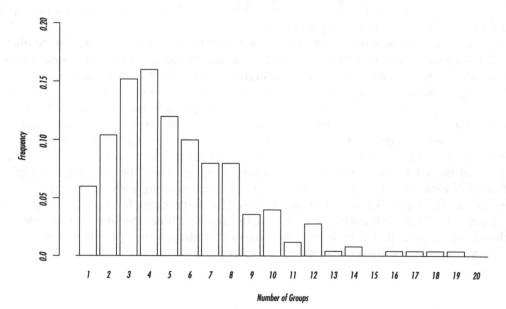

Histogram of Chi-square Values

CHAPTER 21 EXERCISES

1. Run the CHISQUARE program for each sample size and degrees of freedom listed below; use a population mean of 0, standard deviation of 1, and 250 replications. Graph the shape of the distributions and list the modal group. The modal group is the group with the highest relative frequency.

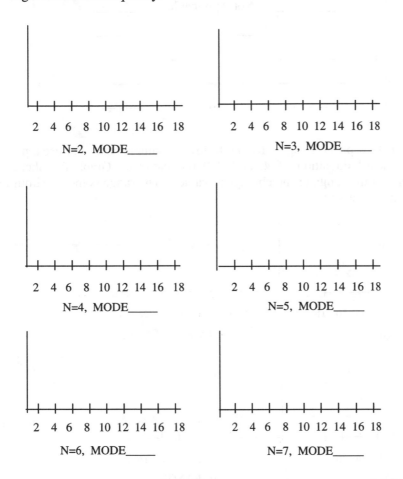

2   4   6   8   10 12 14 16   18

N=2, MODE_____

2   4   6   8   10 12 14 16 18

N=3, MODE_____

2   4   6   8   10 12 14 16   18

N=4, MODE_____

2   4   6   8   10 12 14 16 18

N=5, MODE_____

2   4   6   8   10 12 14 16   18

N=6, MODE_____

2   4   6   8   10 12 14 16 18

N=7, MODE_____

a. Does the shape of the chi-square distribution change as sample size increases?

YES _____ NO _____

b.   List the modal group values from the graphs in the table. The mode of the theoretical chi-square distribution is (DF – 2) when DF > 2. List the theoretical chi-square mode for each sample size. (ERROR = MODAL GROUP - TRUE MODE).

N	DF	MODAL GROUP	TRUE MODE	ERROR
2	1	_____	Not Applicable	_____
3	2	_____	Not Applicable	_____
4	3	_____	_____	_____
5	4	_____	_____	_____
6	5	_____	_____	_____
7	6	_____	_____	_____

2.   Run the CHISQUARE program again for the following sample sizes, but use a population mean of 10, standard deviation of 4, and 250 replications. Graph the shape of the distributions and list the range of the chi-square values. The range is the maximum minus the minimum chi-square value.

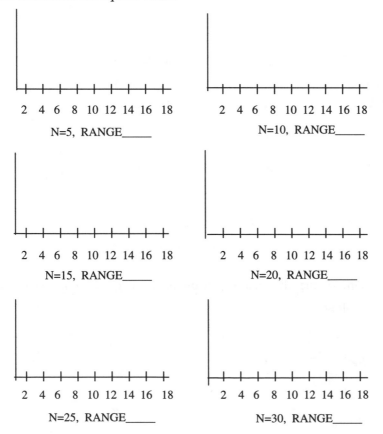

2 4 6 8 10 12 14 16 18	2 4 6 8 10 12 14 16 18
N=5, RANGE_____	N=10, RANGE_____
2 4 6 8 10 12 14 16 18	2 4 6 8 10 12 14 16 18
N=15, RANGE_____	N=20, RANGE_____
2 4 6 8 10 12 14 16 18	2 4 6 8 10 12 14 16 18
N=25, RANGE_____	N=30, RANGE_____

a. Compare these graphs with those in Exercise 1. What differences do you see?

_____

_____

b. The variance of the theoretical chi-square distribution is two times the degrees of freedom
    (2 * df). List the theoretical chi-square variance and standard deviation. Divide the range
    of the chi-square values by four (Range / 4) to approximate the standard deviation of the
    simulated chi-square distribution.

N	σ^2	σ	RANGE / 4	ERROR
5	_____	_____	_____	_____
10	_____	_____	_____	_____
15	_____	_____	_____	_____
20	_____	_____	_____	_____
25	_____	_____	_____	_____
30	_____	_____	_____	_____

c. Does the theoretical standard deviation compare to the estimated standard deviation?
    YES _____ NO _____

TRUE OR FALSE QUESTIONS

T   F   a.   The chi-square distribution is independent of the mean and variance of the
                   normal distribution.

T   F   b.   As the degrees of freedom increases, the variance of the chi-square
                   distribution decreases.

T   F   c.   The location of the mode in a chi-square distribution moves to the left as
                   sample size increases.

T   F   d.   For small degrees of freedom, the chi-square distribution is skewed right.

T   F   e.   Some chi-square values are negative.

CHAPTER 22

F DISTRIBUTION

CHAPTER OBJECTIVES

- To understand the origin of the F distribution.
- To understand the relationship between the normal, t, chi-square, and F distributions.
- To calculate an F ratio of differences between variances from two independent samples.
- To calculate an F ratio of differences between variances of several independent samples.
- To simulate and graph the sampling distribution of the F ratio for different numerator and denominator degrees of freedom.
- To understand the effect of sample size on the shape of the F distribution.

Sir Ronald Fisher was interested in extending our knowledge of testing mean differences to an analysis of the variability of scores, i.e., variance. He was specifically interested in comparing the variance of two random samples of data. For example, if a random sample of data was drawn from one population and a second random sample of data was drawn from a second population, then the two sample variances could be compared by computing an **F ratio**: $F = S^2_1 / S^2_2$. The F ratio is equal to one if the variances of the two random samples are the same. The F-distribution in the appendix reveals this for F values with df = ∞, ∞ in the numerator and denominator. The F ratio could be less than one, depending upon which sample variances were in the numerator and denominator, but F values less than one are not considered, so we always place the larger sample variance in the numerator.

If several random samples of data were drawn from each population and the F ratio computed on the variances for each pair of samples, a sampling distribution of the F's would create the F distribution. Sir Ronald Fisher determined that like the t distribution and chi-square distribution, the F distribution was a function of sample size; specifically the sizes of the two random samples. Consequently, a family of F curves can be formed based on the degrees of freedom in the numerator and denominator. An **F curve** is positively skewed with F ratio values ranging from zero to infinity (∞). If the degrees of freedom for both samples are large, then the F distribution approaches symmetry (bell-shaped).

Example F curves for certain degree of freedom pairs can be illustrated as:

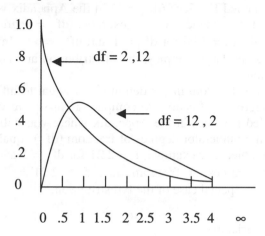

F values

Because there are two degrees of freedom associated with an F ratio, F tables were constructed to list the F values expected by chance with the degrees of freedom for the numerator across the top (column values) and the degrees of freedom for the denominator along the side (row values). The corresponding intersection of a column and row degrees of freedom would indicate the tabled F value. If the computed F value is greater than the tabled F value, we conclude that the two sample variances are statistically different at a specified level of probability, e.g., .05 level of significance.

Relationship of F distribution to t distribution and Chi-square distribution

In previous chapters, sampling distributions of statistics were graphed based on various sample sizes. We learned that with large sample sizes, t values and z values were similar, as were their sampling distributions (frequency distributions). Like the t distribution, the chi-square distribution was also a function of sample size. In fact, as sample size increased, the t, z, and chi-square sampling distributions became symmetrical and bell-shaped (normal). The sampling distributions of the F ratio operate similar to the t, z, and chi-square family of curves based on sample size.

The t distribution with degrees of freedom equal to infinity is the normal distribution. Consequently, t values become equal to z values when sample sizes are large (n > 10,000 to infinity). Check this by referring to the last row of the tabled t values in the Appendix where you will find that the t values are the same as the z values in the normal distribution table. For example, $t = 1.96$ is equal to $z = 1.96$ at the .05 level of significance. The normal distribution can be considered a special case of the t distribution because as sample size increases the shape of the t distribution becomes the same as the normal distribution, i.e., t values = z values.

The **F distribution**, with *one* degree of freedom in the numerator and the same degree of freedom in the denominator as the t-test, is equal to the square of the t distribution value. To check this, refer to the first column of the tabled F values (df $_1$ = 1) in the Appendix where you will find that the F values are the square of the t values in the t-test table (df $_2$ = degrees of freedom for t-test). For example, if F = 3.84, then t = 1.96 for df $_1$ = 1 and df $_2$ = ∞. In fact, since t ^{2} = z ^{2} = F for one degree of freedom given large samples, the t distribution and normal distribution are special cases of the F-distribution.

The F distribution values, with degrees of freedom in the denominator equal to infinity, can be multiplied by the F value numerator degrees of freedom to compute a chi-square value. To check this, refer to the last row of the tabled F values in the Appendix where you will find that the F values multiplied by the corresponding numerator degrees of freedom (df $_1$) equals the chi-square value in the chi-square distribution table. For example, F = 2.21 for df $_1$ = 5 and df $_2$ = ∞, therefore, chi-square = 11.05 with 5 degrees of freedom, i.e., 5 * 2.21 = 11.05! Consequently, the chi-square distribution is also a special case of the F distribution.

Test of Difference Between Two Independent Variances

The sampling distribution of the F ratio of two variances cannot be approximated by the normal, t, or chi-square sampling distributions because sample sizes seldom approach infinity, and unlike the normal and t distributions, F sampling distributions range from zero to infinity rather than from negative infinity to positive infinity. Consequently, the F distribution, named after Sir Ronald A. Fisher, is used to test whether two independent sample variances are the same or different.

If the variances from two randomly drawn samples are equal, then the F ratio equals one (largest sample variance over the smallest sample variance), otherwise it increases positively to infinity. The ratio of the two sample variances is expressed as $F = S^2_1 / S^2_2$, with a numerator and denominator degrees of freedom. For example, the distance *twenty suburban* housewives traveled to the grocery store varied by 2 miles and the distance *ten rural* housewives traveled to the grocery store varied by 10 miles. We want to test if the suburban and rural mileage variance is equal: F = 10 / 2 = 5.0 with df $_1$ = 9 and df $_2$ = 19 (Note: degrees of freedom are one less than the respective sample sizes). We compare this computed F ratio to the tabled F value in the Appendix for a given level of significance, e.g., .01 level of significance. We find the 9 degrees of freedom (df $_1$) across the top of the F table and the 19 degrees of freedom (df $_2$) along the side of the table. The intersection of the column and row indicates an F value equal to 3.52. Since F = 5.0 is greater than tabled F = 3.52, we conclude that the *rural* housewives vary more in their mileage to the grocery store than *suburban* housewives. Another way of saying this is that the sample variances are not homogeneous (equal) across the two groups.

Since we conducted this test for only the larger variance in the numerator of the F ratio, we must make a correction to the level of significance. This is accomplished for any tabled F value by simply doubling the level of significance, e.g., .01 to .02 level of significance. Therefore, F = 5.0 is statistically different from the tabled F = 3.52 at the .02 level of significance (even though we looked up the F value in the .01 level of significance table).

Test of Difference Between Several Independent Variances

      H.O. Hartley extended the F ratio test to the situation in which three or more sample variances were present, which was aptly named the **Hartley F-max test**. A separate F-max distribution table was therefore created (see Appendix). The Hartley F-max test is limited to using equal sample sizes and sample data randomly drawn from a normal population. However, **Henry Winkler** in 1967 at Ohio University compared the Hartley F-max, Bartlett, Cochran, and Levene's tests for equal variances in his master's thesis and concluded that the Hartley F-max test was the most robust (best choice) when sample sizes were equal.

      Extending our previous example, the distance *twenty-one suburban* housewives traveled to the grocery store varied by 2 miles, the distance *twenty-one rural* housewives traveled to the grocery store varied by 10 miles, and the distance *twenty-one urban* housewives traveled to the grocery store varied by 5 miles. The Hartley F-max test is computed for the following example as follows:

Step 1: Calculate the sample variances

Urban	$S^2 = 5$
Suburban	$S^2 = 2$
Rural	$S^2 = 10$

Step 2: Calculate F-max test by placing largest variance over smallest variance

    F-max = 10 / 2 = 5.0

Step 3. Determine the two separate degrees of freedom for the F-max Table

    k = number of sample variances (column values in table)
    k = 3
    df = sample size - 1 (row values in the table)
    df = 21 - 1 = 20

Step 4. Compare computed F-max to tabled F-max values

    F-max = 5.0 is greater than tabled F-max = 2.95 for 3 and 20 degrees of
    freedom at the .05 level of significance. We conclude that the sample
    variances are *not* homogeneous (not the same) across the three groups.

SUMMARY

In this chapter, you should learn that:

- The F distribution is a family of curves based upon sample size.
- The normal (z), t, and chi-square distributions are special cases of the F distribution.
- The F ratio can test whether two independent sample variances are homogeneous.
- The F-max can test whether three or more independent sample variances are homogeneous.
- The F distribution is positively skewed for different numerator and denominator degrees of freedom.
- As sample sizes increase, the shape of the F distribution becomes symmetrical.

How the F DISTRIBUTION program works

The first program, **F Curve** (chap22a.ssc), is a very short and simple program that prints simulated F distributions for given degrees of freedom. It begins by defining the degrees of freedom for the numerator (df1) and denominator (df2) of a F ratio. Next, the number of replications for the simulation is defined and the random F values for that number of replications is taken from an F distribution with the given degrees of freedom. Once the values are saved, the mean is calculated and three standard deviations above the mean (plotTop) is used as the cutoff point for the histogram that is generated. Bars are drawn every 0.1 spaces along the F value scale to give a reasonable histogram representation of the F curve.

The **F Curve** program could be modified by changing the df1 and df2 variables to vectors of matching length with various combinations for the numerator and denominator degrees of freedom. Then an iteration around all of the code after the definition of the number of replications could be written and a histogram created for each pair of degrees of freedom

The second program, **F Ratio** (chap22b.ssc), is longer than the F Curves program, but not more complicated. The group sizes and variances of two groups, as well as, the alpha level for the significance test are defined to begin the program. Next the F ratio is calculated and placed into a display string along with a representation of the actual ratio as a fraction. Then the critical F is determined using the **qf** function, based on the alpha level and degrees of freedom. If the F ratio is greater than the critical F then the decision is set to "reject," otherwise it stays at "accept." Finally, the display string for the F ratio, the critical F value, and the decision are placed into a matrix, labels are applied, and the matrix is displayed.

The F Ratio program can be modified to create vectors of sample size and variance values with a summary table of all of the values and decisions. The summary table should include the sample sizes and variances used for each F ratio, critical F, and decision.

F Curve Program Output

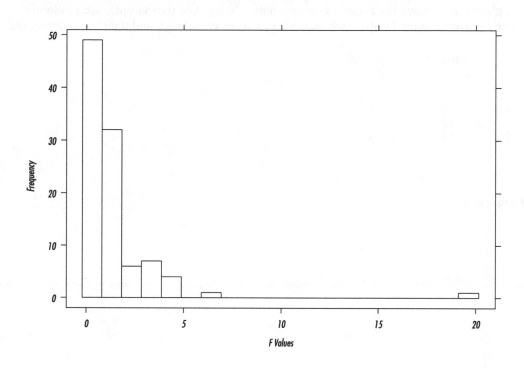

F-Curve with $df_1 = 2$ and $df_2 = 9$

F Ratio Program Output

Given the following values:

```
sampSize1 <- 20
variance1 <- 10
sampSize2 <- 20
variance2 <- 10
alpha <- .01
```

```
|F ratio        |Tabled F       |Decision       |
+---------------+---------------+---------------+
|10/10 = 1      |3.03           |accept         |
+---------------+---------------+---------------+
```

CHAPTER 22 EXERCISES

1.   Run the **F Curve** program for each pair of degrees of freedom listed below based on 100 replications. Graph the F-curves on the chart. Note: The two samples are randomly drawn from a normal population, sample variances calculated, and the F-ratio computed.

	Sample 1 df_1	Sample 2 df_2
Run 1:	5	15
Run 2:	15	15
Run 3	15	5

Frequency

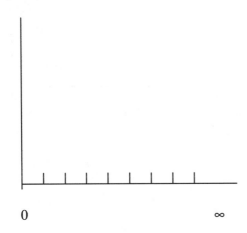

0   ∞

F values

a.   Does the shape of the F curve change based on the numerator and denominator degrees of freedom?   YES _____   NO _____

b.   Are the F values always positive?   YES _____   NO _____

c.   Why are some of the F values below 1.0?

_____

_____

2.   Run the **F Ratio** program for the following pairs of sample variances listed below.
      List the F ratio, Tabled F value, and Decision at the .01 level of significance.
      The *Decision* indicates whether the sample variances are homogeneous.

	Sample 1	Sample 2	F-ratio	Tabled F	Decision
Run1	$n = 20$ $S^2 = 10$	$n = 20$ $S^2 = 10$	_____	_____	_____
Run2	$n = 20$ $S^2 = 10$	$n = 20$ $S^2 = 100$	_____	_____	_____
Run3	$n = 40$ $S^2 = 100$	$n = 20$ $S^2 = 10$	_____	_____	_____
Run4	$n = 20$ $S^2 = 10$	$n = 40$ $S^2 = 100$	_____	_____	_____
Run5	$n = 20$ $S^2 = 100$	$n = 40$ $S^2 = 10$	_____	_____	_____

a. Does the sample size affect the accept or reject decision?

    YES _____ NO _____

b. Can you estimate the sample variance ratio that would yield an F value,
    which would lead to a reject decision?

    YES _____ NO _____

c. Explain how you determined that the ratio of sample variances led to a
    rejection of the Tabled F value.

    _____

    _____

    _____

3. For the following list of sample variances, compute the F-max test.   Find the Tabled
    F-max value at the .01 level of significance. Decide whether sample variances are
    homogeneous. Sample size is n = 31 for each sample.

	Sample 1	Sample 2	Sample 3	F-max	Tabled F	Decision
a.	$S^2 = 10$	$S^2 = 10$	$S^2 = 10$	_____	_____	_____
b.	$S^2 = 10$	$S^2 = 100$	$S^2 = 100$	_____	_____	_____
c.	$S^2 = 40$	$S^2 = 10$	$S^2 = 20$	_____	_____	_____

TRUE OR FALSE QUESTIONS

T   F   a.   The normal(z), t, and chi-square distributions are special cases of the
               F distribution.

T   F   b.   As sample size increases for both samples, the F curve becomes
               symmetrical.

T   F   c.   The F ratio tests whether two sample variances are homogeneous.

T   F   d.   The word "homogeneous" implies that sample variances are different.

T   F   e.   The F distribution ranges from zero to infinity.

T   F   f.   The Hartley F-max test requires equal sample sizes in groups.

T   F   g.   The F Ratio program could be used to compute a Hartley F-max
               test.

T   F   h.   Sample size affects the F ratio test of equal variances.

III

SAMPLING AND INFERENCE

CHAPTER 23

SAMPLING DISTRIBUTIONS

CHAPTER OBJECTIVES

- To learn that there are different types of sampling distributions.
- To understand the properties of estimators.
- To graph the sampling distribution of sample standard deviations.
- To determine sample size effects on the sampling distribution of sample standard deviations.
- To determine whether or not there is a bias in the sample standard deviation when it is used as an estimator of the population standard deviation.
- To understand the standard error of the mean and how it is used in statistics.
- To illustrate how the standard error of the mean is affected by sample size.

In previous chapters, we learned about various statistical distributions that can be studied using the Monte Carlo technique. In this chapter, we will learn that there are many different sampling distributions, each providing an estimate of its corresponding population parameter. In subsequent chapters, we will learn how the sampling distributions of various statistics are used to make inferences and test hypotheses. The **sampling distribution** is a frequency distribution of a statistic created by taking repeated samples of a given size from a population. Consequently, we can create sampling distributions of the mean, variance, standard deviation, range, or median, as well as many other sample statistics, with each providing a sample estimate of a corresponding population parameter.

The statement, "*A statistic is to a sample as a parameter is to a population,*" is a very important concept in statistics. This basic statement reflects the idea behind taking a random sample from a population, computing a statistic, and using that sample **statistic** as an estimate of the population **parameter**. Obviously, if the population parameter were known, e.g., mean or standard deviation, then we would not need to take a sample of data and estimate the population parameter.

All sample statistics have sampling distributions with the variance of the sampling distribution indicating the error in the sample statistic, i.e., the error in estimating the population parameter. When the error is small, the statistic will vary less from sample to sample, thus providing us an assurance of a better estimate of the population parameter. In previous chapters, examples were provided to demonstrate that larger sample sizes yielded smaller error or variance in the sampling distribution, i.e., yielded a more reliable or efficient statistical estimate of the population parameter. For example, the mean and median are both sample statistics that estimate the central tendency in population data, but the mean is the more consistent estimator of the population mean because the sampling distribution of the mean has a smaller variance than the sampling distribution of the median. The variance of the sampling distribution of the mean is called the *standard error of the mean*. It is designated as:

$$\sigma\!\big/\!\sqrt{n}$$

and is estimated in a sample as:

$$S_{\overline{X}} = S\!\big/\!\sqrt{n}$$

In previous chapters, we have seen how the sampling distribution of a statistic is a function of sample size. In the formula, it is easy to see that as sample size n becomes larger, the denominator in the formula becomes larger and the standard error of the statistic becomes smaller; hence the frequency distribution of the statistic or sampling distribution has less variance. This indicates that a more precise sample estimate is achieved. This concept of standard error of a sampling distribution applies to any sample statistic that is used to estimate a corresponding population parameter.

An important concern in using sample statistics as estimators of population parameters is whether the estimates possess certain properties. **Sir Ronald Fisher** in the early twentieth century was the first to describe the properties of estimators. The four desirable **properties of estimators** are 1) *unbiased*; 2) *efficient*; 3) *consistent*; and 4) *sufficient*. If the mean of the sampling distribution of the statistic equals the corresponding population parameter, the statistic is *unbiased*; otherwise it is a biased estimator. If the sampling distributions of two statistics have the same mean, then the statistic with the smaller variance in its sampling distribution is more *efficient* (more precise or less variable) while the other statistic is a less efficient estimator. A statistic is a *consistent* estimator of the population parameter if the statistic gets closer to the actual population parameter as sample size increases. A *sufficient* statistic is one that can't be improved upon using other aspects of the sample data. If several sample statistics compete as an estimate of the population parameter, e.g., mean, median, and mode, the sample statistic that is unbiased, efficient, and consistent is a *sufficient* sample statistic estimate, while the other sample statistics are less sufficient. We are therefore interested in sample estimates of population parameters that are unbiased, efficient, consistent, and sufficient.

The sample mean (**statistic**) is an unbiased, efficient, sufficient, and consistent estimator of the population mean (**parameter**). Sample statistics however don't always possess these four properties. For example, the sample standard deviation is a biased, but consistent estimator of the population standard deviation. The sample standard deviation therefore more closely approximates the population standard deviation as sample size increases, i.e., it is a consistent estimate.

In this chapter, the sampling distributions of sample standard deviations are generated given varying sample sizes. The sample standard deviation is computed as:

$$S = \sqrt{\Sigma(X - Mean)^2 / (N-1)}$$

The frequency distribution of sample standard deviations computed from repeatedly drawing samples from a population generates the sampling distributions of the sample standard deviations. A comparison of the mean of the sampling distribution of sample standard deviations to the population standard deviation will help us to determine if the sample standard deviation is a consistent estimator of the population standard deviation.

The S-PLUS program, DEVIATION, produces the sampling distribution of the sample standard deviations. The program initially specifies a sample size of n = 5 and then 250 replications of that sample size are chosen at random from a uniform distribution between 0 and 100. The sample standard deviation is calculated for each sample and a histogram is printed for these 250 standard deviations. The program generates a single sampling distribution for a given sample size. A different sampling distribution exists for every sample of size N. Consequently, you will need to run the program several times, each time with a different sample size, in order to determine whether the mean of the sampling distribution more closely approximates the population parameter. This basic approach can be used to determine whether any sample statistic is a consistent estimator of a corresponding population parameter. Characteristics common to the sampling distributions based on different sample sizes are the most descriptive information we can obtain about theoretical population distributions.

A statistic that estimates a parameter is unbiased when the average value of the sampling distribution is equal to the parameter being estimated. The sample standard deviation is an unbiased estimator of the population standard deviation if the mean of the sampling distribution is equal to the population standard deviation. In this chapter, you will make a judgment about whether or not the sample standard deviation is a biased or an unbiased estimator of the population standard deviation.

SUMMARY

In this chapter, you should learn that:

- Many different sampling distributions can be generated with the mean of the sampling distribution being an estimator of the population parameter.
- For each sampling distribution of a statistic, the variance of the sampling distribution indicates how precise the statistic is as an estimator.
- The variance of a sampling distribution of a statistic becomes smaller as sample size increases, i.e., the standard error of the statistic.
- The sampling distribution of sample standard deviations is a frequency distribution of sample standard deviations computed from samples of a given size taken from a population.
- The variance of the sampling distribution of sample standard deviations decreases with increased sample size; thus the sample standard deviation is a consistent estimator.
- The mean of the sampling distribution of sample standard deviations is less than the population standard deviation; thus the sample standard deviation is a biased estimator of the population standard deviation.
- The error in the sample standard deviation as an estimate of the population standard deviation decreases with increased sample size.

How the DEVIATION program works

The DEVIATION program is short and simple because no lengthy tables are output. The sample size and number of replications are assigned, and then a vector to hold the values in the frequency distribution of standard deviations is initialized to **NULL**. The main processing loop, which iterates from one to the number of desired replications is listed next. For each replication, a sample of size, *SampleSize,* is drawn from a uniform population ranging from 0 to 100. The standard deviation of each sample is calculated and added to the distribution of standard deviations in the vector. After the completion of the loop, the mean of the distribution of sampling standard deviations is calculated. The mean, the sample size, and the true population standard deviation are affixed to each other by use of the **paste** function and placed into the *HistTitle* variable. Finally, the last line of the program creates a histogram of the distribution of sampling standard deviations ranging from 0 to 100 with histogram bars 5 units wide and a title set to the value of *HistTitle*.

DEVIATION Program Output

Sampling Mean = 27.98 Population Standard Deviation = 28.58

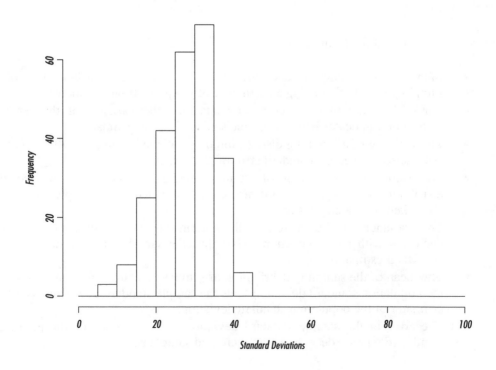

CHAPTER 23 EXERCISES

1. List the four desirable properties of a sample estimate (statistic) for a population parameter.

    a. _____

    b. _____

    c. _____

    d. _____

2. Compare the standard error of the mean from the following two sampling distributions.
    Note: The standard error of the mean is calculated as: $S_{\bar{x}} = S/\sqrt{n}$

    Which sample has the smaller error? _____.

    Sample 1: S = 20, N = 100 _____   Sample 2: S = 10, N = 100 _____

3. Run DEVIATION for the two sample sizes below and draw the histograms.

```
_____              _____
  20    40    60    80                   20    40    60    80
         N = 2                                 N = 100
```

    Sampling Mean _____   Sampling Mean _____
    Population S.D. _____   Population S.D. _____

    a. Are the two graphs the same or different?   Same _____ Different _____
        Why? _____

    b. Which sample size has a Sampling Mean closer to the Population S.D.? _____

4. Run the DEVIATION program for the sample sizes listed below. Record the Sampling Distribution Mean and ERROR for each sample size.

   Note: ERROR = SAMPLING MEAN - POPULATION S.D.

N	SAMPLING MEAN	POPULATION S.D.	ERROR
5	_____	28.58	_____
10	_____	28.58	_____
15	_____	28.58	_____
20	_____	28.58	_____
25	_____	28.58	_____
30	_____	28.58	_____
35	_____	28.58	_____
40	_____	28.58	_____
45	_____	28.58	_____
50	_____	28.58	_____

a. Does the SAMPLING MEAN consistently overestimate the POPULATION S.D.?

   YES _____ NO _____

b. Does the variance of the sampling distribution decrease with increased sample size?

   YES _____ NO _____

c. The mean of the sampling distribution doesn't get any closer to the population standard deviation. What do the signs of the differences lead you to think about the direction of the bias when the sample standard deviation is used as an estimator of the population standard deviation?

   _____

   _____

TRUE OR FALSE QUESTIONS

T   F   a. The sampling distribution of sample standard deviations is symmetrical
             for N = 2.

T   F   b. As sample size increases, the error in the sample standard deviation as
             an estimator of the population standard deviation decreases.

T   F   c. The sample standard deviation is an unbiased, efficient, consistent, and
             sufficient estimator of the population standard deviation.

T   F   d. The sample standard deviation tends to overestimate the population
             standard deviation.

T.   F   e. On the average, the sample standard deviation is equal to the population
             standard deviation.

T   F   f. A consistent estimator is one that more closely approximates the population
             parameter as sample size increases.

CHAPTER 24

CENTRAL LIMIT THEOREM

CHAPTER OBJECTIVES

- To understand the Central Limit Theorem.
- To graph the sampling distribution of the mean for various samples of size N.
- To understand the relationship between the mean of the sampling distribution of the mean and the mean of the population being sampled.
- To understand the relationship between the variance of the sampling distribution of the mean and the variance of the population being sampled.
- To determine the effect of sample size on the shape of the sampling distribution of the mean.

In some instances, the normal distribution may not be the appropriate distribution for studying research variables and/or the population data may not be normally distributed on which we base our statistics. The normal probability distribution however is still useful because of the Central Limit Theorem. The **Central Limit Theorem** state that as sample size increases a sampling distribution of a statistic will become normally distributed even if the population data is not normally distributed. The sampling distribution of the mean of any nonnormal population is approximately normal, given the Central Limit Theorem, but a larger sample size might be needed depending upon the extent to which the population deviates from normality. Typically, a smaller sample size can be randomly drawn from a *homogeneous* population, whereas a larger sample size needs to be randomly drawn from a *heterogeneous* population, to obtain an unbiased sample estimate of the population parameter. If the population data are normally distributed, then the sampling distribution of the mean is normally distributed; otherwise larger samples of size N are required to approximate a normal sampling distribution. The sampling distribution of the mean is a probability distribution created by the frequency distribution of sample means drawn from a population. The **sampling distribution**, as a frequency distribution, is used to study the relationship between sample statistics and corresponding population parameters.

The Central Limit Theorem is useful in statistics because it proves that sampling distributions will be normally distributed regardless of the shape of the population from which the random sample was drawn. For example, a physician is studying the life expectancy of adults after being diagnosed with cancer. She is going to do a statistical analysis on the data concerning age at death and needs a theoretical probability distribution to model the adult ages. Since most of the adults lived to an advanced age due to new cancer treatments, she realizes that the population of ages is skewed to the left (see Figure below).

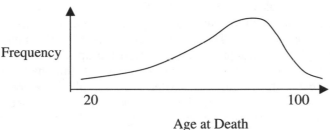

Age at Death

The physician doesn't know whether a mathematical function would best describe this population distribution, but would like to test mean differences in age at death between normal adults and adults with cancer. Fortunately, she can use a sampling distribution of sample means, which doesn't require exact knowledge of the population distribution to test her hypothesis. The Central Limit Theorem, which is based on the sampling distribution of statistics, permits the use of the normal distribution for conducting statistical tests.

In this chapter, the S-PLUS CENTRAL program will graph the sampling distribution of the mean for samples of a given size N. You will be able to observe the shape of this sampling distribution of the mean. The random samples will be taken from one of four different population types: uniform, normal, exponential, or bimodal. The frequency distribution of the sample means can be based on an infinite number of samples, but the initial value in the program is set at 250 samples.

SUMMARY

In this chapter, you should learn that:

- Sampling distributions of the mean from nonnormal populations approach a normal distribution as the sample size increases, which is the definition of the Central Limit Theorem.

- The frequency distribution of sample mean based on samples of size N randomly drawn from a population is called the sampling distribution of the mean.

- The sampling distribution of the mean is a normally distributed probability distribution.

- The mean of the sampling distribution of the mean is equal to the mean of the population being sampled.

- The variance of the sampling distribution of the mean is equal to the variance of the population being sampled divided by the sample size N.

- Sampling distributions of the mean from normal populations are normally distributed.

How the CENTRAL program works

The CENTRAL program uses functions and techniques presented in previous chapters. The output is helpful in understanding the fundamentals of why significance testing works for many different kinds of distributions. The program begins by initializing the user-defined variables, including a numerical representation for the underlying distribution type from which samples are drawn. An initial dialog box displays a selection for the Uniform, Exponential, Normal, and Bimodal distributions. After selecting the distribution type, two vectors are initialized to **NULL** and the main processing loop begins. The main loop iterates for the number of desired replications, creating a sample of the appropriate size from the appropriate distribution. The parameters for the samples are set so that most of the sampling distributions of the mean should fall between 0 and 2 for ease of comparison. After each sample is selected, the mean is calculated and added to the vector of sample means. The entire sample is added to a vector that contains all the raw data from every sample, thereby creating a very large, single sample.

When replications are finished, an output vector is created to display the mean and variance for the population, theoretical sampling distribution, and actual sampling distribution of the mean. This vector is then formatted into a matrix to be output, dimension names are assigned, and the matrix is printed with **print.char.matrix**. Two histograms are graphed, one for the sampling distribution and one for the population distribution. A second dialog box is then displayed to permit choosing "Yes" or "No" to continue. Selecting "Yes" to continue permits selection of other distribution types. Selecting "No" stops the program.

The sampling distributions of the mean approach a normal distribution, as sample size increases. Because of this, you will be able to observe how the underlying data distribution type does not affect the normality of the sampling distribution of the mean. You may want to try different sample sizes and number of replications to observe the appearance of the histograms.

CENTRAL Program Output

Given the following values:

```
SampleSize <- 10
NumReplications <- 250
```

	Uniform	Theoretical	Sampling Distribution
Mean	1.000	1.000	0.998
Variance	0.333	0.033	0.031
	Normal	Theoretical	Sampling Distribution
Mean	1.000	1.000	0.999
Variance	0.111	0.011	0.012
	Exponential	Theoretical	Sampling Distribution
Mean	1.000	1.000	0.972
Variance	1.000	0.100	0.095
	Bimodal	Theoretical	Sampling Distribution
Mean	1.000	1.000	0.990
Variance	0.500	0.050	0.059

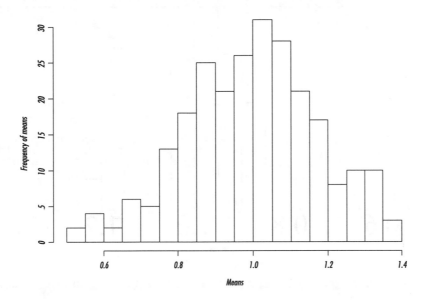

Sampling Distribution of the Mean (Uniform Distribution)

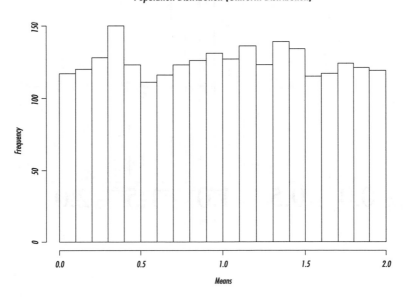

Population Distribution (Uniform Distribution)

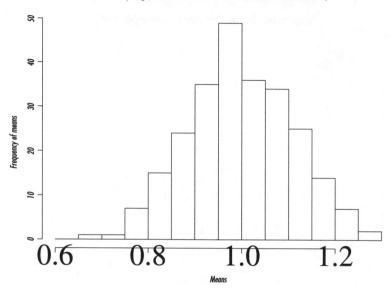

Sampling Distribution of the Mean (Normal Distribution)

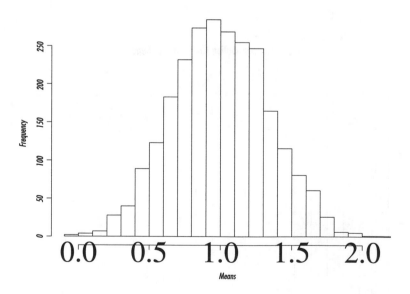

Population Distribution (Normal Distribution)

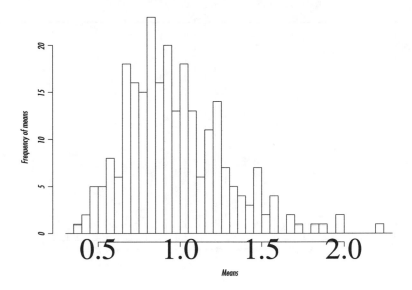

Sampling Distribution of the Mean (Exponential Distribution)

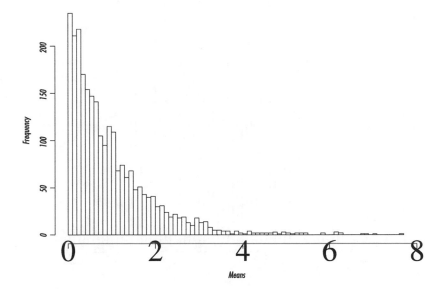

Population Distribution (Exponential Distribution)

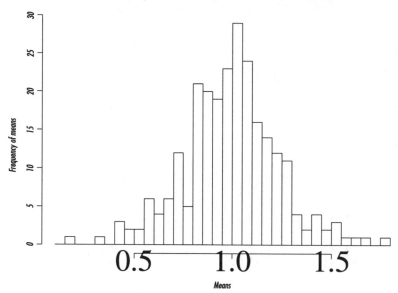

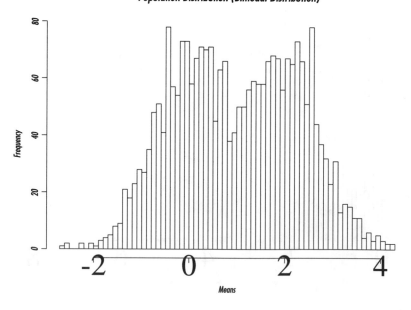

CHAPTER 24 EXERCISES

1. Run CENTRAL for sample size N = 5 for each of the four population types. Enter the tabled output of results below. Print the sampling distribution and population distribution graphs for each of the population distribution types.

UNIFORM

	POPULATION	THEORETICAL	SAMPLING DISTRIBUTION
MEAN	_____	_____	_____
VARIANCE	_____	_____	_____

NORMAL

	POPULATION	THEORETICAL	SAMPLING DISTRIBUTION
MEAN	_____	_____	_____
VARIANCE	_____	_____	_____

EXPONENTIAL

	POPULATION	THEORETICAL	SAMPLING DISTRIBUTION
MEAN	_____	_____	_____
VARIANCE	_____	_____	_____

BIMODAL

	POPULATION	THEORETICAL	SAMPLING DISTRIBUTION
MEAN	_____	_____	_____
VARIANCE	_____	_____	_____

---

a. Which of the sampling distributions are the most like a normal distribution?

_____

b. Which sampling distribution is most different from a normal distribution?

_____

c. Are the sampling distributions approximately normal regardless of the shape of the underlying population? YES _____   NO _____

2.   Run the CENTRAL program for samples of size N=30 for each population type. Draw a rough graph of each sampling distribution of the mean.

_____   _____
         UNIFORM   NORMAL

_____   _____
      EXPONENTIAL   BIMODAL

a.   Are the sampling distributions for sample size N = 5 and N = 30 different?
       YES _____ NO _____

b.   Are the population means and sampling distribution means the same for samples of size N = 30? Note: ERROR = THEORETICAL - SAMPLING.

                                                               ERROR
       Uniform   YES _____ NO _____   _____
       Normal   YES _____ NO _____   _____
       Exponential   YES _____ NO _____   _____
       Bimodal   YES _____ NO _____   _____

c.   Are the population variances and sampling distribution variances the same for samples of size N = 30? Note: ERROR = THEORETICAL - SAMPLING.

                                                               ERROR
       Uniform   YES _____ NO _____   _____
       Normal   YES _____ NO _____   _____
       Exponential   YES _____ NO _____   _____
       Bimodal   YES _____ NO _____   _____

3.   Run the CENTRAL program again, but this time select a sample size of 100.
      Answer the following questions.

      a.   Is a sample size of 100 sufficiently large to produce a sampling distribution of the
            mean that is approximately normal regardless of the population type?
            YES _____ NO _____

      b.   Is the mean of each population type related to the mean of the sampling
            distribution of the mean?
            YES _____ NO _____

      c.   Is the variance of each population type related to the variance of the sampling
            distribution of the mean?
            YES _____ NO _____

      d.   Would the means and variances for a single sample be equal to the mean and
            variance of each population type?
            YES _____ NO _____

TRUE OR FALSE QUESTIONS

T   F   a.   If a population is normal, the sampling distribution of the mean will also
                be normal.
T   F   b.   A frequency distribution of 100 sample means for samples of size N
                drawn from a population is called the sampling distribution of the mean.
T   F   c.   The variance of sampling distribution of mean is equal to the variance of
                the underlying population divided by the sample size.
T   F   d.   The mean of a sampling distribution of mean is not normally distributed if
                the underlying population is not normally distributed.
T   F   e.   A sampling distribution of mean is a probability distribution.

CHAPTER 25

CONFIDENCE INTERVALS

CHAPTER OBJECTIVES

- To compute the confidence interval for the population mean.
- To understand that the standard error of the mean is used to establish a confidence interval around a sample statistic to capture the population parameter.
- To determine the relationship between the sample size and the width of a confidence interval.
- To understand the confidence level of a confidence interval.
- To simulate a number of samples from a known population and determine the confidence intervals of these samples.
- To discover that population means are captured within confidence intervals around the sample statistic for a given confidence level.

Confidence intervals can be computed for many different population parameters by using the standard error of the statistic and the confidence level. The **standard error of a statistic** was described in the previous chapter, e.g., standard error of the mean. The variance of a sampling distribution indicates the amount of error in estimating the population parameter. Smaller sampling variance reflects less error in estimating the population parameter. The standard error of a statistic is computed as the standard deviation of the sampling distribution divided by the square root of the sample size. Consequently, as sample size increases, the standard error of the statistic decreases. A **confidence interval** is computed using the sample statistic and the standard error of the statistic (standard deviation of the statistic in the sampling distribution). The confidence interval around the sample statistic is a range of values that should contain the population parameter. A **confidence level** is used which defines how confident we are that the interval around the sample statistic contains the parameter being estimated. The confidence interval is determined by picking an area in the tail of the sampling distribution in which the value of the statistic is improbable. Recall that a sampling distribution is a frequency distribution; therefore we could pick a 5% probability area, leaving 95% of the sample statistics in the frequency distribution as plausible estimates of the population parameter.

The confidence interval around the sample statistic is computed by using the standard error of the statistic. The **confidence interval** indicates the precision of the sample statistic as an estimate of the population parameter. The confidence interval around the sample statistic is said to include the population parameter with a certain level of confidence. It should be common practice to report confidence intervals for various population parameters such as proportions, means, or correlations. The confidence interval contains a high and low score, above and below the sample statistic, in which we feel confident that the interval contains the population parameter. **Confidence levels** are used to determine the confidence interval width. Commonly used confidence levels are 90%, 95%, or 99%. These confidence levels for sample data are indicated by a critical t value of 1.65 (10% probability area), 1.96 (5% probability area), and 2.58 (1% probability area), respectively, which are given in Table 2 (Distribution of t for Given Probability Levels).

The 95% confidence interval for the population mean is computed as:

$$\overline{X} \pm 1.96(S / \sqrt{n})$$

where S = sample standard deviation and n = sample size. The value of 1.96 corresponds to the t value that contains 5 percent of the sample means in the tail of the sampling distribution that are improbable. This implies that 5 times out of 100 replications, a confidence interval for a sample mean may not contain the population mean. In contrast, 95 times out of 100, the confidence interval around the sample mean will contain the population mean. Stated differently, 5 percent of the time the sample mean will not be a good estimate of the population mean, or conversely, 95 percent of the time we are confident that the sample mean will be a good estimate of the population mean.

If the sample mean was 50, sample standard deviation 10, the sample size 100, and we wanted to be 90 percent confident that the confidence interval captured the population mean, then the confidence interval around the sample mean would range between 51.65 and 48.35. This range of values is computed as:

$$CI_{.90} = \overline{X} \pm t(\frac{S}{\sqrt{n}}) = 50 \pm 1.65(\frac{10}{\sqrt{100}}) = 50 \pm 1.65$$

$$CI_{.90} = (51.65, 48.35)$$

If we replicated our sampling ten times, we would expect the population mean to fall in the range of values approximately 90 percent of the time (9 times out of 10 the confidence intervals would contain the population mean).

In this chapter, the CONFIDENCE program will simulate random samples and compute the confidence intervals around the sample mean (the process is the same for other population parameters because it would be based on the sampling distribution of the statistic). A population with a normal distribution ($\mu = 50$ and $\sigma = 10$) will be sampled. You can enter different sample sizes and confidence levels to see the effect they have on estimating the confidence interval. The program uses the population standard deviation rather than the sample standard deviation in the confidence interval formula because it is known. The 95% confidence interval would be computed as:

$$\overline{X} \pm 1.96(\sigma / \sqrt{N})$$

If the population standard deviation is known, one would use the population standard deviation with a z value for the confidence interval. If the population standard deviation is *not* known, one would use a sample standard deviation estimate with a critical t value for the confidence interval. The sampling distribution of the mean will be based on 20 replications. For each sample mean, the 95% confidence interval around the mean will be computed and the program will check to see whether or not the population mean of 50 is contained in the confidence interval. Due to sampling error, one may not achieve the exact percent of confidence intervals that contain the population mean as indicated by the confidence level, i.e., 95%.

SUMMARY

In this chapter, you should learn that:

- A confidence interval reflects a range of values (high, low) around the sample mean for different levels of confidence, e.g., 90%, 95%, and 99%.
- A confidence interval indicates the precision of a sample statistic as an estimate of a population parameter.
- If a confidence interval has a 95% level of confidence, this indicates that approximately 95 out of 100 confidence intervals around the sample statistic will contain the population parameter.
- If the confidence level remains the same, but the sample size increases, then the width of the confidence interval decreases, indicating a more precise estimate of the population parameter.

How the CONFIDENCE program works

The CONFIDENCE program creates confidence intervals around repeated samples taken from a population and tests to see whether they contain the population mean. The program contains familiar techniques and functions used in other chapter programs. The sample size, population mean, population standard deviation, number of replications and size of the confidence interval can be changed in the program. The confidence interval size is specified as a z-value. Samples are simulated for the number of desired replications. The mean of each sample as well as the confidence intervals are calculated according to the formula given in the chapter. There is a count of the number of times the population mean is captured by the confidence interval for the sample. This is expressed as a percentage based on all the replications at the end of the program, both as a ratio and percent. Individual sample information is output, including the sample means and confidence intervals, which capture the population mean.

You can run the program using different values for sample size, population mean, or population standard deviation to observe the effect on the frequency with which the population mean is contained in the confidence interval. Observe how each variable affects (or doesn't affect) the width of the confidence interval.

You can also run the program for varying sample sizes by commenting out the table of individual sample information and creating a loop in the program to iterate through sample sizes from 5 to 50 by intervals of 5. Create a table specifying what percent of the time the population mean was in the confidence interval around the sample mean for each sample size to better view what effect sample size has on the ability to estimate the population mean.

CONFIDENCE Program Output

Given the following values:

```
SampleSize <- 100
PopMean <- 50
PopStdDev <-10
NumReplications <- 20
Zvalue <- 1.96   [Zvalue=1.65 (90%), Zvalue=1.96 (95%), or Zvalue=2.58 (99%)]
```

Confidence Intervals for Z value = 1.96

Sample Mean	CI (high - low)	Population Mean	Within CI
49.18	47.22 - 51.14	50	Yes
50.59	48.63 - 52.55	50	Yes
49.92	47.96 - 51.88	50	Yes
49.74	47.78 - 51.7	50	Yes
50.99	49.03 - 52.95	50	Yes
48.39	46.43 - 50.35	50	Yes
50.62	48.66 - 52.58	50	Yes
49.79	47.83 - 51.75	50	Yes
48.88	46.92 - 50.84	50	Yes
48.85	46.89 - 50.81	50	Yes
50.34	48.38 52.3	50	Yes
50.86	48.9 - 52.82	50	Yes
51.31	49.35 - 53.27	50	Yes
51.21	49.25 - 53.17	50	Yes
49.33	47.37 - 51.29	50	Yes
52.38	50.42 - 54.34	50	No
50.58	48.62 - 52.54	50	Yes
49.88	47.92 - 51.84	50	Yes
50.36	48.4 - 52.32	50	Yes
50.96	49 - 52.92	50	Yes

Confidence Intervals that Contain Population Mean = 19/20 = 95%

CHAPTER 25 EXERCISES

1. Run the CONFIDENCE program for ten (10) replications with a confidence level of 90% (z = 1.65) and keep the population mean of 50, standard deviation of 10, and sample sizes of 100.

   a. How many of the confidence intervals contained the population mean? _____

   b. What percentage did you expect to contain the population mean? _____

   c. If you increased the number of replications, would you more closely approximate the confidence level percent? Hint: Run CONFIDENCE and change the number of replications to observe what happens. YES _____ NO _____

   d. Why does increasing the number of replications not guarantee a more close approximation to the confidence level percent? _____

2. Run the CONFIDENCE program for fifty (50) replications with a confidence level of 90% (z = 1.65); keep the population mean of 50, standard deviation of 10, and sample sizes of 100.

   a. Do all the confidence intervals have the same width? YES _____ NO _____

   b. What is the width of the confidence interval? _____

   c. Compute the confidence interval width using the population standard deviation and the sample size formula in the chapter. _____

$$\bar{X} \pm 1.65(\sigma / \sqrt{N})$$

   d. Does the formula give the same confidence interval width as the CONFIDENCE program? Note: (1.65 * 2 = 3.30; using the probability area in both tails of the sampling distribution). YES _____ NO _____

3. Run the CONFIDENCE program for each of the sample sizes listed below. Keep the
    population mean of 50, standard deviation of 10, and set the number of replications to 10 for
    a 1.96 confidence level (95%). Record the high and low values for the confidence intervals
    and calculate the width of the confidence interval. Note: You can obtain the confidence
    interval width by subtracting the low value from the high value in the outputted table.

Confidence Interval for Z value = 1.96

Sample Size	CI (High-Low)	CI Width
10	_____	_____
144	_____	_____
256	_____	_____
625	_____	_____

a. As sample size increases, does the confidence interval width that contains the
    population mean become smaller?

    YES _____ NO _____

b. If the confidence interval width becomes smaller as sample size increases, does this
    imply a more accurate estimate of the population mean?

    YES _____ NO _____

4. Run the CONFIDENCE program for each of the confidence levels listed below. Keep the
    population mean of 50, standard deviation of 10, sample size of 100, and set the number
    of replications to 100. Record the CI high and low values and the percent of confidence
    intervals that contained the population mean.

Confidence Level	CI (High-Low)	Percent
90	_____	_____
95	_____	_____
99	_____	_____

a.   Does the confidence interval become wider as the confidence level increases from 90% to 99%?

YES _____ NO _____

b.   If the confidence interval becomes wider, does this imply that we are more confident to have captured a range of values that contains the population mean.

YES _____ NO _____

TRUE OR FALSE QUESTIONS

T   F   a. A 95% confidence interval computed from sample data contains the population parameter approximately 95% of the time.

T   F   b. A confidence interval indicates the precision of a statistic to estimate the population parameter.

T   F   c. As sample size increases, the confidence interval width becomes narrower.

T   F   d. A 95% confidence interval implies that 95 times out of 100 the confidence interval *will not* contain the population parameter.

T   F   e. It is possible that a 95% confidence interval will not contain the population parameter.

T   F   f. As the confidence level increases from 90% to 99%, the width of the confidence interval becomes smaller.

CHAPTER 26

HYPOTHESIS TESTING

CHAPTER OBJECTIVES

- To learn that research questions are transformed into statistical hypotheses that can be tested using probability theory.
- To learn that there are different types of statistical hypotheses depending on the level of measurement.
- To understand directional (one-tailed) and non-directional (two-tailed) tests of statistical hypotheses.
- To understand the level of significance (alpha) and the region of rejection.
- To understand p-values and the region of rejection.
- To understand how TYPE I error and TYPE II error affect hypothesis testing.
- To understand the effect of using the sample standard deviation instead of the population standard deviation.
- To observe a z test of mean differences for different sample sizes and standard deviations.

The scientific community investigates phenomena in the world. The areas for scientific inquiry are many and have led to the creation of numerous academic disciplines, e.g., botany, biology, education, psychology, business, music, and so forth. The first step in any academic discipline that conducts scientific investigation is to ask a research question. Research questions can be expressed in many different ways. For example, "In the upcoming election, who will be elected President of the United States?" or "Which is better, margarine or butter, in lowering cholesterol?" The next important step is to design a study, then gather data and test the research question. This requires converting the research question into a statistical hypothesis. There are many different kinds of statistical hypotheses depending upon the level of measurement (nominal, ordinal, interval, or ratio) and type of research design used in the study. A statistical hypothesis is the cornerstone to testing the two possible outcomes, which are always stated in terms of population parameters, given the kind of data collected (percents, ranks, means, or correlation coefficients). The two possible outcomes of a statistical hypothesis are stated in a null (H_o: no difference) and alternative (H_A: difference exists) format using symbols for the population parameter. The alternative statistical hypothesis is stated to reflect the outcome expected in the research question. This involves either a directional (greater than) or non-directional (difference exists) expression. The null hypothesis is the corresponding opposite expected outcome of less than/equal or no difference, respectively. A research question and statistical hypothesis for each type of data is listed.

Research Question	Data	Statistical Hypothesis
Is the percent of people drinking beer in Texas greater than the national average?	Percents	$H_O : P_{Texas} \leq P_{National}$ $H_A : P_{Texas} > P_{National}$
Is there a difference in the ranking of persons on two different diets for weight gain?	Ranks	$H_O : R_{Diet\,A} = R_{Diet\,B}$ $H_A : R_{Diet\,A} \neq R_{Diet\,B}$
Does my 5th grade class on average score higher than the national average in math?	Means	$H_O : \mu_{Class} \leq \mu_{National}$ $H_A : \mu_{Class} > \mu_{National}$
Is the relationship between music ability and self-esteem in my sample of students different than the population?	Correlation	$H_O : \rho_{Sample} = \rho_{Population}$ $H_A : \rho_{Sample} \neq \rho_{Population}$

Two kinds of errors are associated with our decision to retain or reject the null hypothesis based on the outcome of the statistical test (TYPE I error and TYPE II error). The TYPE I error is specified by selecting a level of significance (probability area) such that if the sample statistic falls in this probability area, then we reject the null hypothesis in favor of our alternative hypothesis. The TYPE II error corresponds to the probability of retaining the null hypothesis when it is false. Chapters 27 and 28 provide more detail about these two kinds of errors. When we state the statistical hypothesis as "greater than," we designate only one-tail of the sampling distribution of the statistic because of the directional nature of the research question. When we state the statistical hypothesis as a "difference exists," we designate both tails of the sampling distribution of the statistic because of the non-directional nature of the research question. Consequently, the probability area corresponds to different "tabled statistics."

Once the probability area is determined for the statistical hypothesis, we can select a tabled statistical value to set our region of rejection. The tabled statistical values were generated using probability theory and created from the sampling distribution of the statistic for different sample sizes (degrees of freedom) and levels of significance. Only the more popular levels of significance (.05, .01, and sometimes .001) are included in the tables due to page length consideration. Consequently, it is common for researchers to select a region of rejection and test statistical hypotheses based on the .05, .01, or .001 levels of significance. The relationship between the level of significance and probability area for the region of rejection (vertical hash marks) can be depicted as follows:

Non-directional (two-tailed) Research Question:

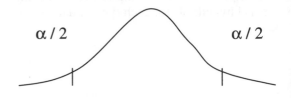

Directional (one-tail) Research Question:

An example research question and corresponding statistical hypothesis will help to illustrate the relationship between the non-direction and/or direction of the question, level of significance, and region of rejection. The research question, " Is the SAT population mean in Texas greater than the SAT population mean for the U.S.," is converted into a null and alternative statistical hypothesis:

$$H_O : \mu_{Texas} \leq \mu_{U.S.}$$
$$H_A : \mu_{Texas} > \mu_{U.S.}$$

This is a directional research question, hence the alternative statistical hypothesis indicates a greater than expression, while the null statistical hypothesis indicates less than or equal to for the population parameters. We test our hypothesis by random sampling of 100 students in Texas, compute the sample mean, and conduct a statistical test at the .05 level of significance. Once we have selected a sample size and level of significance for the study, a tabled statistical value can be selected. Under the normal probability curve in Table 1, a z value of 1.64 corresponds to a probability value (p-value) that indicates an area approximately equal to .05 (probability area beyond z). This z value is used to set the region of rejection for testing our statistical hypothesis: $R_{.05} = z > 1.64$. When we conduct a z test for the difference between the means, a computed z value greater than 1.64 will imply that the population mean in Texas is greater than the population mean in the U.S. In other words, the computed z value falls in the probability area of the sampling distribution of the statistic that we have designated to be a highly improbable outcome. The probability area for the null hypothesis and the alternative hypothesis is therefore depicted along with the tabled z value and level of significance for a directional research question as follows:

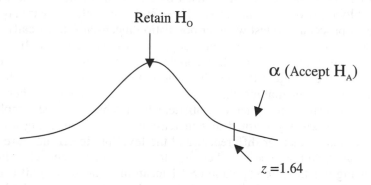

Given our selection of the .05 level of significance, only 5% of the time would we expect a mean difference to exceed $z = 1.64$ if the null hypothesis is true, i.e., the population means are equal. Consequently, if the mean difference is large enough and we compute a z value greater than

1.64, we are 95% confident in our decision to reject the null hypothesis in favor of the alternative hypothesis.

Assume we computed a Texas SAT mean of 530 for the 100 randomly sampled students and the U.S. SAT mean was 500 with a population standard deviation of 100. A one-sample z test to determine the statistical significance of this mean difference is computed as:

$$z = \frac{\overline{X} - \mu}{\sigma / \sqrt{N}} = \frac{530 - 500}{100 / \sqrt{100}} = \frac{30}{10} = 3.0$$

Since the computed $z = 3.0$ is greater than $z = 1.64$, and therefore falls in the region of rejection, we reject the null hypothesis of no difference in favor of the alternative hypothesis that the population SAT mean in Texas is greater than the population SAT mean in the U.S. We are 95% confident in our decision, but also know that 5% of the time our decision might be wrong (TYPE I error). We would answer the research question by stating that the population SAT mean in Texas is statistically significantly higher than the population SAT mean in the U.S.

This example used a z test because the population standard deviation for the SAT was known. In many research studies, the population standard deviation is unknown, so we would use a t test. The t test formula that uses the *sample standard deviation* in place of the population standard deviation is:

$$t = \frac{\overline{X} - \mu}{S / \sqrt{N}}$$

Research questions involving a test of differences in population means are commonplace in several academic disciplines. An engineer needs to know the average weight of vehicles that can safely travel across a bridge. A psychologist needs to test whether a group of clients have an average cognitive ability greater than the national average. A sociologist needs to determine the average family size for different ethnic groups. The auditor of a large oil company wants to know the average amount of error in the bills prepared for customers. A doctor studying the possible reduction in blood pressure caused by a new medicine is concerned about the average reduction in blood pressure for patients. These and many other research questions reflect a need for a statistical procedure to test whether population means are statistically different.

Tests of statistical hypotheses do not provide exact outcomes. Instead, the tests are based on data-gathering evidence to reach a conclusion with some degree of uncertainty. In other words, it is possible to reject the null hypothesis when in fact the null hypothesis is true. We preset the probability of making this kind of error (TYPE I error) when selecting the level of significance and corresponding tabled statistic, which is based on the sampling distribution of the statistic. We have already learned that increasing sample size, using a directional hypothesis, willingness to detect a larger difference, and the level of significance are factors that influence whether the statistical test is powerful enough to detect a difference when in fact one exists.

In testing whether the population SAT mean in Texas was significantly different from the population SAT mean in the U.S., knowledge of the population standard deviation and sample size played a role. A larger random sample of students would dramatically reduce the standard error in the formula, which would result in a larger computed z value, e.g., $z = 30$ if N = 10,000.

A smaller sample size would result in a smaller z value. If the population standard deviation is *not* known, a sample standard deviation as an estimate might produce a very different result.

The HYPOTHESIS TEST program will allow you to specify the true population mean and then test various null and alternative hypotheses. In the program output, you will be able to observe either z tests or t tests for several statistical hypotheses depending upon whether the population standard deviation (z test) or sample standard deviation (t test) is used, without having to do the calculations. The program will select a random sample of size N from the true population, compute the sample mean and variance, compute the appropriate test statistic, the p-value, and indicate the decision outcome. Since you specify the true population mean, you will know whether or not the decision to reject the null hypothesis is correct. The HYPOTHESIS TEST program allows for either the population standard deviation or sample standard deviation to be used in the test statistic. If the population standard deviation is used (set varUse=0, the default), the z-statistic is reported. If the sample standard deviation is used (set varUse=1), the t statistic is reported.

SUMMARY

In this chapter, you should learn that:

- In hypothesis testing, the null hypothesis is retained as true unless the research findings are beyond chance probability (unlikely to have occurred by chance).
- A TYPE I error occurs when a true null hypothesis is rejected erroneously, usually due to an atypical research outcome.
- The region of rejection is specified by the level of significance (α), which indicates the probability of making a TYPE I error.
- If the z value falls in the region of rejection probability area, then the null hypothesis is rejected in favor of the alternative hypothesis.
- For different values of alpha (levels of significance) and sample size, the region of rejection will be indicated by a tabled statistic from the sampling distribution of the statistic.
- A TYPE II error occurs when a false null hypothesis is retained erroneously, usually due to insufficient data.

How the HYPOTHESIS TEST program works

The HYPOTHESIS TEST program uses the **pValue** function within S-PLUS to determine the probability in the tails for either the z test or t test after all the user-defined variables are initialized. The parameters to be passed to the *pValue* function are defined within the parentheses following the **function** command. Based on the direction of the statistical hypothesis for the z test or t test, probability values are determined using the **pnorm** function, which returns the probability value for a mean difference with a given standard deviation. If the sample mean is less than the null hypothesis mean, then **pnorm** is reported; if the sample mean is greater than the null hypothesis mean, then **1-pnorm** is reported. This use of the **pnorm** function results in only the probability area for one-tail of either the normal or t distribution. For a two-tailed test, the probability area (alpha) is divided evenly between the two ends of the distributions. The HYPOTHESIS TEST program specifies the probability area for one- and two-tailed tests using tails = 1 or tails = 2 commands.

After the *pValue* function is defined, the main processing loop begins depending upon whether the population standard deviation (**varUse**=0, the default) or sample standard deviation (**varUse**=1) was selected, and then creates the table of output values. Random samples are generated from a normal distribution and the probability of the mean of each is determined with either the sample standard deviation or the population standard deviation using the *pValue* function defined earlier. Once the probability value has been determined, the decision outcome is labeled retain null or reject null, and the information from the sample is bundled into a vector and added to an output matrix. The program default is p < .05, therefore if the computed p-value is less than .05, the decision is reject the null. If the p-value is greater than .05, the decision is retain the null. The number of statistical tests computed and printed is based upon the value for **numSamples**. The output matrix is given dimension names and printed out.

HYPOTHESIS TEST Program Output

Given the following values:

```
popMean <- 10.5
popVar <- 2
nullMean <- 10
tails <- 1
sampleSize <- 36
alpha <- .05
varUse <- 0
numSamples <- 10
```

Sample Mean	Pop. SD	z statistic	Decision	p value
10.461	1.414	1.957	REJECT NULL	0.026
10.887	1.414	3.765	REJECT NULL	0.001
10.452	1.414	1.918	REJECT NULL	0.028
10.494	1.414	2.097	REJECT NULL	0.018
10.274	1.414	1.163	RETAIN NULL	0.123
10.196	1.414	0.832	RETAIN NULL	0.203
11.035	1.414	4.393	REJECT NULL	0.001
10.045	1.414	0.191	RETAIN NULL	0.425
10.57	1.414	2.419	REJECT NULL	0.008
10.358	1.414	1.519	RETAIN NULL	0.065

Given the following values:

```
popMean <- 10.5
popVar <- 2
nullMean <- 10
tails <- 1
sampleSize <- 36
alpha <- .05
varUse <- 1
numSamples <- 10
```

Sample Mean	Sample SD	t statistic	Decision	p value
10.862	1.382	3.744	REJECT NULL	0.001
10.468	1.426	1.969	REJECT NULL	0.025
10.566	1.07	3.177	REJECT NULL	0.001
10.471	1.44	1.964	REJECT NULL	0.025
10.626	1.34	2.803	REJECT NULL	0.003
10.353	1.356	1.56	RETAIN NULL	0.060
10.245	1.467	1.002	RETAIN NULL	0.159
10.625	1.354	2.771	REJECT NULL	0.003
10.591	1.401	2.53	REJECT NULL	0.006
10.239	1.759	0.815	RETAIN NULL	0.208

CHAPTER 26 EXERCISES

1.   Run the HYPOTHESIS TEST program with the following initial values which defines a
       one-tail test and uses the population variance:

```
popMean <- 10
popVar <- 2
nullMean <- 10
tails <- 1
sampleSize <- 36
alpha <- .05
varUse <- 0
numSamples <- 10
```

Sample	Sample Mean	z statistic	Decision	p value
1				
2				
3				
4				
5				
6				
7				
8				
9				
10				

a.   Is the z statistic correct in the table (Use the formula below to verify)?

       YES _____   NO _____ $z = \dfrac{\overline{X} - \mu}{\sigma / \sqrt{N}}$

b.   Compare each p value to $\alpha = 0.05$. If $p \geq 0.05$, then the decision should be to
       RETAIN the null hypothesis. If $p < .05$, then the decision should be to REJECT
       the null hypothesis. Do all of the decisions correspond to the p values?

       YES _____   NO _____

c.   Since the null hypothesis is actually true, any REJECT NULL decisions are
       errors. This is a TYPE I error. The probability of a TYPE I error is equal to α.
       How many REJECT NULL decisions were there? What percent is this? _____

2.   Run HYPOTHESIS TEST program again using all of the same values, except increase the number of samples to 40 (numSamples <- 40).

    a.   What is the percent of TYPE I errors in the 40 simulations?   _____

    b.   What do you expect this TYPE I error percent to be?   _____

3.   Run HYPOTHESIS TEST program again, except change α to .10 (alpha <-.10).

    a.   How many times was the null hypothesis rejected?   _____

    b.   What do you expect this percent to be?   _____

4.   Run HYPOTHESIS TEST program again, except increase the sample size to 100 (sampleSize <- 100).

    a.   How many times is the null hypothesis rejected?   _____

    b.   Does sample size have an effect on the percent of TYPE I errors?   _____

5.   Run HYPOTHESIS TEST program again, except use the sample variance (varUse<-1). In most cases the proportion of rejections will be much higher because the sample standard deviation is not as good an estimator as the true population standard deviation.

    a.   What is the percent of rejections?   _____

    b.   Does the percent of rejections approximate α?   YES _____NO _____

6.   Run the HYPOTHESIS TEST program in which the null hypothesis is false (The population mean is actually greater than the null mean). Run the program five times using a different sample size each time. Use the following settings:

```
popMean <- 10.5
popVar <- 2
nullMean <- 10
tails <- 1
sampleSize <- 36      (Use different sample sizes: 36, 25, 16, 8, 2)
alpha <- .05
varUse <- 0
numSamples <- 20
```

Record the number of times the null hypothesis was retained or rejected for each run. Compute the percentage of null hypotheses that were retained. This is the probability of a TYPE II error.

Sample Size	Number Rejected	Number Retained	Percent Retained
36			
25			
16			
8			
2			

a.   Which sample size had the greater probability of a TYPE II error?

    36 _____ 25 _____ 16 _____ 8 _____ 2 _____

b.   What effect does sample size have on the probability of a TYPE II error?
Hint: A TYPE II error is when you retain a false null hypothesis.

_____

_____

7. Run the HYPOTHESIS TEST program again in which the null hypothesis is false. Use $\alpha = 0.10$. Run the program five times using the same sample sizes as before. The program settings should be:

```
popMean <- 10.5
popVar <- 2
nullMean <- 10
tails <- 1
sampleSize <- 36        (Use different sample sizes: 36, 25, 16, 8, 2)
alpha <- .10
varUse <- 0
numSamples <- 20
```

Sample Size	Number Rejected	Number Retained	Percent Retained
36			
25			
16			
8			
2			

a. Which sample size had the greater percent retained (probability of a TYPE II error)?

36 _____ 25 _____ 16 _____ 8 _____ 2 _____

b. Did an increase in α from .05 to .10 *decrease* the percent retained (probability of a TYPE

II error)?   YES _____   NO _____

c. Did an increase in α from .05 to .10 *increase* the percent rejected (probability of a TYPE

I error)?   YES _____   NO _____

8. Run the HYPOTHESIS program again, except this time use a two-tailed test. Run the program five times using the same sample sizes as before. The program settings should be:

```
popMean <- 10.5
popVar <- 2
nullMean <- 10
tails <- 2
sampleSize <- 36      (Use different sample sizes: 36, 25, 16, 8, 2)
alpha <- .10
varUse <- 0
numSamples <- 20
```

Sample Size	Number Rejected	Number Retained	Percent Retained
36			
25			
16			
8			
2			

a. Does a two-tailed test in comparison to the previous one-tail test result in more

Null Hypotheses being retained?   YES _____   NO _____

b. Does sample size affect the results?   YES _____   NO _____

TRUE OR FALSE QUESTION

T   F   a.   If the null hypothesis is false, it will be rejected approximately α percent of the time.

T   F   b.   If the null hypothesis is false, it can still be retained.

T   F   c.   The sample standard deviation may be used in place of the population standard deviation in the z test if the sample size is small.

T   F   d.   The probability of a TYPE II error increases if α is decreased.

T   F   e.   If the p-value is greater than α, then the null hypothesis is rejected.

T   F   f.   The region of rejection is denoted by a tabled statistical value for a given sample size and level of significance.

T   F   g.   A directional hypothesis specifies the probability area for rejection of the null hypothesis in both tails of the normal distribution.

T   F   h.   Different kinds of statistical hypotheses are tested depending on the level of measurement of data.

T   F   i.   The level of significance (alpha) determines the probability area for the region of rejection.

CHAPTER 27

TYPE I ERROR

CHAPTER OBJECTIVES

- To understand the nature of TYPE I Error.
- To understand the relationship between the confidence level and the probability of TYPE I Error.
- To investigate the relationship between sample size and the probability of TYPE I Error.
- To observe the relationship between the width of the confidence interval, sample size, and TYPE I Error.
- To observe that population means don't always fall in the confidence interval for different sample sizes and levels of TYPE I Error.

Science, as a way of understanding the world around us, has for centuries encompassed the classification, ordering, and measuring of plants, characteristics of the earth, animals, and humans. Humans by their very nature have attempted to understand, explain, and predict phenomena in the world around them. When individuals, objects, or events are described as a well-defined, infinite population, random sampling and probability statistics can play a role in drawing conclusions about the population. The problem in Science is essentially one of drawing conclusions about the characteristics of infinitely large populations.

The use of a random sample to compute a statistic as an estimate of a corresponding population parameter involves some degree of uncertainty. In previous chapters, we discovered that the sample mean doesn't always fall in the confidence interval and therefore isn't always accurate in the estimation of the population parameter. The number of times the sample mean falls in the confidence interval is called the confidence level (probability of occurrence) and the number of times it doesn't fall in the confidence interval is called the TYPE I Error (probability of non-occurrence). The **TYPE I Error** therefore indicates the amount of uncertainty or probability of error, especially when making a decision about a population parameter. We generally make a decision about a population parameter in the context of a research question.

The research question could be whether or not to use a new experimental drug for the treatment of a disease. In other words, how confident are we that the drug will work. It could also be whether or not to spend money on an innovative math program for High School students. How confident are we that the innovative math program will be better than the traditional math program? In business, the research question of interest could be whether or not to implement a new strategic plan. We conduct research, formally or informally, to answer these types of questions. In simple terms, we ask a question, gather data, and then answer the question. This is the essence of the research process. However, in making our decision to release a drug for public use or spend thousands of dollars on an innovative math program, we can never be 100 percent certain it will work. There is always some uncertainty involved in our decision, just as the sample means in the previous chapter didn't always fall in the confidence interval!

The research process involves the formulation of a question that can be tested, the collection of relevant data, the analysis and presentation of the data, and the answering of the question. This formal research process embodies the use of the following scientific principles:

a.   Statement of the Research Hypothesis
b.   Selection of Sample Size and Sample Statistic
c.   Selection of Confidence Level and Region of Rejection
d.   Collection and Analysis of Data
e.   Statistical test and Interpretation of Findings

In conducting research using random samples from a population, our research hypothesis is related to the probability of whether an event occurs or not. The probability of an event occurring and the probability of an event not occurring are equal to 100 percent (see Chapter 11). As researchers, we accept some level of probability or uncertainty as to whether an event occurs or not. Our statistical test and interpretation of findings are linked to the TYPE I Error in our decision?

The statement of the research hypothesis expresses the outcomes expected in the research question. The outcomes are expressed as a Null Hypothesis and an Alternative Hypothesis. The **Null Hypothesis** is a statement of no difference between the sample mean and population parameter, or in general terms between a sample statistic and a population parameter. The **Alternative Hypothesis** is a statement that a difference exists between the sample mean and population parameter, typically based upon some intervention, treatment, or manipulation of participants, objects, or events. For example, the Null Hypothesis would state *no difference* in the average mathematics test scores of students in a traditional math program versus an innovative math program. The Alternative Hypothesis would state that the average mathematics test score of students in the innovative math program is greater (*statistically different*) than the average mathematics test score of students in the traditional math program.

The sample size and sample statistic chosen to make a comparison between the sample mean and population mean is determined next in the research process. The sample size is an important consideration because as sample size increases the sample statistic more closely approximates the population parameter. The sample statistic is computed by taking the difference between the sample mean and the population mean, or between two sample means, divided by the standard error of the mean difference, which is based on the sampling distribution of the statistic. We will learn more about conducting these types of statistical tests in later chapters.

The confidence level and region of rejection are now established which set the amount of uncertainty we are willing to accept for the two possible outcomes of the research question, i.e., null versus alternative. If we want to be 95% confident in our decision that the innovative math program produced higher average mathematics test scores, then we must also have a 5% level of uncertainty (TYPE I Error) in our decision. This probability of making a mistake (uncertainty) is called the **level of significance** and denoted by the symbol, α. It is the chance we take of rejecting the Null Hypothesis statement when it is true and erroneously accepting the Alternative Hypothesis statement. If we *reject* the Null Hypothesis statement when it is true, and *accept* the Alternative Hypothesis statement, we commit a **TYPE I Error**. If we *retain* the Null Hypothesis statement when it is false, thus *don't accept* the Alternative Hypothesis statement, we commit a **TYPE II Error,** which will be discussed in the next chapter. In either instance, we do so with a level of confidence and a level of error in our decision.

The region of rejection refers to the selection of a statistical value from the sampling distribution that is at the cut-off point for the beginning of the probability area in which we would reject the null hypothesis in favor of the alternative hypothesis. Statistical values for varying sample sizes and different types of sampling distributions for the 90%, 95%, and 99% confidence levels can be found in the appendix of most statistics books. We refer to these statistical values as the "tabled statistic." If the sample statistic computed from the sample data falls in the 5% area, corresponding to a 95% confidence level, then we reject the Null Hypothesis and accept the Alternative Hypothesis. We make this decision knowing that 5% of the time it might not be the correct decision; which is the TYPE I Error.

The research process would now involve randomly sampling students and randomly assigning them to either a traditional math program or an innovative math program. After a semester of study, each group would take the same mathematics test. The sample means and standard deviations for each group would be computed. A statistical test would determine if the means were statistically different for our level of confidence and corresponding level of significance. In this instance, an independent t-test would be computed which will be presented in a later chapter (see Chapter 30).

The final step in the research process is a comparison of the "tabled statistic" (based on the level of significance and region of rejection) and the sample statistic computed from the sample data. If the sample statistic is greater than the tabled statistic, a decision is made to reject the Null Hypothesis and accept the Alternative Hypothesis. If the sample statistic does not exceed the tabled statistic, then a decision is made to retain the Null Hypothesis and reject the Alternative Hypothesis. Our interpretation of the findings of the research process is based on this decision to reject or accept the research question, which relates to the two possible outcomes of the study.

In this chapter, you will further investigate the relationship between the confidence level and the width of the confidence interval, but in the context of TYPE I Error. In addition, you can use different sample sizes to observe the effect of sample size on the width of the confidence interval, the confidence level, and the TYPE I Error. A single sample of size N will be chosen from a normally distributed population with a mean of 50 and a standard deviation of 10. The TYPE I ERROR program will then compute and graph the 90%, 95%, and 99% confidence intervals which correspond to the 10%, 5%, and 1% levels of uncertainty (levels of significance). Since the population standard deviation is known, z values rather than t-values are used to compute the intervals. The tabled z-values that correspond to the levels of significance are 1.65, 1.96, and 2.58, respectively, for 90%, 95%, and 99% confidence levels. The TYPE I ERROR program prints the location of the sample mean so that you can compare it with the true population mean of 50. A statistical comparison of a single random sample to the population mean would use a one-sample t-test (see Chapter 30).

SUMMARY

In this chapter, you should learn that:

- TYPE I Error is the probability of rejecting a Null Hypothesis statement, which is true, and erroneously accepting an Alternative Hypothesis.
- TYPE I Error probability is the same as the level of significance denoted by the symbol, α.
- As the level of confidence is increased, TYPE I Error is decreased, and the width of the confidence interval increases.
- As the sample size is increased, the width of the confidence interval is decreased.
- The sample mean is always in the confidence interval.
- The population mean is sometimes outside of the confidence interval; the percentage of the intervals that contain the population mean is the confidence level, while the percentage of the intervals that don't contain the population mean is the TYPE I error probability.

How the TYPE I ERROR program works

The **TYPE I ERROR** program uses functions and techniques found in earlier chapters, but adds a way to create generic graphs and custom lines. Only a few new functions were added. The user-defined variables are initialized, a sample of data is randomly generated from a normal distribution, and the mean of that sample is calculated. Next, a dummy variable is created and used as the target for the generic **plot** function. The **plot** function creates a graph with values from 0 to 80 on the x-axis and titles listing the sample mean and sample size. Next, the **lines** function creates a line running from the x-axis to the top of the graph at the point of the sample mean. The first vector within the **lines** function specifies the x values for the ends of the line and the second vector specifies the y values for the ends of the line. During the main processing loop of the program, the lower bound and upper bound, as well as the width of each confidence interval is calculated and added to its respective vector. Each limit is then graphed on the generic plot using the **lines** function. The vertical lines, starting with the two inside lines, indicate the 90%, 95%, and 99% confidence intervals, respectively. Finally, a matrix is created, assigned dimension names, and outputted using **print.char.matrix**.

TYPE I ERROR Program Output

Given the following values:

```
SampleSize <- 10
PopMean <- 50
PopStdDev <- 10
Zvalues <- c(1.645, 1.96, 2.576)   # 90%, 95%, & 99% confidence intervals
numReplications <- 100
```

Confidence Level	Percent In Error	Confidence Interval	Interval Width
90%	7%	50.5 - 40.1	10.4
95%	4%	51.5 - 39.1	12.4
99%	1%	53.5 - 37.2	16.3

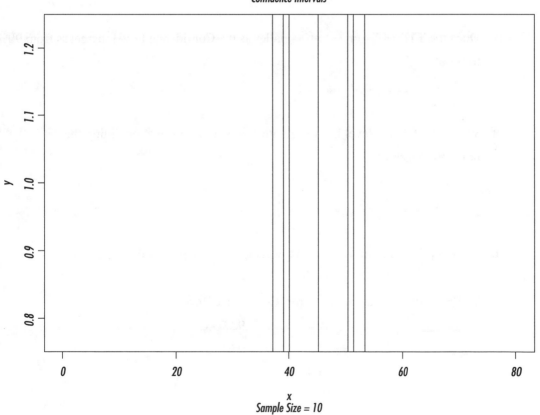

Sample Mean = 45.31
Confidence Intervals

CHAPTER 27 EXERCISES

1.   Run the TYPE I ERROR program for a sample size of 100; keep the other values the same. Record the confidence interval, interval width and TYPE I Error.

Confidence Level	Confidence Interval	Interval Width	TYPE I Error
90%	_____	_____	_____
95%	_____	_____	_____
99%	_____	_____	_____

a.   Does the Interval Width become larger as the Confidence Level increases from 90% to 99%?

   YES _____   NO _____

b.   Does the TYPE I Error become smaller as the Confidence Level increases from 90% to 99%?

   YES _____   NO _____

c.   Which confidence level has the greatest probability of *not* containing the population mean?

   90% _____   95% _____   99% _____

d.   Were the TYPE I Error percents the same as the Expected Error percents?

TYPE I Error	Expected Error	Confidence Level
_____	10%	90%
_____	5%	95%
_____	1%	99%

2.   Run the TYPE I ERROR Program for the sample sizes listed below. Record
the Confidence Interval Width and TYPE I Error for each sample size and
confidence level.

90% Confidence Level

Sample Size	Interval Width	TYPE I Error
10	_____	_____
100	_____	_____
500	_____	_____
1000	_____	_____

95% Confidence Level

Sample Size	Interval Width	TYPE I Error
10	_____	_____
100	_____	_____
500	_____	_____
1000	_____	_____

99% Confidence Level

Sample Size	Interval Width	TYPE I Error
10	_____	_____
100	_____	_____
500	_____	_____
1000	_____	_____

a. Does the confidence interval width become smaller as sample size
increases for 90%, 95%, and 99% confidence levels.

YES _____   NO _____

b. In comparing the results for large versus small sample sizes across the
three confidence levels, do the confidence interval widths get narrower as
sample size increases?

YES _____   NO _____

c. Is it possible for the sample mean to be outside of the confidence interval?

YES _____   NO _____

TRUE OR FALSE QUESTIONS

T   F   a.   A Confidence Level and TYPE I error probability equals 100%

T   F   b.   If the confidence level increases, the TYPE I error decreases.

T   F   c.   As sample size increases, the confidence interval width decreases.

T   F   d.   A TYPE I error is the probability of rejecting the Null Hypothesis when it is true and falsely accepting the Alternative Hypothesis.

T   F   e.   The sample mean is always inside the confidence interval.

T   F   f.   The population mean sometimes falls outside of the confidence interval.

T   F   g.   With all other factors remaining constant, a 90% confidence interval would be narrower than a 99% confidence interval.

CHAPTER 28

TYPE II ERROR

CHAPTER OBJECTIVES

- To understand the nature of TYPE II error.
- To understand the relationship between level of significance (α) and the probability of a TYPE II error.
- To understand the relationship between the directionality of the research question and the probability of a TYPE II error.
- To understand the relationship between sample size and the probability of a TYPE II error.
- To understand the relationship between population variance and the probability of a TYPE II error.
- To understand the relationship between the hypothesized difference between a population parameter and sample statistic (effect size) and the probability of a TYPE II error.
- To understand the relationship between the probability of a TYPE II error and power.

The research process begins with the formulation of a research question. The research question is then stated in a form that can be tested which is called a statistical hypothesis. The two possible outcomes of the statistical hypothesis are termed a **null hypothesis** and an **alternative hypothesis**. The null hypothesis is stated as "no difference" between population parameters and indicates, "to be nullified." The alternative hypothesis reflects the outcome expected by the research question. Consequently, the alternative hypothesis can be stated in either a directional or non-directional format. A **directional** hypothesis states that one population parameter is greater than the other population parameter. A **non-directional** hypothesis states that the two population parameters "are different," but doesn't specify which is greater than the other population parameter. In the previous chapter we assumed a non-directional hypothesis because we used the probability area in both tails (both sides) of the normal bell-shaped probability curve. It is also important to point out that statistical hypotheses are stated in the form of population parameters.

An example of both the non-directional and directional statistical hypotheses will help to visualize how they are presented using population parameters. The **non-directional** hypothesis in both Null Hypothesis (H_O) and Alternative Hypothesis (H_A) form, stating that Company A and Company B have the same average sales, would be indicated as:

$$H_O : \mu_{CompanyA} = \mu_{CompanyB}$$

$$H_A : \mu_{CompanyA} \neq \mu_{CompanyB}$$

The Null Hypothesis indicates that the population means for the two companies are equal. The Alternative Hypothesis indicates that the population means for the two companies are different.

The **directional** hypothesis in both Null Hypothesis (H_O) and Alternative Hypothesis (H_A) form, stating that Company A had greater average sales than Company B, would be indicated as:

$$H_O : \mu_{CompanyA} \leq \mu_{CompanyB}$$

$$H_A : \mu_{CompanyA} > \mu_{CompanyB}$$

The Null Hypothesis indicates that the population mean for Company A is less than or equal to the population mean for Company B. The Alternative Hypothesis indicates that the population mean for Company A is greater than the population mean for Company B, thereby only testing a specific directional difference in the population means of the companies.

The probabilities related to the two possible outcomes, Null Hypothesis and Alternative Hypothesis, are given the name TYPE I error and TYPE II error. A **TYPE I error** is when the null hypothesis is rejected, but in fact it is true. This means that you gathered evidence (data) and concluded that the evidence was strong enough to accept an alternative hypothesis, but did so erroneously. A **TYPE II error** is when the null hypothesis is accepted, but in fact it is false. This means that you gathered evidence (data) and concluded that the evidence wasn't strong enough to reject the null hypothesis, so you retained the null hypothesis, but did so erroneously. Not rejecting the null hypothesis was due to a lack of sufficient evidence (data). Neither decision, to reject or retain the null hypothesis, is one hundred percent certain; therefore we make our decision with some amount of uncertainty. Whether the TYPE I error or TYPE II error is more important depends on the research situation and the type of decision made. An example will help to clarify the TYPE I and TYPE II errors and possible outcomes.

A corporation is going to use data from a sample of people to test a research question of whether or not a new product design will increase the average sales above that of the current product design. Using the current product design, the company sold an average of 85 cars. The company, in planning the study, realizes that two types of error are possible in the study. If the new product design is used, the average sales of the product may not be greater than 85 cars, but the analysis could incorrectly lead to the conclusion that the average sales were higher, a TYPE I error. If the new product design was used and the average sales did exceed 85 cars, but the statistical analysis failed to indicate a statistically significant increase, then a TYPE II error will occur.

When planning this study, the company can control the probability of a TYPE I error by setting the level of significance (α) to a stringent probability level. For example, setting the level of significance to .05 implies that 95 times out of 100 replications of the study, a correct decision would be made, and 5 times out of 100 an incorrect decision would be made. Setting the level of significance to .01 implies that 99 times out of 100 a correct decision would be made, and only 1 time out of 100 an incorrect decision would be made. These probabilities for a correct decision and an incorrect decision are applicable only when the Null Hypothesis is true. Therefore, we set the TYPE I error to a probability level that instills confidence in our decision to reject the null hypothesis (no difference) and accept an alternative hypothesis (difference exists). A TYPE II error requires a further concern for many other factors in the study. The probability of a TYPE II error depends on the level of significance (α), the direction or non-direction of the research question, the sample size, the population variance, and the difference between the population parameters we want to be able to detect (effect size). These concerns determine how powerful our test will be to detect a difference when it actually exists in the population(s) we study. In planning the study, the company needs to be concerned about both TYPE I and TYPE II errors, as well as the consequences of the decision made based on the outcome of the decision.

In testing hypotheses, four possible outcomes exist with regard to the decision made. They are:

		Actual Population Condition	
		Null Hypothesis is True	Null Hypothesis is False
Decision	Reject Null Hypothesis	TYPE I ERROR (Probability = α)	CORRECT DECISION (Probability = 1 – β)
	Retain Null Hypothesis	CORRECT DECISION (Probability = 1 – α)	TYPE II ERROR (Probability = β)

The probability of making a TYPE I error in the Null Hypothesis is denoted by the symbol alpha, α, and referred to as the level of significance, with the probability of a correct decision 1 – α. The probability of making a TYPE II error in the Alternative Hypothesis is denoted by the symbol Beta, β, with the power of the test given by 1 – β; the probability of making a correct decision. The relationship between TYPE I error and TYPE II error is typically graphed using vertical hash marks to denote the area for the region of rejection. The two graphs below indicate the probability areas for the four decision outcomes.

Distribution under Null Hypothesis   Distribution under Alternative Hypothesis

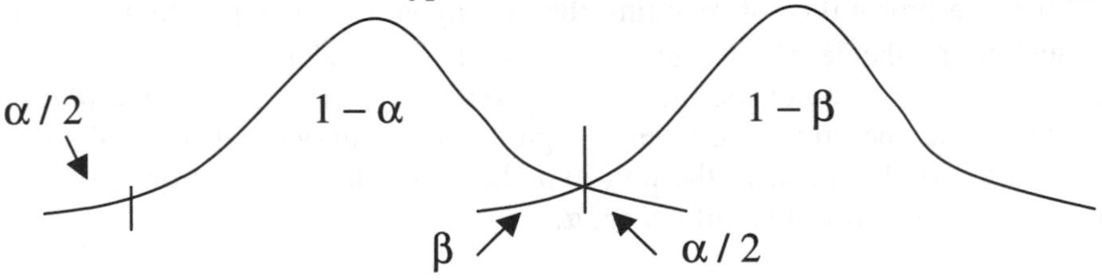

The probability in the tails of the distributions can change because the null and alternative hypotheses can be stated in directional or non-directional forms. In this example, the hypotheses are in a non-directional form, i.e., Is there a statistically significant mean difference between boys and girls on the mathematics test? If the level of significance is .05, then one-half or .025 would be the probability area in the tails of the distribution. If we chose only the one tail ($p = .025$), then the alternative research question would be stated as directional, e.g., Will the girls on average score higher than the boys in mathematics achievement? The statistical tables in the appendix adjust for the directional versus non-directional nature when selecting a "tabled statistic" value.

The basic concern in selecting a TYPE II error is the value for power, which is $1 - \beta$. **Power** is the probability of *not* committing the error. In conducting research in education, psychology, business, and other disciplines, we are concerned about the power of our statistical test to detect a difference in the population parameters. A graph of the power values against different population parameter values will result in *power curves* for different levels of significance and sample size. The resulting power curves provide an adequate determination of the power of a test for all alternative values of the population parameter.

The concerns in research for having an adequate sample size, the nature of TYPE I and TYPE II errors, power of a test, and selection of alternative values for the population parameters, called effect size, form the basis of hypothesis testing. The hypothesis testing theory, known as the *Neyman-Pearson* hypothesis-testing theory, formulates the relationship between these concerns. In practice, we might select power equal to .80, use a .05 level of significance, and a directional hypothesis to test our statistical hypothesis. The **effect size** or magnitude of difference between the population parameters also affects the power of the test. If a small difference must be detected, then the sample size, level of significance, and power must be increased. We also generally know that the power of a test increases as sample size increases, and the power of a test increases as the level of significance is decreased, i.e., .01 to .05. Basically, all of these values are inter-related such that increasing or decreasing one affects the others. There are software programs available on the Internet that help in selecting sample size or power for different statistical tests, given values for the other criteria.

In this chapter, how the probability of a TYPE II error is affected by four criteria (α, sample size, population variance, and effect size) will be simulated using the TYPE II ERROR program in S-PLUS. The TYPE II ERROR program chooses a sample of the size you specify from a true population and determines whether or not to reject the null hypothesis. The TYPE II ERROR program is initially repeated 100 times. The relative frequency of occurrence with which a false null hypothesis is retained is an approximation of the probability of a TYPE II error, β. The power of the test is calculated as 1 minus this relative frequency. Power is equal to $1 - \beta$ when the null hypothesis is false. The theoretical values for the probability of retaining the null hypothesis and power are also given. If the true mean is equal to the mean in the null hypothesis, then the probability of retaining the null hypothesis is equal to $1 - \alpha$. In this case, power is equal to α, the level of significance.   The hypothesis testing in the program is directional to determine whether the mean of a population with a normal distribution is greater than a specified value, therefore, the level of significance is in one tail of the distribution. You will be able to specify the mean in the null hypothesis, the true population mean and variance, the sample size, and the level of significance, α.

SUMMARY

In this chapter, you should learn that:

- A TYPE II error implies that a null hypothesis has been accepted, but is false.
- The probability of a TYPE II error is denoted by the symbol β.
- The probability of a TYPE II error, β, decreases as:

1) α increases (e.g., .01 to .05),
2) N increases,
3) the population variance decreases,
4) the effect size is larger (true mean is farther from the hypothesized mean in the direction of the alternative hypothesis).

- When a TYPE II error decreases, power increases.
- Power is the probability of rejecting a null hypothesis that is false.
- When the null hypothesis is false, power is equal to $1 - \beta$.
- When the null hypothesis is true, power is equal to α.

How the TYPE II ERROR program works

In the TYPE II ERROR program, samples are drawn for a given number of replications instead of for a single sample. A **p-value function** determines the probability area based on a directional one-tail test. The number of times the null hypothesis is rejected based on the p-value is tallied. This tally is used along with the total number of replications to calculate the estimated probability of retaining the null hypothesis and estimated power. Next, the critical value for the test is determined by using a new function called **qnorm**, which takes a probability, mean and variance and returns the number of standard deviations above or below the mean. This is multiplied by the standard deviation and added to the mean to obtain the raw score value that equates to a cutoff point for the region of rejection in the tail of the distribution. This cut-off value is used to obtain the true probability of retaining the null hypothesis and true power for the given number of replications. The rest of the program uses familiar techniques to format and output the calculated information. Two separate tables are output, one table for the null mean difference, population mean difference, population variance, sample size, and alpha; and one table for the estimated probability of retaining the null mean difference, estimated power, true probability of retaining the null mean difference, and true power. Experiment with different values in the program. Be sure that you are aware of the direction of your test and the relative position of the population mean with respect to the mean in the null hypothesis.

TYPE II ERROR Program Output

```
Table of Means, Variance, Sample Size, and Alpha

|Null Mean Diff.|Pop Mean Diff. |Pop Variance  |Sample Size   | Alpha        |
+---------------+---------------+---------------+---------------+---------------+
|0             |0             |1             |5             |0.05          |
+---------------+---------------+---------------+---------------+---------------+


Table of Estimated Null Mean Diff. % and Power with True Null % and Power

|Retain Null % |Power Estimate |True Null %   |True Power    |
+---------------+---------------+---------------+---------------+
|0.920         |0.080         |0.950         |0.050         |
+---------------+---------------+---------------+---------------+
```

CHAPTER 28 EXERCISE

1.   Run the TYPE II ERROR program for the values indicated in the following table for 100 replications.

Null Mean Difference	Population Mean	Population Variance	Sample Size	Alpha	Retain Null %	Power Estimate	True Null %	True Power
0	0.0	1.0	10	.05				
0	1.0	1.0	10	.10				
0	1.0	1.0	10	.05				
0	1.0	1.0	10	.025				
0	1.0	1.0	10	.01				
0	1.2	1.0	10	.05				
0	1.5	1.0	10	.05				
0	2.0	1.0	10	.05				
0	1.0	1.5	10	.05				
0	1.0	2.0	10	.05				

a.   In the first run, the Null Mean equals the Population Mean (Null Hypothesis is true), so does the True Power equal Alpha?

YES _____ NO _____.

b.   In runs 2 - 5, α decreases from .10 to .01 with other factors held the same, so does β increase (Retain Null %)?

YES _____ NO _____.

c.   In runs 2 - 5, α decreases from .10 to .01 with other factors held the same, so does Power decrease (Power Estimate)?

YES _____ NO _____.

d.   Does β (Accept Null %) and $1 - \beta$ (Power Estimate) equal 100 %?

YES _____ NO _____.

e.   In runs 6 - 8, the Population Mean is increasingly different from the Null Mean, that is
     the population mean is getting farther away from the null mean in the direction of the
     alternative hypothesis (effect size), so with other factors held constant does power
     increase?

     YES _____   NO _____.

f.   In runs 9 - 10, the Population Variance is increased, so does Power decrease?

     YES _____   NO _____.

g.   Try to summarize the relationships between alpha, β (Retain Null %), 1 - β (Power
     Estimate), and effect size in examples **a** to **f** above.

     _____

     _____

     _____

     _____

     _____

     _____

2. Run TYPE II ERROR program with the following sample sizes: 10, 20, 30, and 40.

    Keep the other values the same in the program:

```
nullMean <- 0
popMean <- 1
popVar <- 1
sampleSize <- 10
alpha <- .05
tails <- 1
numReplications <- 100
```

a.   As sample size increases with the other factors held constant, does β approach zero?

     YES _____   NO _____

b.   As the sample size increases with the other factors held constant, does Power increase?

     YES _____   NO _____

c. What is the region of rejection for the directional hypothesis where the null hypothesis will be rejected? Note: Tabled Statistic = Mean + (z * Standard error of the statistic).

_____

d. Using the Tabled Statistic in 2c, draw two overlapping normal curves and indicate the areas that represent α, 1- α, β, and 1 - β.

```
         0                    1
        Null              Population
```

3. Run TYPE II ERROR again using the following factors:

```
nullMean <- 0
popMean <- -1
popVar <- 1
sampleSize <- 4
alpha <- .05
tails <- 1
numReplications <- 100
```

a. What is the true probability of retaining the null hypothesis? _____

b. What is the true power? _____

e. Why do you get these values for true probability and power? Hint: You are conducting a directional hypothesis, which only uses the probability area in one tail of the normal curve.

_____

_____

_____

TRUE OR FALSE QUESTIONS

T   F   a.   As α increases, the power of the test increases.

T   F   b.   Larger sample sizes will yield more powerful tests.

T   F   c. β is the probability of rejecting a true null hypothesis.

T   F   d.   Small effect sizes are difficult to detect.

T   F   e. β decreases for larger sample sizes.

T   F   f.   As sample size increases, power increases

T   F   g.   An acceptable value for power is .80

T   F   h.   Power is the probability of rejecting a null hypothesis that is false.

T   F   i.   A TYPE I error refers to rejecting the null hypothesis when it is true.

T   F   j.   A TYPE II error refers to retaining the null hypothesis when it is false.

T   F   k.   Effect size refers to the difference between TYPE I and TYPE II errors.

T   F   l.   A non-directional hypothesis indicates no difference between population parameters.

T   F   m.   A directional hypothesis indicates that one population parameter is greater than the other population parameter.

V

HYPOTHESIS TESTING IN RESEARCH

CHAPTER 29

z TEST STATISTIC FOR PROPORTIONS

CHAPTER OBJECTIVES

- To test research questions involving differences in proportions (percentages).
- To understand differences in research designs involving independent and dependent proportions.
- To calculate the z test statistic for testing differences in independent proportions.
- To calculate the z test statistic for testing differences in dependent proportions.
- To interpret the z test statistic.
- To calculate a confidence interval around the z test statistic.

The previous chapters have presented information on sampling distributions, Central Limit Theorem, confidence intervals, Type I error, Type II error, and hypothesis testing. This information is useful in understanding how the statistics presented in the following chapters are used to test differences between population parameters. The statistical tests presented in this and subsequent chapters depend upon the level of measurement and type of research design.

Many research questions involve testing differences between two population proportions (percentages). For example, Is there a significant difference between the proportion of girls and boys who smoke cigarettes in high school? Is there a significant difference in the proportion of foreign and domestic automobile sales? or Is there a significant difference in the proportion of girls and boys passing the Iowa Test of Basic Skills? These research questions involve testing the differences in population proportions between two independent groups. Other types of research questions can involve differences in population proportions between related or dependent groups. For example, Is there a significant difference in the proportion of adults smoking cigarettes before and after attending a stop smoking clinic? Is there a significant difference in the proportion of foreign automobiles sold in the U.S. between years 1999 and 2000? or Is there a significant difference in the proportion of girls passing the Iowa Test of Basic Skills between the years 1980 and 1990?. Research questions involving differences in independent and dependent population proportions can be tested using a z **test** statistic. Unfortunately, these types of tests are not available in most statistical packages, and therefore you will need to use a calculator or spreadsheet program to conduct the test.

Independent Samples

A practical example using the hypothesis testing approach outlined in Chapter 28 will help to illustrate the z test for differences in proportions between two independent groups. The research question for our example will be: Do a greater proportion of high school students in the population smoke cigarettes in urban rather than rural cities? This is a directional research question. A step-by-step outline will be followed to test this research question.

Step 1. State the directional research question in a statistical hypothesis format.

$$H_0: P_1 \leq P_2 \quad (\text{or } P_1 - P_2 \leq 0)$$
$$H_A: P_1 > P_2 \quad (\text{or } P_1 - P_2 > 0)$$

> Notice that the "H" stands for hypothesis with the subscripts "0" for the null statistical hypothesis and "A" for the alternative statistical hypothesis. The alternative statistical hypothesis is stated to reflect the research question. In this example, the alternative statistical hypothesis indicates the directional nature of the research question. Also, P_1 is the population proportion of high school students who smoke in an urban city and P_2 is the population proportion of high school students who smoke cigarettes in a rural city.

Step 2. Determine the criteria for rejecting the null hypothesis and accepting the alternative hypothesis.

Given $\alpha = .01$, we select the corresponding z value from Table 1 (see appendix) which is the closest to 1% of the area under the normal curve. If our computed z test statistic is greater than this tabled z value, we would reject the null hypothesis in favor of the alternative hypothesis. This establishes our region of rejection, R, or the probability area under the normal curve where differences in sample proportions are unlikely to occur by random chance.

$$R: \ z > 2.33$$

> Notice that in Table 1 (see appendix), the first column indicates z = 2.3 with the other column indicating the 3 in the hundredths decimal place. Also, notice that the percentage = .4901 is the closest to 49%, which leaves 1% area under the normal curve. In Table 1, only one-half of the normal curve is represented, so 50% is automatically added to the 49% to get 99%, which reflects the one-tail probability for the directional alternative statistical hypothesis.

Step 3. Collect the sample data and compute the z test statistic

A random sample of 20 percent of all high school students from both an urban and a rural city was selected. In the urban city, 20,000 high school students were sampled with 25% smoking cigarettes ($n_1 = 5,000$). In the rural city, 1,000 high school students were sampled with 15% smoking cigarettes ($n_2 = 150$). The proportions were:

$P_1 = .25$ (25% of the boys in the sample of high school students smoke cigarettes)
$P_2 = .15$ (15% of the girls in the sample of high school students smoke cigarettes)

The standard deviation of the sampling distribution of the differences in independent sample proportions is called the standard error of the difference between independent sample proportions. This value is needed to compute the z test statistic. The formula is:

$$S_{P_1-P_2} = \sqrt{\frac{pq}{N}}$$

where:

$p = (n_1 + n_2 / N) = (5,000 + 150 / 21,000) = .245$
$q = 1 - p = 1 - .245 = .755$
n_1 = number in first sample = 5,000
n_2 = number in second sample = 150
N = total sample size taken = (20,000 + 1,000) = 21,000

$$S_{P_1-P_2} = \sqrt{\frac{.245(.755)}{21000}} = .003$$

The z test can now be computed as:

$$z = \frac{P_1 - P_2}{S_{P_1-P_2}} = \frac{.25 - .15}{.003} = \frac{.10}{.003} = 33.33$$

> We have learned from previous chapters that to test a statistical hypothesis, we need to know the sampling distribution of the statistic. The sampling distribution of the difference between two independent proportions is normally distributed when sample sizes are greater than five. Thus, we can use the normal distribution z statistic to test our statistical hypothesis.

Step 4. Compute the confidence interval around the z test statistic

A confidence interval is computed by using the percent difference between the two independent groups ($P_1 - P_2 = .10$), the tabled z value corresponding to a given alpha level for   a two-tailed region of region (z = 2.58), and the standard deviation of the sampling distribution or standard error of the test statistic ($S_{P1 - P2} = .003$).

$CI_{99} = .10 +/- (2.58)(.003)$
$CI_{99} = .10 +/- (.008)$
$CI_{99} = (.092, .108)$

> Notice that the tabled z value selected for determining the confidence interval around the computed z test statistic is not the same because the confidence interval is based on a two-tailed interpretation. The alternative statistical hypothesis was one-tail because of the directional nature of the research question.

Step 5. Interpret the z test statistic results

Our interpretation is based upon a test of the null hypothesis and a 99% confidence interval around the computed z test statistic. Since the computed z = 33.33 is greater than the tabled z value, z = 2.33 at the .01 level of significance, we reject the null statistical hypothesis in favor of the alternative statistical hypothesis. The probability that the observed difference in the sample proportions of 10% would have occurred by chance is less than .01. We can therefore conclude that the urban city had a greater percentage of high school students smoking cigarettes than the rural city. The Type I error was set at .01, so we can be fairly confident in our interpretation.

The confidence interval was computed as .092 to .108, indicating that we can be 99% confident that this interval contains the difference between the population proportions from which the samples were taken. Moreover, the narrowness of the confidence interval gives us some idea of how much the difference in independent sample proportions might vary from random sample to random sample. Consequently, we can feel fairly confident that a 9% (.092) to 11% (.108) difference would exist between urban and rural city high school students smoking cigarettes upon repeated sampling of the population.

Dependent Samples

The null hypothesis that there is no difference between two population proportions can also be tested for dependent samples using the z test statistic. The research design would involve obtaining percentages from the same sample or group twice. The research design would therefore have paired observations. Some examples of when this occurs would be:

1) Test differences in proportions of agreement in a group before and after a discussion of the death penalty.
2) Test differences in percent passing for students who take two similar tests.
3) Test differences in the proportion of employees who support a retirement plan and the proportion that support a company daycare.

The research design involves studying the impact of diversity training on the proportion of company employees who would favor hiring foreign workers. Before and after diversity training, employees were asked whether or not they were in favor of the company hiring foreign workers. The research question could be stated as: Are the proportions of company employees who favor hiring foreign workers the same before and after diversity training?. This is a non-directional research question. A step-by-step approach to hypothesis testing will be used.

Step 1. State the non-directional research question in a statistical hypothesis format.

$$H_O: P_1 = P_2 \quad (\text{or } P_1 - P_2 = 0)$$
$$H_A: P_1 \neq P_2 \quad (\text{or } P_1 - P_2 \neq 0)$$

Notice in this example that we are interested in testing the null hypothesis of no difference between the population proportions against the non-directional alternative hypothesis, which indicates that the proportions are different. The alternative statistical hypothesis is stated to reflect the non-directional research question. Also, P_1 is the proportion of employees in favor before diversity training and P_2 is the proportion of employees in favor after diversity training.

Step 2. Determine the criteria for rejecting the null hypothesis and accepting the alternative hypothesis.

Given $\alpha = .05$, we select the corresponding z value from Table 1 which is the closest to 5% of the area under the normal curve (2.5% in each tail of the normal curve). If our computed z test statistic is greater than this tabled z value, we would reject the null hypothesis and accept the alternative hypothesis. This establishes our region of rejection, R, or the probability areas under the normal curve where differences in sample proportions are unlikely to occur by random chance.

$$R: \ z \pm 1.96$$

Notice that in Table 1 (see appendix), the first column indicates $z = 1.9$ with the other column indicating the 6 in the hundredths decimal place. Also, notice that the percentage $= .4750$ indicates .025 probability area under the normal curve in only one tail. In Table 1, only one-half of the normal curve is represented, but .025 in both tails of the normal curve would equal 5%. If we add $.4750 + .4750$, it would equal .95 or 95%, which indicates the remaining percent under the normal curve. The region of rejection indicates two z values, $+1.96$ and -1.96, for rejecting the null hypothesis, which reflects testing a non-directional research question.

Step 3. Collect the sample data and compute the z test statistic

A random sample of 100 employees from a high-tech company were interviewed before and after a diversity training session and asked whether or not they favored the company hiring foreign workers. Their sample responses were as follows:

After Diversity Training

		No	Yes	
Before Diversity Training	Yes	10 (.10)	20 (.20)	30 (.30)
	No	50 (.50)	20 (.20)	70 (.70)
		60 (.60)	40 (.40)	100 Total

The sample data indicated the following proportions:

P_1 = proportion in favor before diversity training = .30 or 30%
P_2 = proportion in favor after diversity training = .40 or 40%

Notice the order of the data entry in the cells of this table. This was done so that certain cells indicate disagreement or dissimilar responses before and after diversity training.

The standard deviation of the sampling distribution of the differences in dependent sample proportions is called the standard error of the difference between dependent sample proportions. This value is needed to compute the z test statistic. The formula is:

$$S_{P_1 - P_2} = \sqrt{\frac{P_{11} + P_{22}}{N}}$$

where:

P_{11} = percent change from before to after training (yes→ no) = .10
P_{12} = percent change from before to after training (no→ yes) = .20
N = total sample size = 100

$$S_{P_1 - P_2} = \sqrt{\frac{.10 + .20}{100}} = .055$$

The z test can now be computed as:

$$z = \frac{P_1 - P_2}{S_{P_1 - P_2}} = \frac{.30 - .40}{.055} = \frac{-.10}{.055} = -1.82$$

> We have learned from previous chapters that to test a statistical hypothesis, we need to know the sampling distribution of the statistic. The sampling distribution of the difference between two dependent proportions is normally distributed when the sum of the sample sizes in the diagonal cells are greater than ten. Thus, we can use the normal distribution z statistic to test our statistical hypothesis.

Step 4. Compute the confidence interval around the z test statistic

A confidence interval is computed by using the percent difference between the two independent groups (P_1 - P_2 = .10), the tabled z value corresponding to a given alpha level for a two-tailed region of region (z = ±1.96), and the standard deviation of the sampling distribution or standard error of the test statistic ($S_{P1 - P2}$ = .055).

CI_{99} = .10 +/- (1.96)(.055)
CI_{99} = .10 +/- (.108)
CI_{99} = (-.008, .208)

> Notice that the tabled z value selected for determining the confidence interval around the computed z test statistic is the same because the confidence interval is also based on a two-tailed interpretation. Also, the null hypothesized parameter of zero (no difference in proportions) is contained in the confidence interval, which is consistent with not rejecting the null hypothesis.

Step 5. Interpret the z test statistic results

Our interpretation is once again based upon a test of the null hypothesis, but this time using a 95% confidence interval around the computed z test statistic because of the non-directional nature of the research question. Since the computed z = -1.82 is less than the tabled z value, z = -1.96 at the .05 level of significance, we retain the null statistical hypothesis. The probability that the observed difference in the sample proportions of 10% would have occurred by chance is greater than .05. We therefore cannot conclude that the percent of company employees in favor of hiring foreign workers was different before and after diversity training. The Type I error was set at .05, so we can be fairly confident in our interpretation.

The confidence interval was computed from -.008 to .208, indicating that we can be 95% confident that this interval contains the null hypothesis parameter of zero difference between the population proportions from which the sample was taken. Moreover, the spread in the confidence interval gives us some idea of how much the difference in the dependent sample proportions might vary from random sample to random sample. Consequently, we should be sensitive to a research design factor that may have impacted the statistical test, which is the duration and intensity of the diversity training. Obviously a one-hour training session involving watching a short slide presentation might have less of an impact on employees than a six-week training session involving role modeling with foreign workers on the job.

SUMMARY

In this chapter, you should learn that:

- A *z* test statistic can be used to answer research questions concerning differences in proportions between independent samples or groups.
- A *z* test statistic can be used to answer research questions concerning differences in proportions between dependent samples or groups.
- A statistically significant difference in proportions indicates that, beyond a random chance level, two groups differ in their proportions.
- A confidence interval around the z test statistic indicates the amount of difference in the group proportions one can expect upon repeated sampling.
- The confidence interval captures the null hypothesis parameter of zero when proportions are not statistically significantly different.

How the ZTEST programs work

The ZTEST-IND program begins by assigning a critical z value based on the alpha level and directional nature of the test. Next, *size1* and *size2* are set to the respective sample sizes and *num1* and *num2* are set to the number of positive cases in each sample. After this, the proportion of positive cases for each sample are computed as well as the overall *p* and *q*, which represent the overall proportion of positive cases and negative cases, respectively. Next, the standard error of the difference(*s*) is computed as well as the *z* statistic. The individual proportions of positive cases, the critical z value, and the standard error of the difference are then used to calculate the confidence interval around the proportion differences and all relevant values are printed to the screen.

The ZTEST-DEP program is similar to the ZDIFF-IND program with a few differences in how some intermediate values are calculated. It starts by assigning a critical z value, but then assigns numbers to the variables *num11*, *num12*, *num21*, and *num22*, where *num11* and *num22* represent changes from one outcome to the other and *num12* and *num21* represent cases where the outcome was the same. Next, the total number of outcomes are calculated by adding the cells and then the proportion of changes of both types (*num11* and *num22*) are calculated. The proportions of cases with a positive outcome from each group or occasion are calculated next. The standard error of the difference is determined using the proportion of changed outcomes and the total number of outcomes, and the z statistic is determined from the difference in positive outcomes between the two groups or occasions and the standard error of the difference. Finally, the upper and lower bounds of a confidence interval around the difference in dependent proportions is calculated and all relevant values are output using the **cat** command.

ZTEST-IND Program Output

Given the following values for two independent sample proportions:

```
zCrit <- 2.576   # 90%=1.645, 95%=1.96, & 99%=2.576 confidence intervals (two-
tailed)
size1 <- 20000
size2 <- 1000
num1 <- 5000
num2 <- 150
```

The z test results for the difference between two independent proportions is:

```
Difference in proportions= 0.1
Standard Error of Diff= 0.003
z Statistic= 33.3333
Confidence Interval=( 0.0923 , 0.1077 )
```

ZTEST-DEP Program Output

Given the following values for two dependent sample proportions:

```
zCrit <- 1.96   # 90%=1.645, 95%=1.96, & 99%=2.576 confidence intervals (two-
tailed)
num11 <- 10
num12 <- 20
num21 <- 50
num22 <- 20
```

The z test results for the difference between two independent proportions is:

```
Difference in proportions= -0.1
Standard Error of Diff= 0.0548
z Statistic= -1.8248
Confidence Interval=( -0.0074 , 0.2074 )
```

CHAPTER 29 EXERCISES

1. Run ZTEST for the independent sample proportions in the following example.
    The research question is: Do Democrats and Republicans differ in their percent
    agreement on handgun control? Test the research question at the .01 level of
    significance. The following sample data was collected:

    Democrats: 50,000 with 24,000 (.48) or 48% in favor of handgun control
    Republicans: 50,000 with 12,000 (.24) or 24% in favor of handgun control

    a. What is the percent difference between the two independent groups?_____
    b. What is the standard error of the difference between the independent percents?

        _____

    c. What is the z test statistic value?_____
    d. What are the confidence interval values? (_____ , _____)
    e. What decision is made based on the z test and confidence interval?
        Retain Null _____ Reject Null_____
    f. What percent of the time would you expect the null hypothesis to be rejected by
        mistake? _____.
    g. What is the name of this type of error? _____

2. Run ZTEST for the dependent sample proportions in the following example.
    The research question, Is the proportion of students passing the first exam the same as the
    proportion of students passing the second exam?, will be tested at the .05 level of
    significance. The following sample data was collected (fill in the missing information):

    Pass Second Exam

		No	Yes	
Pass	Yes	20 ( )	50 ( )	__ ( )
First Exam	No	15 ( )	15 ( )	__ ( )
		__ ( )	__ ( )	100

a. What is the percent passing difference between the exams? ____

b. What is the standard error of the difference between the dependent percents? _____

c. What is the z test statistic value? _____

d. What are the confidence interval values? (_____ , _____)

e. What decision is made based on the z test and confidence interval? Retain Null ____ Reject Null____

f. What percent of the time would you expect the null hypothesis to be rejected by mistake? _____

g. What is the name of this type of error? _____

TRUE OR FALSE QUESTIONS

T　　F　　a.　　A z test statistic is used *only* with independent sample percents.

T　　F　　b.　　The null hypothesis in the z test corresponds to no difference in the proportions of either independent or dependent proportions.

T　　F　　c.　　The z test statistic will be large if there are large differences between the sample proportions relative to the standard error.

T　　F　　d.　　A Type I error may occur when using the z test statistic.

T　　F　　e.　　The z test statistic can be negative or positive in value.

T　　F　　f.　　The z test statistic can *only* be used with directional hypothesis testing.

T　　F　　g.　　The tabled z value used in forming the confidence interval around the z test statistic is always based upon two tails under the normal curve.

CHAPTER 30

CHI-SQUARE TEST STATISTIC

CHAPTER OBJECTIVES

- To test research questions involving categorical variables.
- To understand observed versus expected frequencies in the cross-tabulation of data.
- To calculate the chi-square test statistic for testing the independence of two categorical variables.
- To interpret chi-square results for significance, variance account for, and contribution of each cell to the chi-square statistic.
- To understand the meaning of α in interpreting the chi-square test of independence.
- To understand the meaning of a TYPE II error in interpreting the chi-square test of independence.
- To understand the relationship between the probability of a TYPE II error and the amount of deviation from independence.

A popular statistic for testing research questions involving categorical data is the chi-square test statistic. The chi-square statistic was developed by **Karl Pearson** to test whether two categorical variables were independent of each other. A typical research question involving two categorical variables can be stated as, "Is drinking alcoholic beverages independent of smoking cigarettes?" A researcher would gather data on both variables in a "yes-no" format, then cross tabulate the data. The cross-tabulation of the data for this research question would look like the following:

Do you drink alcoholic beverages?

	Yes	No
Yes		
No		

Do you smoke cigarettes?

Individuals would be asked both questions and their separate responses recorded. The cross-tabulation of the data would permit an indication of the number of people who *did* smoke cigarettes and *did* drink alcoholic beverages, the number of people who *did* smoke cigarettes and *did not* drink alcoholic beverages, the number of people who *did not* smoke cigarettes and *did* drink alcoholic beverages, and the number of people who *did not* smoke cigarettes and *did not* drink alcohol. Consequently, four possible outcomes are represented by the cross-tabulation of the yes/no responses to the two questions.

228

The **chi-square statistic** is computed by taking the sum of the observed frequency minus the expected frequency squared divided by the expected frequency in each of the four cells. The chi-square formula is expressed as:

$$\chi^2 = \sum \left(\frac{(O-E)^2}{E} \right)$$

Multiplying the respective row and column sums and dividing by the total number of individuals yields the expected frequencies in each of the four cells. The calculation of the difference between what is observed and what is expected by chance alone forms the basis for the test of independence between two categorical variables. The *expected cell frequencies* are based on the two categorical variables being independent. An example will help to illustrate how to calculate the expected frequencies and the chi-square statistic.

A school district is interested in having parents pass a bond referendum to build a new high school. The superintendent decides to conduct a preliminary poll of the voters to see if they might favor passing the bond. The superintendent is also concerned about whether men and women would vote differently on the bond referendum. Consequently, 200 parents (100 men and 100 women) in the district were randomly selected and telephoned to collect the data. Each parent was asked their gender and whether they favor or oppose a bond to build a new high school. The responses are cross-tabulated below.

Gender	Favor		Oppose		Total
Men	40	(60)	60	(40)	100
Women	80	(60)	20	(40)	100
Totals	120		80		200

The observed values indicate 40 out of 100 (40%) men and 80 out of 100 (80%) women are in favor of the bond, while 60 out of 100 (60%) men and 20 out of 100 (20%) women are opposed to the bond. If the null hypothesis is true (no difference in the percent between men and women in favor of the bond), then we would expect the percentages to be the same for both men and women, i.e., of the 120 observed in favor, one-half or 60 individuals would be expected in each gender cell. The expected cell frequencies are what would be expected if gender and voting were independent. The most convenient way to calculate the expected cell values is to multiply the corresponding row and column sums and divide by the total sample size. For men, the first expected cell value is: (100 x 120) / 200 = 60. The other expected cell value is: (100 x 80) / 200 = 40. For women, the first expected cell value is: (100 x 120) / 200 = 60. The other expected cell value is: (100 x 80) / 200 = 40. The expected cell values are in parentheses in the table. The expected cell values should always add up to the total for each row and/or column, respectively.

The chi-square statistic compares the corresponding observed and expected values in the cells of the table under the assumption that the categorical variables are independent, i.e., the null hypothesis is true. If the row and the column variables are independent, then the proportion observed in each cell should be similar to the proportion expected in each cell. Is the difference between what we observed and expected in the four cells statistically different or due to random chance (expected values)? A decision about the null hypothesis is made on the basis of the chi-square statistic, which is computed as follows:

$$\chi^2 = \sum \left(\frac{(40-60)^2}{60} + \frac{(60-40)^2}{40} + \frac{(80-60)^2}{60} + \frac{(20-40)^2}{40} \right)$$

$$\chi^2 = \sum (6.67 + 10 + 6.67 + 10) = 33.34$$

The computed chi-square value is compared to a tabled chi-square value in the appendix for a given degree of freedom. The degrees of freedom are always determined by the number of rows minus one (r-1) times the number of columns minus one (c-1). This can be expressed as: df = (r-1)(c-1). Since there are two rows and two columns, the degree of freedom is: df = (2-1)(2-1) = 1. The tabled chi-square value for df = 1 and a .05 level of significance is 3.84. Since the computed chi-square value of 33.34 is greater than the tabled chi-square value of 3.84, we reject the null hypothesis in favor of the alternative hypothesis that men and women differ in the percent favoring a bond for building a new school.

The chi-square value is computed over all the cells and therefore a significant chi-square doesn't specify which cells may have contributed to the significance of the overall chi-square value. Our interpretation of the overall chi-square result is greatly enhanced by realizing that each cell value is itself a chi-square value! Consequently, we can interpret each cell value individually and compare it to the tabled chi-square value of 3.84 with df = 1. Since each cell value is greater than 3.84 (6.67, 10, 6.67, and 10), we would conclude that each cross-tabulated cell significantly contributed to the overall chi-square. Also, each expected cell frequency should be greater than five to meet the assumption for computing the chi-square statistic.

Another helpful approach to interpreting chi-square results is to take each individual chi-square value (cell value) as a percent of the overall chi-square value. This provides a variance accounted for interpretation. In our example, 6.67/33.34 = 20%, 10/33.34 = 30%, 6.67/33.34 = 20%, and 10/33.34 = 30%. The sum of these cell percents must always equal 100%. Our interpretation would then be based on which cell or cells contributed the most to the overall chi-square.

The chi-square statistic will be small if there are small differences between the observed and the expected values, and it will be large if there large differences. The chi-square statistic for a two-by-two table is distributed as a theoretical chi-square sampling distribution with 1 degree of freedom. Therefore, the theoretical chi-square distribution can be used to determine the region of rejection for the null hypothesis. The region of rejection includes any chi-square statistic greater than the 1-α percentile of the theoretical chi-square distribution with degree of freedom = (r-1)(c-1). Consequently, the chi-square test of independence can be performed on tables of any dimension, i.e., varying numbers of rows and columns for categorical variables.

In this chapter, we only demonstrate the chi-square statistic for two-by-two tables. The CROSSTAB program will allow you to select row and column values that are independent or dependent. If the rows and columns are independent, you will be able to observe the variability in the observed values that occur because of random sampling. A TYPE I error will occur when the rows and columns are independent, i.e., the null hypothesis will be rejected when it is true. If the rows and columns are dependent, you will be able to observe TYPE II errors, i.e., the null hypothesis is retained. As in previous programs, the probability of a TYPE II error will depend on how much the true situation differs from the null hypothesis. If the rows and columns are almost independent, then the probability of a TYPE II error will be high.

In the CROSSTAB program, you must select four percents for the true population and the sample size. The program will then select a random sample of size N from this population. The percents you selected will be printed in a table along with the observed and expected values. A chi-square statistic will be computed and printed along with the degrees of freedom and probability value. You will make a decision about whether to retain or reject the null hypothesis based on the probability value being $p < .05$. You should try both small and large differences between the observed and expected values to better understand the magnitude of the chi-square value. You may want to examine each individual cell chi-square value for significance and hand calculate the percent contribution to the overall chi-square value.

SUMMARY

In this chapter, you should learn that:

- A chi-square statistic can be used to test research questions involving cross-tabulated categorical variables.
- An overall chi-square statistic is computed by summing the individual cell values (chi-squares) in a cross-tabulated table.
- The degrees of freedom for a cross-tabulated table are row minus one times column minus one, i.e., $df = (r-1)(c-1)$.
- The chi-square test of independence can be used for any number of rows and columns, as long as the expected cell frequency is greater than five.
- A chi-square test of independence is used to determine whether or not the rows and columns are independent (null hypothesis).
- If the null hypothesis is true, it is still possible that the chi-square test could lead to a rejection of the null hypothesis (TYPE I error).
- If the null hypothesis is false, it is still possible that the chi-square test could lead to retaining the null hypothesis (TYPE II error).
- The ratio of each cell value to the overall chi-square value provides a variance accounted for interpretation of how much each cell contributed to the overall chi-square value.

How the CROSSTAB program works

The CROSSTAB program makes extensive use of matrices to represent cross-tabulated categorical variable tables. The program first defines the true proportions within each cell (the numbers are arranged by the first row followed by the second row) and then the sample size.

Next, random data are generated from a discrete population of data from 1 to 4, simulating categorization into a cell of the table. The vector of data is factored and tabled in order to get counts for each outcome and then placed into a matrix. The table of expected values is built from the sample data by taking the sum of the values for column 1 and dividing it by the sample size to determine the proportion of total outcomes that fall within the first column, then multiplying it by the total number of responses for row 1. This gives the expected value for cell (1,1). The process is repeated for the other three cells and the results are fitted into a matrix and rounded to two digits. Three matrices are then printed: True Population Proportions, Observed Proportions, and Expected Proportions. Finally, the function **chisq.test** is performed on the *testMatrix* object in order to do the actual chi-square test. The chi-square value, degrees of freedom, and p-value are printed by default.

The program is simplified for sample data in a 2 x 2 table. Most of the program commands create output matrices for the true and expected values in the table, which are not necessary for the **chisq.test** function. The **chisq.test** function uses the Yates correction, which uses real limits around numbers, e.g. real limits of 5 is 4.5 to 5.5. You may wish to run the program several times to familiarize yourself with the output and check the accuracy of the expected values by hand calculation. Also, cell proportions rather than cell frequencies are output for ease of understanding.

CROSSTAB Program Output

Given the following values:

```
cellProbs <- c(.10,.15,.30,.45)
sampleSize <- 100
```

```
Population Proportions      Observed Proportions      Expected Proportions

      X     Y                     X     Y                     X     Y
A 0.10  0.15                A 0.15  0.17                A 0.14  0.18
B 0.30  0.45                B 0.30  0.38                B 0.31  0.37
```

```
Pearson's chi-square test with Yates' continuity correction
Chi-square = 0.0019, df = 1, p-value = 0.9656
```

Given the following values:

```
cellProbs <- c(.70,.10,.10,.10)
sampleSize <- 100
```

```
Population Proportions      Observed Proportions      Expected Proportions

      X     Y                     X     Y                     X     Y
A 0.70  0.10                A 0.65  0.12                A 0.59  0.18
B 0.10  0.10                B 0.12  0.11                B 0.18  0.05
```

```
Pearson's chi-square test with Yates' continuity correction
Chi-square = 8.6544, df = 1, p-value = 0.0033
```

CHAPTER 30 EXERCISES

1.   Run CROSSTAB using the Population proportions below with a sample size of 100.

        Population Proportions

.50	.20
.10	.20

        Observed Proportions

        Expected Proportions

        a.   Are the expected values in the cells computed correctly?   YES____ NO____
        b.   Is the chi-square statistic computed correctly?   YES____ NO____
        c.   What is the chi-square value?   _____
        d.   What is the statistical decision?   Retain Null ____ Reject Null____
        e.   Does the decision agree with the true percent?   YES____ NO____
        f.   What percent of the time would you expect the null hypothesis to be
                rejected by mistake? _____
        g.   What is the name of this type of error? _____

2.   Run CROSSTAB using the Population proportions below with a sample size of 100.

Population Proportions

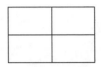

| .16 | .32 |
| .28 | .24 |

Observed Proportions

Expected Proportions

a. Are the expected values in the cells computed correctly?   YES_____ NO_____
b. Is the chi-square statistic computed correctly?   YES_____ NO_____
c. What is the chi-square value?   _____
d. What is the statistical decision?   Retain Null _____ Reject Null_____
e. Does the decision agree with the true percent?   YES_____ NO_____
f. What percent of the time would you expect the null hypothesis to be rejected
    by mistake? _____
g. What is the name of this type of error? _____

TRUE OR FALSE QUESTIONS

T   F   a.   A chi-square statistic is used with ordinal data.

T   F   b.   The null hypothesis in the chi-square test corresponds to no difference in the row and column categories.

T   F   c.   The chi-square statistic will be large if there is a large difference between the observed and the expected values in the cells.

T   F   d.   If the true population has independent rows and column, then a TYPE I error may occur.

T   F   e.   The chi-square statistic can be negative.

T   F   f.   The overall chi-square value indicates which cells contributed to a statistically significant finding.

T   F   g.   The tabled chi-square value is 3.84 with one degree of freedom at the .05 level of significance.

CHAPTER 31

t Test for Mean Differences

CHAPTER OBJECTIVES

- To understand the sampling distribution of the mean.
- To apply the sampling distribution of the mean to test statistical hypotheses.
- To compute the one sample t-test for the mean given small sample sizes.
- To understand the sampling distribution of the difference between the means of two independent samples given small sample sizes.
- To compute the two sample independent t-test.
- To understand the sampling distribution of the difference between the means of two related (dependent) samples given small sample sizes.
- To compute the dependent t-test.

Sampling distributions are frequency distributions of a statistic, which are generated to make an inference between the sample statistic and its corresponding population parameter. The average (mean) statistical value in the sampling distribution is the expected value of the population parameter. The variance of the sampling distribution is used to calculate the standard error of the statistic. The standard error of the statistic is a function of sample size and is used to calculate confidence intervals around the sample statistic, which provides the basis for testing statistical hypotheses.

The distribution theory that led to a solution of the problem of estimating the population mean, μ, when the population variance was unknown, σ^2, was due to **William S. Gossett**, a chemist, who in 1908 wrote under the pseudonym of "Student." William S. Gossett, who worked for a brewery, in Dublin, Ireland determined that when the sample size was large, the sampling distribution of the z statistic was normal, however, when the sample size was small, the sampling distribution was leptokurtic or peaked. He referred to this slightly non-normal distribution as the t distribution (see Chapter 20). W. S. Gossett further discovered that as he increased the sample sizes, the sampling distribution became normal, and therefore the t values equaled the z values. W. S. Gossett signed his pivotal work, "Student," and today small sample tests of mean differences are referred to as the "student t-test," or simply the t-test. **Sir Ronald Fisher**, using the early work of "Student," extended his ideas into modern day analysis of variance techniques (see Chapter 32).

One-sample t-test

The sampling distribution of the mean can be used to determine the expected value of the population mean and variance when they are unknown. The Central Limit Theorem supports this assumption because as sample size increases, the sampling distribution of the mean becomes

236

a normal distribution with the mean = μ, and variance = σ^2/N. Knowledge of this permits one to test whether the sample mean is statistically different from a population mean. The test is called a **one-sample t-test**, which is computed by:

$$t = \frac{\overline{X} - \mu}{\sqrt{\dfrac{S^2}{N}}} = \frac{\overline{X} - \mu}{S/\sqrt{N}}$$

Suppose a class of 25 students was given instruction using a new, enriched mathematics curriculum and then took a nationally standardized math achievement test. If the new, enriched mathematics curriculum leads to better learning in the population, then this sample of 25 students should perform better on the math achievement test than students in the larger population who learned mathematics under the traditional mathematics curriculum. Assume the 25 students had a mean math achievement test score of 110 with a standard deviation of 15. The mean math achievement test score for students in the population taking the traditional math curriculum was 100. What is the probability that a random sample of this size would have a sample mean of 110 or higher? This research question can be tested using a one-sample t-test. The one-sample t-test is computed as:

$$t = \frac{110 - 100}{\sqrt{\dfrac{15^2}{25}}} = \frac{10}{\sqrt{\dfrac{225}{25}}} = \frac{10}{3} = 3.33$$

If we were to examine the probability area in the tails of the normal distribution for a z value of 3.33, we would find a probability area equal to .0004 (.4996 + .0004 = .5000). However, since the probability area in the tails of the normal distribution are not the same as the t distribution, given small sample sizes, we need to examine the probability area in the tails of the t distribution *not* the normal distribution. We therefore use the t-table in the appendix, where we find the degrees of freedom, *df*, (df = n -1 = 24) and a probability area depending upon a directional (one-tail) or non-directional (two-tailed) test. For *df* = 24 and *p* = .0005 (one-tail test), we find a tabled t value equal to 3.745. Since the computed *t* = 3.33 is less than the tabled *t* = 3.745, we retain the null hypothesis. We would conclude that there is no difference in the mean math achievement test scores at the *p* = .0005 level of statistical significance.

Because the t distribution is leptokurtic or peaked for small samples, the probabilities in the tails of the t distribution are greater than the probabilities in the normal distribution. When W. S. Gossett discovered this, he made an adjustment for small sample sizes by entering larger tabled t values from the sampling distribution of the t values. By adjusting the t values, he compensated for the greater probability area under the sampling distributions. If you examine the last row in the t table in the appendix, you will find t values that are equal to the z values under the normal distribution because when sample sizes are large *t* = *z*. In practice, we use the t test rather than the z test for testing means because it applies to both small and large samples.

Independent t-test

 The sampling distribution of the difference between the means of two independent samples provides the basis for the testing of a mean difference hypothesis between two groups. Taking a random sample from one population, a second random sample from another population, and then computing the difference in the means, provides the basis for the sampling distribution. The process is repeated several times and the mean differences are graphed in a frequency distribution. Under the assumption of no difference between the means (null hypothesis), the mean of this sampling distribution is zero.

 A typical research situation in which one would use the independent t-test might involve one group of employees receiving sales training and the second group of employees *not* receiving any sales training. The number of sales for each group is recorded and averaged. The null hypothesis would be stated as, "The average sales for the two groups are equal." An alternative hypothesis would be stated as, "The group receiving the sales training will on average have higher sales than the group that did not receive any sales training." If the sample data for the two groups were recorded as 1) Sales Training: mean = 50, standard deviation = 10, n = 100, and 2) No Sales Training: mean = 40, standard deviation = 10, n = 100; then we could compute an **independent t-test** as:

$$t = \frac{\overline{X}_1 - \overline{X}_2}{S_{\overline{x}_1 - \overline{x}_2}}$$

 The numerator of the independent t-test formula computes the difference between the means of the two independent groups. The denominator of the independent t-test formula computes the standard error of the statistic (standard deviation of the sampling distribution), which is computed as:

$$S_{\overline{x}_1 - \overline{x}_2} = \sqrt{\frac{(n_1 - 1)s_1^2 + (n_2 - 1)s_2^2}{n_1 + n_2 - 2}\left(\frac{1}{n_1} + \frac{1}{n_2}\right)}$$

This equation uses information from both samples to estimate a common population variance, which is referred to as "pooling the variances" or "averaging" the sample variances. The square root of this "pooled variance" estimate is the standard error of the statistic (or sampling distribution of the statistic).

 The independent t-test for the mean difference between the two groups would be computed as follows:

$$t = \frac{50 - 40}{1.41} = 7.09$$

Referring to the table of t values in the appendix, we find that the computed t value = 7.09 exceeds the tabled t value of 3.291, for df = 198 (df = ∞) and p = .0005 (one-tailed test). This is considered a statistically significant finding because a mean difference this large is beyond a chance occurrence. We would conclude that the group who received sales training on average had higher sales than the group that received no sales training. This result is an important finding if the company is spending a substantial amount of money on its employees for sales training and wished to know if the sales training was effective in increasing sales.

Dependent t-test

Drawing one random sample, taking two measures on each person, subtracting these two related measures, and graphing the difference generates the sampling distribution of the difference between the means of two related samples. The expected average difference between the related measures is zero under the null hypothesis. The **dependent t-test** is sometimes referred to as the paired t-test or correlated t-test because it uses two sets of scores on the same individuals.

A typical research situation that uses the dependent t-test involves a repeated measure design with one group. For example, a psychologist is studying the effects of a certain motion picture upon attitudes toward violence. The psychologist hypothesizes that viewing the motion picture will cause the students' attitudes to be more violent. A random sample of ten students is given an attitude toward violence inventory before viewing the motion picture. Next, the ten students view the motion picture, which contains graphic violence portrayed as acceptable behavior. The ten students are then given the attitude toward violence inventory after viewing the motion picture. The average attitude toward violence score for the students before viewing the motion picture was 67.5, but after viewing the motion picture was 73. There are ten pairs of scores so ten score differences are squared and summed to calculate the sum of square differences. The standard error of the dependent t-test is the square root of the sum of squared differences divided by N (N-1).

The **dependent t-test** to investigate whether the students' attitudes toward violence changed after viewing the motion picture would be computed as:

$$t = \frac{\overline{D}}{S_D}$$

The numerator in the formula is the average difference between the post- and pre- mean scores on the attitude toward violence inventory, which is 73-67.5 = 5.5. The denominator is calculated as:

$$S_D = \sqrt{\frac{\Sigma(D-\overline{D})^2}{N(N-1)}}$$

The repeated measure sample data are given below. There are ten pairs of student scores.

Student	Pre	Post	D	D^2
1	70	75	+ 5	25
2	60	70	+10	100
3	85	80	- 5	25
4	50	65	+15	225
5	65	75	+10	100
6	80	70	- 10	100
7	90	95	+ 5	25
8	70	80	+10	100
9	40	55	+15	225
10	65	65	0	0

$$\overline{D}_1 = 67.5 \qquad \overline{D}_2 = 73.0 \qquad \Sigma D = 55 \qquad \Sigma D^2 = 725$$

NOTE: $\Sigma (D - \overline{D})^2 = \Sigma D^2 - (\Sigma D)^2 / N = 725 - (55)^2/10 = 422.5$

$S_D = 2.17$ and $\overline{D} = 5.5$

The dependent t-test is calculated as: t = 5.5 / 2.17 = 2.53. This value is compared to a tabled t value for df = 9 and p = .01 (probability value), which is t = 2.82. Since the computed t = 2.53 does not exceed the tabled t = 2.82, we retain the null hypothesis. We conclude that watching the motion picture did not change students' attitudes toward violence.

Notice in calculating the dependent t-test that the sum of the differences between the pre- and post-test scores took into account whether the difference was positive or negative. Also notice that a computation formula makes the calculation of the sum of squares for the difference scores much easier to calculate. The importance of the standard error of the sampling distribution in determining whether the sample statistic is significant should be apparent.

SUMMARY

In this chapter, you should learn that:

- The sampling distribution of a statistic is important in making inferences about the corresponding population parameter.
- The standard error of the sampling distribution of a statistic is important in testing whether the sample statistic is statistically different from the population parameter.
- The t distribution is not normally distributed for small sample sizes.
- The t values in the t distribution become equal to z values in the normal distribution when sample sizes are infinitely large.
- Different sampling distributions are created for different statistical tests.
- The one-sample t-test is useful for testing whether a sample mean from a population is statistically different from the population mean.
- The two sample independent t-test is useful for testing whether the means of two independent groups are identical.
- The single sample dependent t-test is useful for testing whether the means before and after some intervention in a single group are statistically different.
- A table of t values has been created for various sample sizes (degrees of freedom) and probability areas under the t distribution.

How the STUDENT program works

The STUDENT program shows the versatility of the S-PLUS t-test function by utilizing it for a one sample t-test, a two sample independent t-test, and a dependent t-test. This is accomplished by changing parameters in the **t-test** function call. The greatest complexity occurs in determining the values for the user-defined variables based on the type of test. How the different variables are used for each test is described in the header of the script. Once these variables are defined, two samples are drawn (only the second sample is actually used for the one sample t-test) from normal distributions with the prescribed means and standard deviations. Next, the type of test desired determines which block of code is used to perform the test and produce the output. For the one sample t-test, only *sampleTwo* is passed to the function along with a **mu** equal to *meanOne*. The results of the t-test are saved to the *tResults* object for later use and output appropriate to the one sample test is appended to the *outputText* vector. For the two sample independent t-test, both samples are passed along with the **paired** keyword set to false. Again, appropriate output is created for this test. Finally, the dependent t-test looks exactly like the independent t-test except **paired** is set to true. All tests have the keyword **alternative** set to **two.sided** because the alternate hypothesis in all cases is for a difference in either direction, instead of a directional hypothesis. After the test type specific functions are performed, the output from the t-test that is common to all test types is extracted from the *tResults* object by use of **$statistics** and **$p.value** components. Once these values are appended to the output, the output vector is formatted into a matrix and the matrix is printed with the **print.char.matrix** function.

STUDENT Program Output

Given the following values:

```
sampleSize <- 20
meanOne <- 50        (Note: For one-sample test this is the population mean)
stdDevOne <- 10
meanTwo <- 50
stdDevTwo <- 10
testType <- 1
```

```
+------------------------------+------------------------------+
|One sample t-test             |Sample size= 20               |
+------------------------------+------------------------------+
|Sample Mean= 48.8             |Sample Std Dev= 12.19         |
+------------------------------+------------------------------+
|Population Mean= 50           |Population Std Dev= 10         |
+------------------------------+------------------------------+
|t-test= -0.44                 |p-value= 0.663                |
+------------------------------+------------------------------+
```

For testType <- 2

```
+------------------------------+------------------------------+
|Two sample independent t-test |Sample size= 20               |
+------------------------------+------------------------------+
|Sample One Mean= 51.92        |Sample One Std Dev= 12.24     |
+------------------------------+------------------------------+
|Sample Two Mean= 48.1         |Sample Two Std Dev= 7.74      |
+------------------------------+------------------------------+
|t-test= 1.18                  |p-value= 0.245                |
+------------------------------+------------------------------+
```

For testType <- 3

```
+------------------------------+------------------------------+
|Dependent t-test              |Number of paired scores= 20   |
+------------------------------+------------------------------+
|Pre Mean= 49.42               |Post Mean= 52.75              |
+------------------------------+------------------------------+
|Sum of differences= 66.48     |Sum Diff Squared= 3024.82     |
+------------------------------+------------------------------+
|t-test= 1.22                  |p-value= 0.236                |
+------------------------------+------------------------------+
```

CHAPTER 31 EXERCISES

1. Run the STUDENT program for a one-sample t-test. Record the values in the table.

   Use the following values:

   ```
   sampleSize <- 30
   meanOne <- 50      (In one-sample t-test equals population mean.)
   stdDevOne <- 20    (In one-sample t-test equals population s.d.)
   meanTwo <- 60
   stdDevTwo <- 10
   testType <- 1
   ```

One-sample t-test	Sample size =
Sample Mean =	Sample SD =
Population Mean =	Population SD =
t-test =	p-value =

   a. Is the sample mean statistically different from the population mean?

      YES _____ NO _____

   b. Was the one-sample t-test calculated correctly?

      YES _____ NO _____

   c. Would you obtain the same one-sample t-test using the sample standard deviation as the population standard deviation?

      YES _____ NO _____

   d. Interpret the results of the one-sample t-test. What would you conclude?

      _____

      _____

2.   Run the STUDENT program for the two sample independent t-test. Record the values in
       the table. Use the following settings:

```
sampleSize <- 30
meanOne <- 50
stdDevOne <- 20
meanTwo <- 60
stdDevTwo <- 10
testType <- 2
```

Two sample independent t-test	Sample size =
Sample One Mean =	Sample One SD =
Sample Two Mean =	Sample Two SD =
t-test =	p-value =

a. Are the two sample means statistically different?

    YES _____ NO _____

b. Was the two sample independent t-test calculated correctly?

    YES _____ NO _____

c. Would you obtain different results if you ran the STUDENT program a second time?

    YES _____ NO _____

    Why? _____

d. Interpret the results of the two sample independent t-test. What would you conclude?

    _____

    _____

3.   Run the STUDENT program for the dependent t-test. Record the values in the table

below. Use the following settings:

```
sampleSize <- 30
meanOne <- 50
stdDevOne <- 20
meanTwo <- 60
stdDevTwo <- 10
testType <- 3
```

Dependent t-test	Number of paired scores=
Pre Mean =	Post Mean =
Sum of differences =	Sum Diff Squared=
t-test =	p-value =

a. Was the group statistically different from pre to post?

YES _____ NO _____

b. Was the dependent t-test calculated correctly?

YES _____ NO _____

c. Would you obtain different results if you ran the STUDENT program a second time?

YES _____ NO _____

Why? _____

d. Interpret the results of the dependent t-test. What would you conclude?

_____

_____

TRUE OR FALSE QUESTIONS

T   F   a. The sampling distribution of a statistic is useful for making an inference about the population parameter.

T   F   b. The standard error of a statistic provides the basis for testing hypotheses.

T   F   c. The t distribution is normally distributed.

T   F   d. The one-sample t-test may or may not be significant depending upon which probability value is selected from the t table.

T   F   e. The t values and z values become equal as sample size increases.

T   F   f. A z test is preferred over the t test for hypothesis testing.

T   F   g. The independent t-test is used to test whether two independent sample means are statistically different.

T   F   h. The dependent t-test is used to test whether two groups differ after receiving some type of intervention.

CHAPTER 32

ANALYSIS OF VARIANCE

CHAPTER OBJECTIVES

- To understand the one-way and repeated measures analysis of variance procedure.
- To compute the sum of squared deviations of scores around the sample mean.
- To compute the sum of squared deviations of sample means around the grand mean.
- To understand the partitioning of the sum of squared deviation scores.
- To understand the degrees of freedom associated with different sum of squared deviation scores.
- To calculate mean square (average sum of squared deviation scores).
- Be able to table the between group, within group, and total sum of squared deviation scores, degrees of freedom, mean of the squared deviation scores, and F test.
- To interpret the results of between and within sum of squared deviation scores for hypothesis testing.
- To understand that a post-hoc test determines the significance of mean differences between groups after conducting an analysis of variance procedure.
- Be able to table results of Scheffe post-hoc tests.

Sir Ronald Fisher, upon discovering the work of **W. S. Gossett** (developed a test of mean differences between two groups, "student t-test," or simply the t-test), extended it into his idea for an **analysis of variance** (ANOVA) technique. The analysis of variance technique was based on the idea that variance could be used to indicate whether sample means differed. For example, if three groups had the same average math score, then the variance (standard deviation) of the means would be zero, implying that the sample means do not vary (differ). As the sample means become more different, the variance increases. When sample means are similar in value they are called *homogeneous*, when they become more different in value they are called *heterogeneous*.

The basic idea of variance indicating sample mean differences can be understood using the following two sets of mean scores, which indicate similar grand means but different variances:

Population	SET A	SET B
Sample Mean 1	4	3
Sample Mean 2	4	4
Sample Mean 3	4	5
Grand Mean	4	4
Variance	0	1

The sample means are all the same in SET A; hence the variance is zero. The sample means are different in SET B; hence the variance is greater than zero. As sample means become different in value, the variance will become larger.

Fisher determined that the variance of sample means around a common mean (grand mean) could be calculated by determining the sum of squared deviations (SS_B) of the sample means around the grand mean divided by the degrees of freedom (number of groups minus one). Fisher called this average variance a **mean square between groups**; therefore $MS_B = SS_B/df_B$. The variance of scores within a group can be calculated by determining the sum of squared deviations (SS_W) of the scores around the group mean divided by the degrees of freedom (number of scores in a group minus one). Fisher determined that the sum of squares for each group could be averaged across three or more groups. He called this average variance a **mean square within groups**; therefore $MS_W = SS_W/df_W$.

Fisher developed a test, named the F test after him, to indicate a ratio of the variance of sample means around the grand mean to the variance of scores around each sample mean. The F test was computed as $F = MS_B / MS_W$. The F test has an expected value of one (based on sampling error only being present), however in practice if all sample means are identical, the variance of sample means around the grand mean (MS_B) would be zero, and $F = 0$. In some situations, more variance exists within the groups (MS_W) than between the groups (MS_B), which result in F values being greater than zero, but less than one ($0 < F < 1$). Obviously, these are not the expected results when testing for group mean differences, rather we expect the F test (ratio) to yield larger positive values as group means become more different. F summary tables, which give expected F values for various combinations of degrees of freedom between groups (df_B) and degrees of freedom within groups (df_W), are in the Appendix. These F tables are used to determine if the F value you calculate from sample data is larger than expected by chance. If your F value is larger than the tabled value, the group means are significantly different.

Two basic examples will be presented to illustrate how analysis of variance is an extension of both the independent t-test (two mutually exclusive groups) and the dependent t-test (same subjects measured twice).

One-way Analysis of Variance

The **one-way analysis of variance** extends the independent t-test comparison of two group means to three or more group means. For example, the number of customers who visited three different clothing stores on a weekly basis can be compared to determine if they are significantly different. The number of customers for each clothing store was:

Week	Store A	Store B	Store C	Grand Mean (Total Customers)
First	30	25	15	
Second	30	20	20	
Third	40	25	25	
Fourth	40	30	20	
Sum	140.00	100.00	80.00	320.00
Mean	35.00	25.00	20.00	26.67
SD	5.77	4.08	4.08	7.79

The number of customers on average for Store A is higher than Store B; likewise Store B had more customers on average than Store C. The analysis of variance procedure can test (F test) whether the mean differences in customers between the stores are statistically significant. To calculate the F test, we must first compute the variance of the sample means around the grand mean using the following steps (Note: n_i = number of weeks and j = number of stores):

1. $SS_B = n_i$ (Store Mean - Grand Mean)^2
2. $SS_B = 4(35 - 26.67)^2 + 4(25 - 26.67)^2 + 4(20 - 26.67)^2$
3. $SS_B = 466.67$
4. $df_B = (j - 1) = (3 - 1) = 2$
5. $MS_B = SS_B / df_B = (466.67 / 2) = 233.33$

The sum of squares between the stores (SS_B) indicates the sum of the deviation from the grand mean (common mean for all the sample means) which is squared and weighted (multiplied by the sample size) for each store (Steps 1-3 above). The degree of freedom is simply the number of stores minus one (Step 4 above). The mean square between the stores, which is used in the F test to indicate mean differences in the stores, is the average sum of squares between the groups (Step 5 above).

Next, we must compute the variance of the number of customers around each store mean using the following steps (Note: j = number of stores):

1. $SS_W = \Sigma j [(\text{Number of Customers - Store Mean})^2]$

2. $SS_W = [(30 - 35)^2 + (30 - 35)^2 + (40 - 35)^2 + (40 - 35)^2 +$
$(25 - 25)^2 + (20 - 25)^2 + (25 - 25)^2 + (30 - 25)^2 +$
$(15 - 20)^2 + (20 - 20)^2 + (25 - 20)^2 + (20 - 20)^2]$

3. $SS_W = 200.00$

4. $df_W = (\text{sample size} - j) = (12 - 3) = 9$

5. $MS_W = SS_W / df_W = 22.22$

The sum of squares within the stores (SS_W) indicates the sum of the customer number deviation from the store mean which is squared (Steps 1-3 above). The degree of freedom equals the total sample size minus the number of stores (Step 4 above). The mean square within the stores, which is used in the F test to indicate the variance of within the stores, is the average sum of squares within the groups (Step 5 above). This "averaging" of the sum of squares within the stores is sometimes referred to as "pooling" the sum of squares within the groups, i.e., stores.

The **F test** (ratio) can now be calculated as $F = MS_B / MS_W = 233.33 / 22.22 = 10.50$. This F test indicates the *ratio* of the variance between the stores over the variance within the stores. If the store means are more different (vary more between stores) than the scores vary within the stores, the F test ratio would be greater than an F value expected by chance. We therefore compare the computed $F = 10.50$ to a tabled F value in the Appendix for $df_B = 2$ and $df_W = 9$ at the .05 chance level (5% chance our comparison might not yield a correct decision). The computed $F = 10.50$ is greater than the tabled $F = 4.26$ (value expected by chance), which indicates that the average number of customers per store are significantly different.

The results of all these calculations can be neatly organized in an ANOVA Summary Table. The ANOVA Summary Table indicates that both of the sums of squared deviations can be added together yielding a total sum of squared deviations for all scores ($SS_T = SS_B + SS_W$). Likewise, the degrees of freedom from both calculations can be added together yielding the sample size minus one ($df_T = N - 1$). The SS_T divided by df_T yields the total customer variance, which has been "partitioned" into the variance between groups and the variance within groups. The total number of customer variance is therefore computed as $SS_T / df_T = 666.67 / 11 = 60.61$. The total number of customer standard deviation is simply the square root of this variance, which is equal to 7.79 (see summary statistics above). This reveals to us that the sum of squares total divided by the sample size minus one is actually the variance of all the scores. The square root of this variance is the standard deviation of all the scores. The key point is that the analysis of variance procedure "partitions" the variance of *all* the scores.

ANOVA SUMMARY TABLE

Source	Sum of Squares (SS)	Degrees of Freedom (df)	Mean Square (MS)	F
Between Groups	466.67	2	233.33	10.50
Within Groups	200.00	9	22.22	
Total	666.67	11		

Multiple Comparison Tests

The F test doesn't reveal *which* store means are different, only that the store means are different. Consequently, a multiple comparison test is needed to determine which store means are different. There are many different types of multiple comparison tests depending upon whether the group sizes are equal or unequal, whether all group means are compared (pairwise) or combinations of group means are compared (complex contrasts), and whether group mean differences are specified in advance (a priori planned comparison) or after the statistical test (posterior comparison). We will only focus on one type of multiple comparison test called a *post-hoc* test named after **Henry Scheffe**. Post-hoc tests are named "post hoc" because they are calculated after the ANOVA *F* test indicates that the group means are significantly different. The **Scheffe post-hoc test** can be used in most situations because it is *not* limited to equal sample sizes and pairwise comparisons of group means, and maintains the same probability as that used for determining the significance of F (Tabled $F = 4.26$ at 5% chance level). The Scheffe post-hoc test uses the common variance term (pooled variance) from all the groups in the denominator of the formula based on MS_w in the ANOVA Summary Table.

Given three stores, three Scheffe post-hoc tests can be computed using the following steps.

Store A vs. Store B

1. Scheffe $= $ (Store A Mean - Store B Mean)^2 / MS_w $(1/n_A + 1/n_B)$ (j-1)
2. Scheffe $= (35 - 25)^2$ / 22.22 (1/4 + 1/4) (3-1)
3. Scheffe $= (100)$ / 22.22 (1/2) (2)
4. Scheffe $= 4.50$

Store A vs. Store C

1. Scheffe $= $ (Store A Mean - Store C Mean)^2 / MS_w $(1/n_A + 1/n_C)$ (j-1)
2. Scheffe $= (35 - 20)^2$ / 22.22 (1/4 + 1/4) (3-1)
3. Scheffe $= (225)$ / 22.22 (1/2) (2)
4. Scheffe $= 10.13$

Store B vs. Store C

1. Scheffe $= $ (Store B Mean - Store C Mean) / MS_w $(1/n_B + 1/n_C)$ (j-1)
2. Scheffe $= (25 - 20)^2$ / 22.22 (1/4 + 1/4) (3-1)
3. Scheffe $= (25)$ / 22.22 (1/2) (2)
4. Scheffe $= 1.13$

The Scheffe post-hoc test results can be summarized in a Scheffe Post-Hoc Summary Table. Comparing the Scheffe results to the Tabled $F = 4.26$ reveals that Store A had on average the most customers which was significantly higher than both Store B and Store C. Store B and Store C average number of customers did not differ significantly.

Scheffe Post-Hoc Summary Table

	Store		
	A	B	C
Store A			
Store B	4.50*		
Store C	10.13*	1.13	

* Scheffe exceeds Tabled $F = 4.26$
at the .05 chance level.

Repeated Measures Analysis of Variance

The **repeated measures analysis of variance** technique extends the dependent t-test to three or more groups. The dependent t-test is appropriate in research settings where you only measure the same subjects twice and test whether scores change, i.e., increase or decrease in a hypothesized direction. In the case of repeated measures ANOVA, subjects are measured on three or more occasions (typically over time or different experimental conditions) with the same idea of testing whether scores change in a hypothesized direction. An example will illustrate the repeated measures ANOVA technique.

The average number of children per family (X) in four regions was measured over a three-year period by a researcher to test whether birth rate was increasing, decreasing, or remaining the same. The following data were collected:

Average number of children per family (X)

Region	1995	1996	1997	Total
Northern State	2	5	5	12
Southern State	2	7	5	14
Eastern State	3	2	6	11
Western State	1	2	4	7
n	4	4	4	N = 12
Sum	8	16	20	T = 44
Mean	2	4	5	

The repeated measure ANOVA "partitions" the total sum of squared deviations around the grand mean into three component variances: REGION, YEAR, and remaining ERROR variance. The steps needed to calculate each are as follows:

TOTAL Sum of Squares

1. $SS_{TOTAL} = \Sigma [(X)^2] - [(T)^2 / N]$

2. $SS_{TOTAL} = \Sigma [(2^2) + (2)^2 + (3)^2 + (1)^2 \ldots\ldots + (4)^2] - [(44)^2 / 12]$

3. $SS_{TOTAL} = 202 - 161.33 = 40.67$

REGION Sum of Squares

4. $SS_{REGION} = \Sigma [(Total)^2 / j] - [(T)^2 / N]$

5. $SS_{REGION} = \Sigma [(12)^2 / 3] + [(14)^2 / 3] + [(11)^2 / 3] + [(7)^2 / 3] - [(44)^2 / 12]$

6. $SS_{REGION} = \Sigma [48 + 65.33 + 40.33 + 16.33] - [161.33]$

7. $SS_{REGION} = 169.99 - 161.33 = 8.66$

YEAR Sum of Squares

1. $SS_{YEAR} = \Sigma [(Sum)^2 / n] - [(T)^2 / N]$

2. $SS_{YEAR} = \Sigma [(8)^2 / 4] + [(16)^2 / 4] + [(20)^2] / 4] - [(44)^2 / 12]$

3. $SS_{YEAR} = \Sigma [16 + 64 + 100] - 161.33$

4. $SS_{YEAR} = 180 - 161.33 = 18.67$

ERROR Sum of Squares

1. $SS_E = SS_{TOTAL} - SS_{REGION} - SS_{YEAR}$

2. $SS_E = 40.67 - 8.66 - 18.67$

3. $SS_E = 13.34$

These results can be neatly summarized in the table below:

REPEATED MEASURES ANOVA SUMMARY TABLE

Source	Sum of Squares (SS)	Degrees of Freedom (df)	Mean Squares (MS)	F
Region	8.66	3	2.89	
Year	18.67	2	9.33	4.20
Error	13.34	6	2.22	
Total	40.67	11		

The F test in this repeated measures design is *only* calculated for the variable that is measured over time. In this case, the F test is a test of whether the average birth rate is different over the three years. We would compare the computed F = 4.20 to a tabled F in the appendix with df = 2, 6 at the .05 level of significance; which is F = 5.14. Since the computed F= 4.20 is not greater than the tabled F = 5.14, we conclude that the average birth rate across the three years does not differ. We do notice that the average birth rate increased from 2 per family to 4 per family from 1995 to 1996, but to only 5 per family in 1997. The mean birth rate increased across the years, but not enough to warrant a beyond chance statistically significant conclusion.

SUMMARY

In this chapter, you should learn that:

- The one-way analysis of variance procedure is an extension of the independent t-test for testing the differences in three or more sample means.
- The repeated measures analysis of variance procedure is an extension of the dependent t-test for testing the differences in three or more sample means over time.
- The sum of squared deviations of sample means around the grand mean is called the sum of squares between groups.
- The sum of squared deviations of sample scores around each sample mean is called the sum of squares within.
- The sum of squares total is equal to the sum of squares between groups plus the sum of squares within groups.
- The total variance of all scores is partitioned into the sum of squares between groups and the sum of squares within groups.
- The degrees of freedom for the sum of squares between groups are the number of groups minus one.
- The degrees of freedom for the sum of squares within groups are the total sample size minus the number of groups.
- The F test is computed as a ratio of the mean square between over the mean square within.
- Analysis of Variance Summary Tables neatly organize the between group, within group, and total sum of squared deviation scores, degrees of freedom, mean of the squared deviation scores, and F test.
- A Scheffe post-hoc test determines which sample means are different between groups after conducting an analysis of variance procedure.

How the Analysis of Variance Programs Work

ONEWAY Program

The **ONEWAY** program (chap32a.ssc) begins by defining the data for three groups. Each set of group data is then summarized and put into a matrix as the group size, group mean, and standard deviation of the group. Labels are assigned to the matrix to indicate the groups and the summary statistic headings. Next, the grand mean for all of the groups is calculated and the individual group means and sample sizes are combined into vectors for later use. Then the sum of squares between groups (SSB), mean squares between groups (MSB), sum of squares within groups (SSW), degrees of freedom within groups (dfW), and mean squares within groups (MSW) are calculated. These numbers are used to determine the total sum of squares (SST) and the total degrees of freedom (dfT).

Once all of the preliminary calculations are completed, the F ratio is calculated by dividing the mean squares between by the mean squares within. The probability associated with the F ratio is determined using the **pf function** and the degrees of freedom above. The ONEWAY ANOVA summary table information is placed into rows and then into a matrix. The previous group summary matrix is output followed by the ONEWAY ANOVA summary table.

REPEATED Program

The **REPEATED** program (chap32b.ssc) begins by defining the data for four individuals at occasions on four successive years. These are combined into a matrix for later manipulation. The summary information for years is placed into a matrix, stating the number of samples for the year, the sum of values for the year, and the mean value for the year and labels are applied to describe the matrix. Next, the total number of values for all individuals (N) is calculated along with the total sum of values (TotSum). After that begins the calculations of the sum of squares, degrees of freedom, and mean squares for individual, year, total, and error components.

The sum of squares total (SST) and total degrees of freedom (dfT) are quickly calculated, but the sum of squares for the individuals (SSI) takes a few iterations through the data and the creation of the intermediate variable IndSqrDev in order to complete the calculation. The degrees of freedom for the individual (dfI) and mean squares for the individual (MSI) are then easily calculated. Next, the year component is determined in much the same manner as the individual component with the aid of the intermediate variable YearSqrDev. The values then make it possible to determine the sum of squares error (SSE), degrees of freedom error (dfE), and mean squares error (MSE).

Now that all of the components have been determined, the F ratio is calculated along with the associated probability value. The summary table information is placed into a matrix, just as in the ONEWAY program, and the previous year data summary table is output along with the total data information and the REPEATED MEASURES summary table.

ONEWAY Program Output

ONEWAY ANALYSIS OF VARIANCE

	Group A	Group B	Group C
Samp Size	4.00	4.0	4.00
Samp Mean	14.50	11.5	17.50
Std Dev	4.43	4.2	6.19

Source	SS	df	MS	F	p
Between	72	2	36	1.43	0.289
Within	227	9	25.22		
Total	299	11			

REPEATED Program Output

REPEATED MEASURES ANALYSIS OF VARIANCE

	Year 1	Year 2	Year 3	Year 4
Samp Size	4.0	4.00	4.00	4.0
Samp Sum	30.0	31.00	55.00	70.0
Samp Mean	7.5	7.75	13.75	17.5

N = 16 , T = 186

Source	SS	df	MS	F	p
Individual	25.25	3	8.42		
Year	284.25	3	94.75	13.27	0.001
Error	64.25	9	7.14		
Total	373.75	15			

CHAPTER 32 EXERCISES

1. Run the ANOVA program (chap32a.ssc) for comparing differences in the means of
   three groups.

Group A	Group B	Group C
10	16	18
12	9	14
20	7	12
16	14	26

   Record the sample size, sample mean and sample standard deviation for each group.

	A	B	C
a. Sample Sizes	_____	_____	_____
b. Sample Means	_____	_____	_____
c. Standard Deviations	_____	_____	_____

   Place the sum of squares deviation results in the ANOVA Summary Table.   Test whether
   the computed F is statistically different from the tabled F at the .05 level of significance.

   ANOVA Summary Table

Source	SS	df	MS	F
Between				
Within				
Total				

   What do you conclude?

   _____

   _____

2. Run the ANOVA program (chap32b.ssc) for comparing repeated measures across four years.

Year 1	Year 2	Year 3	Year 4
8	9	10	12
7	6	14	18
9	6	15	22
6	10	16	18

n   N =

Sum   T =

Mean

Record the sample size (n), sum, and sample mean above. Also, record the total number of scores (N), and total sum of scores (T).   Place the sum of squares deviation results in the ANOVA Summary Table.   Test whether the computed F is statistically different from the tabled F at the .05 level of significance.

REPEATED MEASURES ANOVA Summary Table

Source	SS	df	MS	F
Individual				
Year				
Error				
Total				

What do you conclude?

_____

_____

TRUE OR FALSE QUESTIONS

T F a. The one-way analysis of variance and the repeated measures analysis of variance are the same procedure.

T F b. The analysis of variance procedure "partitions" the total variance of the scores.

T F c. The one-way ANOVA procedure uses an F test to determine if three or more group means are significantly different.

T F d. The Scheffe post-hoc test determines specifically which group means are statistically different.

T F e. The sum of squares between groups in the one-way ANOVA procedure is computed by summing the squared deviations of each score from the sample means.

T F f. The sum of squares total (SS_T) divided by the degree of freedom (df_T) is the variance of all the scores.

T F g. The repeated measures analysis of variance procedure conducts an F test of whether sample means increase over time.

T F h. The Scheffe post hoc test should *not* be used with unequal sample sizes.

CHAPTER 33

CORRELATION

CHAPTER OBJECTIVES

- To learn how the bivariate correlation coefficient originated.
- To calculate the correlation coefficient between two continuous variables.
- To interpret the magnitude and direction of a correlation coefficient.
- To interpret the significance of the correlation coefficient.
- To graph a scatter plot of the bivariate correlation relationship.
- To interpret the squared correlation coefficient as the amount of variance explained in one variable by knowledge of another.
- To distinguish the population correlation coefficient ρ from the sample correlation coefficient r.
- To illustrate the shape of the scatter plot for data drawn from a bivariate normal population with a specified value of ρ.
- To observe the variability in different samples of data points chosen from the bivariate normal population.
- To investigate the slope of the least squares line relative to ρ.

Sir Francis Galton in Great Britain was interested in studying individual differences based on the work of his cousin, **Charles Darwin**. In 1869, Sir Francis Galton demonstrated that the mathematics scores of students at Cambridge University and the admissions exam scores at the Royal Military College were normally distributed. In 1889, Francis Galton published an essay suggesting the idea for examining how two traits varied together (covaried). This effort resulted in the first use of the term "regression." **Karl Pearson** in 1898, based on the suggestions made by Sir Francis Galton, investigated the development of a statistical formula that would capture the relationship between two variables.

The idea was to determine the degree to which two things went together, i.e., how two things varied together. The concept was simple enough in principle, take measurements on two variables, order the measurements of the two variables, and determine if one set of measurements increased along with the second set of measurements. In some cases, maybe the measurements of one variable decreased while the other increased. The basic assumption Karl Pearson made was that the measurements needed to be linear or continuous. He quickly determined that how two things covaried divided by how they individually varied would yield a statistic that was bounded by +1 and -1, depending on the relationship of the two measurements. The conceptual formula he developed, which took into account the covariance between two variables divided by the variance of the two variables, was defined as:

$$r = \frac{\text{Covariance XY}}{(\text{Var X})(\text{Var Y})}$$

In 1927, after **L. L. Thurstone** developed the concept of a **standard score** (z score) as the deviation of a raw score from the mean, divided by the standard deviation, the **correlation** formula was further defined as the average product of standard scores:

$$r=\frac{\sum z_x z_y}{N}$$

An example of the relationship between two continuous variables will better illustrate how the bivariate (two variable) correlated relationship is established.   A typical research question for a group of students can be stated as "Is there a significant relationship between the amount of time spent studying and exam scores?" The data for these two continuous variables, ordered by time spent studying, is listed below.

Time spent	Exam Score
1 hour	75
1 hours	80
2 hours	75
3 hours	90
3 hours	85
4 hours	95
4 hours	85
5 hours	90
5 hours	95
6 hours	90

A computational version of the correlation formula makes the calculation easier and uses the following summary values:

$$\sum X = 34$$

$$\sum X^2 = 142$$

$$\sum Y = 860$$

$$\sum Y^2 = 56800$$

$$\sum XY = 3015$$

The computational correlation coefficient formula is:

$$r = \frac{SP}{\sqrt{SS_x SS_y}}$$

The expression, SP, is defined as the sum of cross products for X and Y. The expression, SS_x, is the sum of squares X, and the expression Ss_y is the sum of squares Y.

These values are computed for each expression in the correlation coefficient formula as:

$SP = \Sigma XY - \dfrac{(\Sigma X)(\Sigma Y)}{N}$	$= 3015 - \dfrac{(34)(860)}{10} = 91$
$SS_X = \Sigma X^2 - \dfrac{(\Sigma X)^2}{N}$	$= 142 - \dfrac{(34)^2}{10} = 26.40$
$SS_Y = \Sigma Y^2 - \dfrac{(\Sigma Y)^2}{N}$	$= 56800 - \dfrac{(860)^2}{10} = 490$

These values are substituted in the Pearson correlation coefficient:

$$r = \frac{SP}{\sqrt{SS_x SS_y}} = \frac{91}{\sqrt{26.4(490)}} = +.80$$

The value of r = +. 80 indicates a positive relationship between the two variables implying that as the amount of study time increases, exam scores increase. The correlation coefficient also indicates the magnitude of the relationship since the r value is approaching + 1.0, which would indicate a perfect relationship.

The correlation coefficient can be interpreted in several different ways. First we can test it for significance using tabled correlation values for different sample sizes (degrees of freedom). Second, we can square the correlation coefficient to obtain a variance accounted for interpretation. Third, we can graph the relationship between the data points in a scatter plot to visually see the trend of the relationship.

To test the significance of the correlation coefficient, we use our standard hypothesis testing approach:

Step 1: State the Null and Alternative Hypothesis using Population Parameters

H_0: $\rho = 0$ (no correlation)

$H_{A:}$ $\rho \neq 0$ (correlation exists)

Step 2: Choose the appropriate statistic and state the sample size obtained

Pearson correlation coefficient for continuous variables

Sample Size, N = 10

Step 3: State the level of significance, direction of alternative hypothesis and region of rejection

Level of Significance (α) = .05

Alternative Hypothesis: Non-directional (Two-tailed test)

For N = 10, df = N-1 = 9

R: $r_{tabled} > .602$

Step 4: Collect Data and Calculate Sample Correlation Statistic

Continuous Variables: Time spent studying and exam scores

N = 10 pairs of data

r = .80

Step 5: Test statistical Hypothesis, make decision, and interpret results

Since the computed r = .80 is greater than the tabled r of .602 at the .05 level of significance for a two- tailed test, reject the null hypothesis and accept the alternative hypothesis. There is a statistically significant relationship between the amount of time spent studying and exam scores.

The second approach to interpreting the Pearson correlation coefficient is to square the sample correlation value. The r^2 value is $(.80)^2 = .64$. This implies that 64% of the variability in exam scores can be explained by knowledge of how much time a student spent studying. This also implies that 36% of the variability in the exam scores is due to other variable relationships or unexplained variance. The average number of hours spent studying was 3.4 hours with a standard deviation of 1.71. The average exam score was 86 with a standard deviation of 7.38. The interpretation is linked to the variance of the exam scores, hence $(7.38)^2 = 54.46$. We would state that 64% of 54.46 is explained variability and 36% of 54.46 is unexplained variability given knowledge of how much time a student spent studying. We can also depict this relationship using a *Venn* or *Ballentine* diagram.

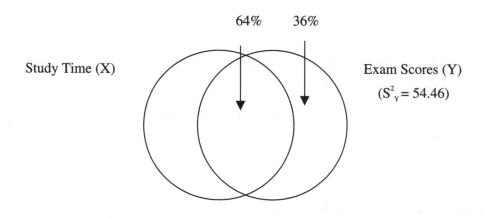

The third approach to interpreting the correlation coefficient obtained from sample data is to graph the data points of the two variables. The scatter plot is used for this purpose. We draw a Y-axis for the exam scores and an X-axis for the amount of time spent studying. We label and scale these two axes to provide a grid such that the pairs of data points can be graphed. A visual look at the "trend" of the pairs of data points helps in interpreting whether the positive direction of the correlation coefficient exists. Scatter plots can display an upward trend (positive relationship), downward trend (negative relationship), or a curvilinear trend (one-half positive and the other half negative). If a curvilinear relationship exists, one-half cancels the other half out, so the correlation coefficient would be zero and the interpretation of the correlation coefficient meaningless. This is why Karl Pearson made the assumption of linear data. A scatter plot of the data points visually reveals the positive upward trend expected from $r = +.80$.

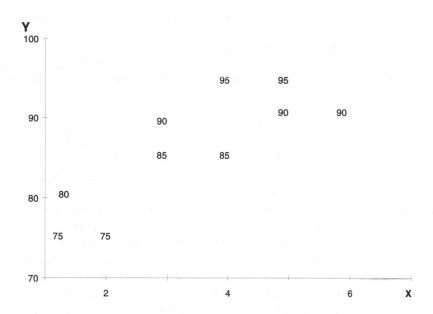

The Pearson correlation coefficient in determining whether or not there is a linear relationship between two continuous variables provides both a measure of the strength of the relationship, as well as, the direction of the relationship. In our example, the number of hours a student spent studying was related positively to the exam score. The strength of the relationship was indicated by a value close to 1.0 and the direction of the relationship by the positive sign. We are also able to explain the variability in the exam scores by squaring the correlation coefficient. In other words, why didn't all the students get the same score, because some students studied more! This can be presented in a diagram and depicted as a percent of the variance of the exam scores that can be explained. A scatter plot is the best visual aid to understanding the trend in the pairs of scores in regards to both magnitude and direction.

Karl Pearson's correlation coefficient was one of the most important discoveries in the field of statistics because numerous other statistical techniques such as multiple regression, path analysis, factor analysis, cluster analysis, discriminant analysis, canonical correlation, and structural equation modeling are based on this coefficient and interpretative understanding. Over one hundred years later, the examination of variable relationships is the singular most important analysis conducted in education, psychology, business, medicine, and numerous other disciplines. The correlation approach assumes that both the X and the Y variables are random, and have a distribution known as the bivariate normal distribution. In the bivariate normal distribution, for any given X value the Y values have a normal distribution in which the mean and the standard deviation depend on the value of X and the strength of the relationship between X and Y. The strength of the relationship between X and Y is measured by a population parameter ρ (pronounced "rho"), which can range between -1 and 1 inclusive. If $\rho = 0$, there is either no relationship between X and Y, or a curvilinear relationship which the Pearson correlation coefficient doesn't detect. If $\rho = 1$, there is a perfect *positive* linear relationship between the two variables, and if $\rho = -1$, there is a perfect *negative* linear relationship between the variables. A value of ρ close to zero indicates a weak relationship (assuming linear data), and a value close to either +1 or −1 indicates a strong relationship.   Consequently, r = -.90 is a stronger relationship than r = +. 50 for the same sample size. Because the Pearson correlation values form an ordinal scale, we do not directly compare the distances between two correlation values. For example, if a correlation of r = + .50 was obtained in one sample and a correlation of r = +.60 obtained in a second sample, you *would not* indicate that the second correlation was .10 higher than the first because they are on an ordinal scale!

In this chapter, the Pearson correlation coefficient will be calculated using the bivariate normal distribution. The CORRELATION program will permit the value of ρ to be specified in the population. The program will then select X at random from a normal distribution with mean of 10 and standard deviation of 3.   Next, a random Y will be selected from the normal distribution that is determined by the random X variable, given ρ that you selected and the mean and standard deviation of Y, which are 5 and 1, respectively. A loop will repeat this 20 times, then a scatter plot will be drawn.   The program will plot a line (least squares line) on the scatter plot, which is discussed in the next chapter on linear regression, and print the sample correlation coefficient, r.   By varying ρ in the CORRELATION program, you can observe the different scatter plots of data points that arise when ρ has different values in the population. You will also be able to see how the least squares line is related to ρ and observe how well the sample correlation coefficient estimates the true ρ.   Other correlation coefficients have been developed since 1898 to establish the relationship between nominal and ordinal data, but are not presented in this chapter, i.e., phi-coefficient (nominal data), Spearman-coefficient (ordinal data).

SUMMARY

In this chapter, you should learn that:

- In a bivariate normal distribution, both X and Y are random variables.
- The Pearson correlation coefficient indicates the linear relationship between two continuous variables.
- The Pearson correlation coefficient indicates both the magnitude and direction of the relationship between two linear continuous variables.
- A Pearson correlation coefficient of r = 0 indicates no linear relationship between two variables.
- The correlation coefficient can be interpreted in three ways: test of significance, variance accounted for, and a diagram of trend in the paired data points.
- The sample correlation coefficient, r, is an estimate of the population correlation coefficient ρ (rho).
- If ρ = 0, then the sample data points will have a random scatter plot, and the least squares line will be horizontal.
- As ρ approaches + 1 or − 1, the sample data points are closer to the least squares line.
- If ρ = + 1 or - 1, then the sample points will lie on the least squares line.

How the CORRELATION program works

The CORRELATION program simulates random samples of data from a population with a known bivariate correlation between two variables. The user specifies the population correlation, known as *rho*, along with the desired sample size. A sample of X values is randomly drawn from a normal distribution with a mean of 10 and standard deviation of 3. The accompanying Y values are calculated based on a random normal clustering around the sample least squares line that is determined by *rho*. The **lsfit** function is used to retrieve the coefficients for the sample least squares line, which are placed into their respective variables. The **cor** function is used to find the sample Pearson correlation, which is placed into a label to be used later along with a label for the *rho* value. The limits of the X and Y axes are set before plotting the pairs of data points so that no plotted points fall outside the axes. Finally, the sample data points are plotted in a scatter plot with the labels for the sample correlation and *rho*. The least squares line is then drawn through the scatter plot. The x-axis is automatically scaled in the graph each time the program is run. The last program line prints out the sample correlation label and the equation for the regression least squares line.

CORRELATION Program Output

Given the following values:

```
rho <- .60
sampleSize <- 20
```

```
r is: 0.72
Least squares fit line is: y = 2.85 + 0.23x
```

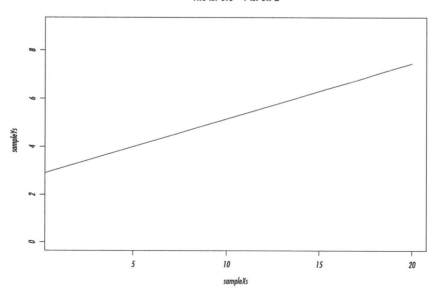

CHAPTER 33 EXERCISES

1.   Run CORRELATION program for the following values of rho. Plot the data values and
        least squares line of fit on the graph. Record the correlation coefficient r and the least
        squares fit line.

rho $= + .5$

r = _____

Least squares fit line:

_____

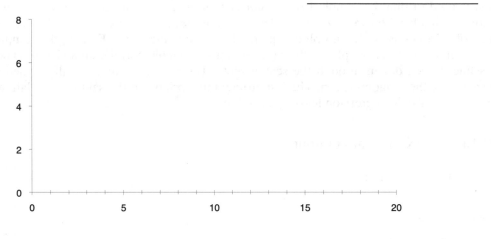

rho $= - .5$

r = _____

Least squares fit line:

_____

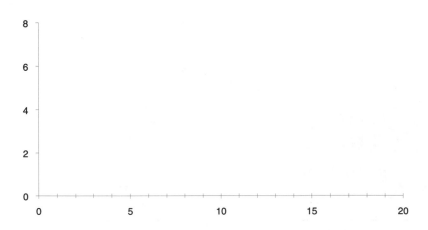

rho = 0.0

r = _____

Least squares fit line:

_____

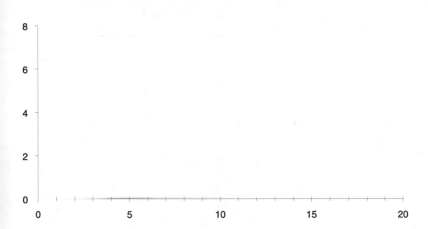

a. For rho = +.5, does the Least squares fit line increase upward?

YES _____ NO _____

b. For rho = -.5, does the Least squares fit line decrease downward?

YES _____ NO _____

c. For rho = 0.0, is the Least squares fit line horizontal?

YES _____ NO _____

2.   Run CORRELATION program for the following values of rho. Plot the data values and
        least squares line of fit on the graph. Record the correlation coefficient r and the least
        squares fit line.

rho = +1.0

r = _____

Least Squares fit line:

_____

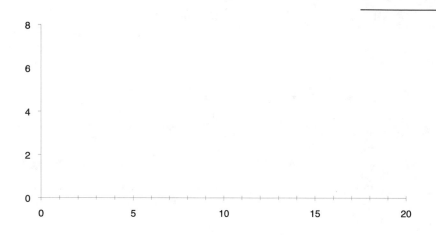

rho = - 1.0

r = _____

Least Squares fit line:

_____

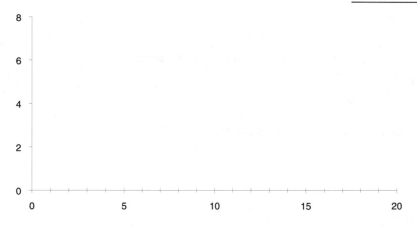

a.   Describe the scatter plot for the data points when rho = 1.
_____
_____

b.   Describe the scatter plot for the data points when rho = -1.
_____
_____

c.   Describe the scatter plot for the data points when rho = 0.
_____
_____

d.   Describe the least squares line when rho = 0. _____

e.   Why does a horizontal line (slope) indicate no relationship between X and Y?
_____
_____

TRUE OR FALSE QUESTIONS

T   F   a.   The Pearson correlation coefficient indicates the relationship between two
                     linear continuous variables.

T   F   b.   A correlation of r = .60 is greater than a correlation of r = − .80.

T   F   c.   A correlation of r = 0 implies no relationship between two variables.

T   F   d.   If no linear relationship exists between two variables, the least squares line
                     will be approximately horizontal.

T   F   e.   If rho is − .5, the scatter plot of data points will indicate an upward trend.

T   F   f.   If r = .80, then 64% of the variability in one variable is explained by
                     knowledge of the other variable.

T   F   g.   If rho = 0, then r = 0.

T   F   h.   rho is a parameter, and r is a statistic.

T   F   i.   Data points will fall on the least squares line when r = 1.0.

CHAPTER 34

LINEAR REGRESSION

CHAPTER OBJECTIVES

- To present a linear equation for predicting Y from knowledge of X.
- To illustrate the simple linear regression equation.
- To interpret the regression equation.
- To calculate the standard error of prediction.
- To observe the variability of Y around predicted Y values for different values of X.
- To interpret the least squares line in a scatter plot of the bivariate correlation between two variables.
- To distinguish between the least squares line and the population regression line.
- To investigate the amount of error between the equation of the least squares line and the equation of the true regression line.
- To use the simple linear regression approach for prediction.

In the late 1950s and early 1960s, the mathematics related to solving a set of simultaneous linear equations was introduced to the field of statistics. In 1961, **Franklin A. Graybill** published a definitive text on the subject, *An Introduction to Linear Statistical Models*, which piqued the curiosity of several scholars. A few years later in 1963, **Robert A. Bottenberg** and **Joe H. Ward, Jr.**, who worked in the Aerospace Medical Division at Lackland Air Force Base in Houston, Texas, developed the linear regression technique using basic algebra and the Pearson correlation coefficient. **Norman R. Draper** and **Harry Smith, Jr.** in 1966 published one of the first books on the topic, *Applied Regression Analysis*. In 1967, under a funded project by the U.S. Department of Health, Education, and Welfare, **W. L. Bashaw** and **Warren G. Findley** invited several scholars to the University of Georgia for a symposium on the general linear model approach to the analysis of experimental data in educational research. The five invited speakers were: **Franklin A. Graybill**, **Joe H. Ward, Jr.**, **Ben J. Winer**, **Rolf E. Bargmann**, and **R. Darrell Bock**. Dr. Graybill presented the theory behind statistics, Dr. Ward presented the regression models, Dr. Winer discussed the relationship between the general linear regression model and the analysis of variance, Dr. Bargmann presented applied examples which involved interaction and random effects, and Dr. Bock critiqued the concerns of the others and discussed computer programs that would compute the general linear model and analysis of variance. Since the 1960s, numerous textbooks and articles in professional journals have painstakingly demonstrated that the linear regression technique, presented by Bottenberg and Ward, is the same as the analysis of variance. In recent years, multiple regression techniques have proven to be more versatile than analysis of variance in handling nominal and ordinal data, interaction effects, and non-linear effects.

The **linear regression** equation developed by Bottenberg and Ward was expressed as: Y = a + bX + e. The Y variable represented a continuous measure, which was referred to as the dependent variable. The X variable represented a continuous measure, which was called an independent variable, but later referred to as a predictor variable. The value *a* was termed the "intercept" and represented the value on the Y axis where the least squares line crossed. The *b* value was a "weight," later referred to as a regression weight or coefficient. The value of *e* was referred to as prediction error, which is calculated as the difference between the Y variable and the predicted Y value (Yhat) from the linear regression equation, given values for the intercept and regression weight. An example will illustrate the logic behind the linear regression equation.

Given the following data pairs on the amount of recyclable aluminum in ounces (Y) and the number of aluminum cans (X), a linear regression equation can be created: Y = a + bX + e.

Recyclable Aluminum (Y)	Number of Aluminum Cans (X)
1	2
2	4
3	6
4	8
5	10
6	12
7	14

The regression intercept (*a*) indicates the point on the Y-axis where the least squares line crosses in the scatter plot. The "rise" and "run" or regression weight (*b*) determines the rate of change, which can be seen by the slope of the least squares line in the scatter plot. It is important to understand that a linear regression equation only refers to the range of values for the pairs of Y and X scores. Given the linear regression equation: Y = a + bX + e, the **intercept** and **regression weight** (slope) for the data can be calculated as:

$$b = r_{XY} \frac{S_Y}{S_X}$$

$$a = \bar{Y} - b\bar{X}$$

The correlation coefficient for these data is r = + 1.0, the mean of Y = 4 and the mean of X = 8. The standard deviation of Y = 2, and the standard deviation of X = 4. Placing these values in the intercept and regression weight formula results in: *a* = 2 - (2/4) 4 = 0 and *b* = 1 (2/4) = .5, with a linear regression equation: Y = 0 + (1/2) X. Since the intercept is zero, the equation is simply Y = .5X. An inspection of the data reveals that 2 aluminum cans yields 1 ounce of recyclable aluminum, 4 aluminum cans yields 2 ounces of recyclable aluminum, and so forth because one-half the number of aluminum cans equals the number of ounces. A scatter plot of these data would indicate the "rise" and "run" of this relationship with the least squares line intersecting the Y axis at *a* = 0. Notice that there is no error in the prediction since every Y value is perfectly predicted by knowledge of X, i.e., $e = Y - Yhat = 0$.   Perfect relationships like this don't often occur with real data!

A more realistic example will help to demonstrate the linear regression equation, least squares line, and error of prediction. The data for twenty student math achievement scores (Y) and days absent during the week from school (X) are summarized below.

Student	X	Y	X^2	Y^2	XY
1	2	90	4	8100	180
2	4	70	16	4900	280
3	3	80	9	6400	240
4	5	60	25	3600	300
5	1	95	1	9025	95
6	2	80	4	6400	160
7	5	50	25	2500	250
8	3	45	9	2025	135
9	2	75	4	5625	150
10	4	65	16	4225	260
11	5	45	25	2025	225
12	1	80	1	6400	80
13	4	80	16	6400	320
14	5	60	25	3600	300
15	1	85	1	7225	85
16	0	90	0	8100	0
17	5	50	25	2500	250
18	3	70	9	4900	210
19	4	40	16	1600	160
20	0	95	0	9025	0
Σ	59	1405	231	104575	3680

The summary statistics for these data can be hand calculated as follows:

$$\bar{X} = \frac{\Sigma X}{N} = \frac{59}{20} = 2.95 \qquad S_X = \sqrt{\frac{SS_X}{N-1}} = \sqrt{\frac{56.95}{19}} = 1.73$$

$$\bar{Y} = \frac{\Sigma Y}{N} = \frac{1405}{20} = 70.25 \qquad S_Y = \sqrt{\frac{SS_Y}{N-1}} = \sqrt{\frac{5873.75}{19}} = 17.58$$

$$r = \frac{SP}{\sqrt{SS_x SS_Y}} = \frac{-464.75}{\sqrt{56.95(5873.75)}} = -.804$$

Recall from the previous chapter that the sum of products and sum of squares X and sum of squares Y were used in computing the correlation coefficient:

$$SP = \Sigma XY - \frac{(\Sigma X)(\Sigma Y)}{N} = 3680 - \frac{(59)(1405)}{20} = -464.75$$

$$SS_Y = \Sigma Y^2 - \frac{(\Sigma Y)^2}{N} = 104575 - \frac{(1405)^2}{20} = 5873.75$$

$$SS_X = \Sigma X^2 - \frac{(\Sigma X)^2}{N} = 231 - \frac{(59)^2}{20} = 56.95$$

The intercept (a) and slope (b) in the linear regression equation can now be computed as:

$$b = r_{XY} \frac{S_Y}{S_X} = -.804\left(\frac{17.58}{1.73}\right) = -8.16$$

$$a = \bar{Y} - b\bar{X} = 70.25 - [(-8.16)(2.95)] = 70.25 + 24.07 = 94.32$$

These values will closely approximate (within rounding error) those output by a computer program. The prediction of Y given knowledge of X is then possible using the intercept and slope values in the following linear regression equation:

$$\hat{Y} = 94.32 + -8.16X$$

To determine the predicted Y values (Yhat) we would substitute each value of X into the linear regression equation. The resulting Y, Yhat, and errors of prediction are given below.

Y	Yhat	e (Y-Yhat)
90	78.00	12.00
70	61.68	8.32
80	69.84	10.16
60	53.52	6.48
95	86.16	8.84
80	78.00	2.00
50	53.52	- 3.52
45	69.84	-24.84
75	78.00	- 3.00
65	61.68	3.32
45	53.52	- 8.52
80	86.16	- 6.16
80	61.68	18.32
60	53.52	6.48
85	86.16	- 1.16
90	94.32	- 4.32
50	53.52	- 3.52
70	69.84	.16
40	61.68	-21.68
95	94.32	.68

The error of prediction for the first student is computed as follows:

Step 1

$$Yhat = a + bX$$
$$Yhat = 94.32 + (-8.16 * 2) = 78$$

Step 2

$$e = Y - Yhat$$
$$e = 90 - 78 = 12$$

Check on linear equation:

$$Y = a + bX + e$$
$$90 = 94.32 + (-16.32) + 12.00$$

In this data example, the correlation coefficient is negative ($r = -.80$), which indicates that as days absent during the week increases (X), the math achievement scores decrease. This relationship would be depicted as a downward line in the data points on a scatter plot. Also notice that the data points go together (covary) in a negative or inverse direction as indicated by the negative sign for the sum of products in the numerator of the correlation coefficient formula. We square the correlation coefficient value to obtain a variance accounted for interpretation, i.e., if $r = -.80$, then $r^2 = .64$. Knowledge of the number of days absent accounts for 64% of the variance in the math achievement scores.

The errors of prediction also serve to identify the accuracy of the regression equation. Notice that some of the errors are positive and some of the errors are negative, consequently the sum (and mean) of the errors should be zero. We expect the Y scores to be normally distributed around Yhat for each value of X so that the variability of these errors indicate the standard deviation of the Y scores around Yhat for each value of X. The standard deviation of the Y scores around Yhat is called a standard error of estimate. It is computed as:

$$S_{Y.X} = \sqrt{\frac{\Sigma e^2}{n-2}} = \sqrt{\frac{2081.08}{18}} = 10.75$$

Another approach using the standard deviation of Y, the correlation coefficient, and sample size is computed as:

$$S_{Y.X} = S_Y \sqrt{1-r^2} \sqrt{n-1/n-2} = 17.58\sqrt{1-(-.804)^2} \sqrt{20-1/20-2} = 10.75$$

A graph of the Y score distribution around each individual X score will help to better understand the interpretation of the standard error of estimate and the concept of homoscedasticity (equal variance of Y scores around Yhat for each X score along the line of least squares). For each value of X, there is a distribution of Y scores around each Yhat value.

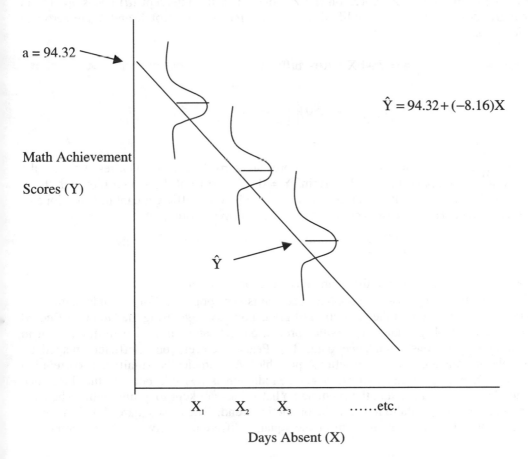

$a = 94.32$

$\hat{Y} = 94.32 + (-8.16)X$

Math Achievement

Scores (Y)

$\hat{Y}$

X_1　X_2　X_3　......etc.

Days Absent (X)

The $S_{Y.X} = 10.75$ is the standard deviation of the Y scores around the predicted Yhat score for each X score. This standard deviation is assumed to be the same for each distribution of Y scores along the least squares line, i.e., homoscedasticity of variance along the least squares line. The predicted Yhat is the mean of the distribution of Y scores for each value of X. The standard error of estimate is therefore calculated as the square root of the sum of the squared differences between Y and Yhat, i.e., $(Y\text{-}Yhat)^2$, divided by N - 2. Since it is assumed that different values of Y vary in a normal distribution around Yhat, the assumption of equal variance in Y across the least squares line is important because you want an accurate mean squared error!

In some instances the Y and X scores are converted to z scores or standard scores to place them both on the same measurement scale. This permits an equivalent "rise" to "run" interpretation of the z values. The standard scores (z scores), as they are sometimes called, can be converted back to their respective raw score. The z score formula subtracts the mean from each score and divides by the standard deviation. The formula you may recall is:

$$z = \frac{X - \overline{X}}{S}$$

As a result of placing Y and X scores on the z score scale, the intercept (a) and slope (b) in the linear regression equation are simplified because the mean values for X and Y are zero and standard deviations for X and Y are one:

$$a = \overline{Y} - b\overline{X} = (0) - b(0) = 0$$

$$b = r_{XY}\frac{S_Y}{S_X} = -.804\left(\frac{1}{1}\right) = -.804$$

Because the mean and standard deviation of z scores are zero (0) and one (1), respectively, the least squares line would pass through the origin (Y = 0 and X = 0) of the scatter plot with the Y and X axes labeled in z-score units. Notice that the correlation coefficient captures the slope of the least squares line. The regression equation in z score form is written as:

$$Z_Y = \beta Z_X$$

with $\beta = -.804$, which is the value of the Pearson correlation coefficient.

The use of linear regression in applied research is very popular. For example, admission into graduate school is based on the prediction of grade point average using the Graduate Record Exam (GRE) score. Colleges and Universities predict budgets and enrollment from one year to the next based on previous attendance data. The Pearson correlation coefficient played an important role in making these predictions possible. A statistically significant correlation between Y and X will generally indicate a good prediction is possible because the difference between the observed Y values and the predicted Yhat values are kept to a minimum. The least squares line is fitted to the data to indicate the prediction trend. The least squares line is a unique regression line, which minimizes the sum of the squared differences between the observed Y's and the predicted Y's, thus keeping prediction error to a minimum by the selection of values for the intercept (*a*) and slope (*b*). In the regression formula using z-scores, we see the unique role that the Pearson correlation coefficient plays.

In this chapter, a true population linear regression equation is formed on the basis of the amount of overtime worked (X) and bonus points received (Y). The true population linear regression equation can be expressed as: $Y = 3 + .25X + e$. This equation indicates that if there are no overtime hours worked (X = 0), the number of bonus points is 3.0, plus some random error (*e*) that is due to chance, which can be either positive or negative. The bonus points are increased by .25 for each hour of overtime worked. It is assumed that for each X, the Y values are normally distributed around Yhat, their mean on the line $Y = 3 + .25X$, and that these normal distributions of Y's around their Yhats have the same variance. The data will be selected at random from a normal population. The scatter plot, linear regression equation, and least squares line will be given for the data each time you run the REGRESSION program.

SUMMARY

In this chapter, you should learn that:

- The *a* in the regression equation is the intercept of the least squares line.
- The *b* coefficient in the regression equation is the slope of the least squares line.
- The intercept in the regression equation is called the Y intercept; the point at which the least squares line crosses the Y axis.
- In the linear regression equation, X is the independent variable and Y the dependent variable.
- The linear regression equation using z scores for X and Y, has a slope equal to the Pearson correlation coefficient.
- The intercept and slope of the least squares line from sample data are estimates of the population intercept and slope.
- The purpose of linear regression is to predict Y from knowledge of X using a least squares criterion to select an intercept and slope that will minimize the difference between Y and Yhat.

How the REGRESSION program works

The REGRESSION program uses the least squares function within S-PLUS to calculate the intercept and slope of the regression equation and plot the results. The program first specifies the intercept and slope of the true regression equation in the population, and defines the sample size. Next, a random sample of x values is chosen from a uniform population ranging from 1 to 10. Then corresponding random y values are created within certain constraints by adding a value extracted from a normal distribution with a mean of 0 and standard deviation of 1 to the true regression y value at point x, thereby creating a roughly normal distribution of y values around the true regression line. These x and y values are then entered into a matrix and printed out for verification and reference by the user.

The next line performs the least squares function, creating a **htest** object named *sampleReg*. The coefficients resulting from the function are extracted and placed into b*Sample* and a*Sample* by use of the **coef [ ]** qualifier. Full descriptions of the least squares fit line and the true regression line are assigned to variables for later output. The limits of the y-axis for the scatter plot are then determined based on the largest and smallest values of the sample data. The plot is created with the title being the description of the least squares equation. After the scatter plot is created, the least squares fit line is drawn on the plot with the **lines** function and both the true and sample least squares equations are output. The correlation coefficient is printed to reference the slope for a regression equation using standard scores for Y and X.

REGRESSION Program Output

```
ScatterPlot Data Points

+-----------+-----------+-----------+-----------+-----------+
|(7.7,2.61) |(2.13,4.26)|(8.88,5.23)|(1.02,4.05)|(1.11,4.45)|
+-----------+-----------+-----------+-----------+-----------+
|(2.55,1.88)|(3.22,3.97)|(3.64,3.88)|(6.14,6.36)|(2.67,3.82)|
+-----------+-----------+-----------+-----------+-----------+
|(9.22,5.29)|(1.6,4.71) |(2.49,2.7) |(8.1,4.77) |(5.11,5.64)|
+-----------+-----------+-----------+-----------+-----------+
|(2.55,4.45)|(6.32,6.48)|(2.77,3.81)|(9.23,6.09)|(6.95,4.87)|
+-----------+-----------+-----------+-----------+-----------+

True regression line is: y = 3 + 0.25x
Least squares fit line is: y = 3.52 + 0.2x
r = 0.48 (slope using standard scores for X and Y)
```

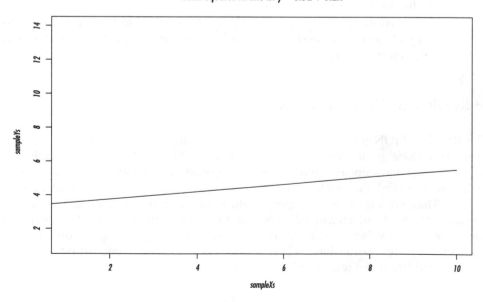

Least squares fit line is: y = 3.52 + 0.2x

CHAPTER 34 EXERCISES

1. Run REGRESSION and enter the 20 pairs of observations in the following spaces.

   _____   _____   _____   _____   _____

   _____   _____   _____   _____   _____

   _____   _____   _____   _____   _____

   _____   _____   _____   _____   _____

   a. What is the equation for the true population least squares line? _____

   b. What is the equation of the sample least squares line?   _____

   c. What is the slope of the equation if using z scores? (Correlation coefficient)_____

   d. Print the scatter plot produced by the S-PLUS REGRESSION program.

2. Run REGRESSION program five more times, and record the sample regression equations.

   TRUE REGRESSION EQUATION: $Y = 3 + .25X$

   SAMPLE EQUATION: Run 1 _____

                      Run 2 _____

                      Run 3 _____

                      Run 4 _____

                      Run 5 _____

   a. What is the slope of the true regression equation?   _____

   b. What is the Y intercept of the true regression equation? _____

   c. Calculate the error in the estimates of the sample slopes and intercepts for the five runs.

       Enter the values in the table below.   (Error = Sample Estimate - True Population Value)

RUN	ERROR IN SLOPE	ERROR IN INTERCEPT
1	_____	_____
2	_____	_____
3	_____	_____
4	_____	_____
5	_____	_____

d. Are the errors in the slopes in the same direction (positive versus negative)?

YES _____ NO _____

e. Are the errors in the Y intercepts in the same direction (positive versus negative)?

YES _____ NO _____

3. Run the REGRESSION PROGRAM and determine for a given value of X (overtime hours worked), what is the bonus received (Y)? Use the following values:

```
bTrue <- .50
aTrue <- 10
sampleSize <- 100
```

a. If X = 4, find the bonus (predicted Y) using the true population regression equation.

_____

b. If X = 4, find the bonus (predicted Y) using the sample equation.

_____

TRUE OR FALSE QUESTIONS

T   F   a. If the equation of a least squares line is Y = 4 – .5X, then the slope of the line is 4.

T   F   b. Prediction of Y given knowledge of X is the purpose of linear regression analysis.

T   F   c. The slope of the linear regression equation in z score form is the Pearson correlation coefficient.

T   F   d. A regression equation from sample data will usually differ from the true population regression equation.

T   F   e. Y values are normally distributed around their Yhat means on the least squares line and the Y distributions have the same variance.

VI

REPLICABILITY OF FINDINGS

REPLICABILITY OF STUDIES

CHAPTER 35

CROSS VALIDATION

CHAPTER OBJECTIVES

- To understand the importance of replicating research findings.
- To understand sample size effects when using the cross-validation approach.
- To apply the regression equation obtained from one randomly split sample to the other randomly split sample.
- To interpret the research findings given similar results from one cross-validation sample to the other.
- To interpret the research findings given dissimilar results from one cross-validation sample to the other.

The various parts of this book have covered statistical theory, probability, sampling distributions, statistical distributions, hypothesis testing, and various statistical tests based on the level of measurement and type of research design. This next section addresses an important area of research related to replicating our findings. Research for many decades involved carrying out a single study, i.e., collection of a single random sample of data from the population. Researchers today are becoming more concerned with validating their research results. Many different approaches have been taken which are discussed in this chapter and subsequent chapters.

Everyday we ask ourselves important questions. It could be as simple as what route to take to a new job. In the process of answering the question, we gather information or data. This could include asking co-workers, driving different routes, and examining an area roadmap. Once we feel that sufficient information has been collected, we answer the question for ourselves and often share the answer with others. Trying the route to work we selected validates our findings or conclusion. The process of asking a question, gathering data, answering the question, and validating the conclusion is the key to the research process

Once we have asked an important question, gathered data, and answered the question, others may ask whether the same results would occur if the process were repeated. In other words, could the research findings be replicated? In order to repeat the same process, we must first document the methods and procedures used in the original research. Then, another person can replicate the research process and report their findings. If the research findings are valid and consistent, then others should report findings similar to the original research.

In numerous academic disciplines, research findings are reported along with the methods and procedures used in the study. Unfortunately, not many research studies are replicated. This is due primarily to the time, money, and resources needed to replicate research studies. Instead, other approaches have been developed which don't require conducting the study again. These methods include cross-validation, jackknife, bootstrap, and meta-analysis. The cross-validation approach will be presented in this chapter while subsequent chapters will present the jackknife, bootstrap, and meta-analysis approaches.

The cross-validation approach involves taking a random sample of data from a population. Typically we would compute a sample statistic for the sample data of size N where the sample statistic is our estimator of the population parameter. In the **cross-validation** approach, the original sample data are randomly split into two equal halves. A sample statistic is computed using one half of the sample data and applied to the other half of the sample data. If the sample statistics for the two randomly split data halves are similar, we assume the research findings would be replicable. Otherwise the findings are not consistent and probably could not be replicated. A large random sample is generally needed to provide two randomly split data halves that are of sufficient sample size so as not to affect the sample statistics. For example, a sample of size N = 1000 randomly drawn from a population would be randomly split into equal halves; each cross-validation sample size would be N = 500.

The essence of the cross-validation technique is the computing of a sample statistic on the first set of sample data and applying it to the second set of sample data. This technique is different from other approaches in statistics. We are not comparing sample means from two random samples of data drawn from different populations and testing whether the means are similar or dissimilar (independent t-test for mean differences). We are not testing two sample proportions to determine if they are similar or dissimilar (z-test for differences in proportions). We are not comparing a sample mean to a population mean (one sample t-test). It should be noted that if the original sample statistic was not a good estimator of the population parameter, the cross-validation results would not improve the estimation of the population parameter.

In this chapter, a random sample will be drawn from a population. The sample data will be randomly split into two equal halves of size, N/2. The **linear regression** equation, $Y = a + bX + e$, will be computed using the first one-half sample. The regression equation will then be applied to the second one-half sample. The regression weights and R-square values will be compared. A smaller R-squared value in the second one-half sample is expected because the regression equation was "optimized" to fit the first one-half sample data. This phenomenon is called *shrinkage* of the R-squared value. The second program will yield results to determine the amount of expected shrinkage in the second one-half sample regression statistics. In the S-PLUS program, separate regression equations are calculated for each randomly selected one-half samples of data.

SUMMARY

In this chapter, you should learn that:

- Replicating research results involves conducting another study using the same methods and procedures.
- When unable to replicate another study, researchers apply the cross-validation approach to a single sample of data randomly drawn from the population.
- The cross-validation approach involves randomly splitting a random sample into two equal halves, then computing a sample statistic on one sub-sample and applying it to the other sub-sample.
- The cross-validation approach is not the same as other statistical tests, which randomly sample from a population and test sample estimates of the population parameter.

- The cross-validation approach does not improve the sample statistic as an estimate of the population parameter.
- A comparison of two regression equations from two equal halves of sample data will indicate the stability of the intercept and regression weight.

How the CROSS VALIDATION program works

In this chapter, there are two separate programs that perform cross-validation exercises. The first program will be described in full with only the differences in the second program presented. The first program, **CROSSVALIDATION1** (chap34a.ssc), uses the traditional method of cross validation whereby a regression equation is created on one randomly chosen half of a sample and applied to the data in the second half to compare stability of regression weights and check for R-squared shrinkage. The second program, **CROSSVALIDATION2** (chap34b.ssc), creates separate independent regression equations on each randomly split half and compares the regression weights and R-squared values. Both programs begin by assigning values for the intercept and slope of the true population regression equation, the sample size, and the number of replications. A replication in the program refers to the splitting of the sample size into random halves and applying the particular method of cross validation. For each replication, a full sample is split into two new random halves, so the same full sample from the population is used for all replications within the same run of the program.

Random X values are taken from a uniform population ranging from 1 to 10. The Y values are assigned based on the population regression parameters with a normal distribution of values centered along the true population least squares line. Once all the points for the full sample have been determined, a regression is run on the data using the **lsfit** function and the results assigned to the *sampleReg* object. This object is then passed to the **ls.print** function in order to create a least squares summary object from which components may be extracted. The R-squared value for the full sample is assigned to *sampleR2* and the regression weight is assigned to b*Sample*.

The main processing loop of the program performs the replications and begins by determining the size of one-half the sample and randomly chooses that number of points for the first random half of data points. A regression is run on these points just as it was for the full sample and the same components are extracted, with the addition of the intercept value. Next, the other half of the sample is assigned to vectors to be analyzed using the vector notation of [-*halfPoints*], which means all points that were not in the first vector of random values. The predicted Y-values are then determined from the X-values of the second half using the slope and intercept determined by the regression of the first half of the sample, the sum of squared errors for the regression, the total sum of squared error Y-values and the predicted Y-values. The first sample half regression weight and the R-squared values for both halves are added to an output vector to finish the processing loop. After all replications are completed, the output vector is moved into a matrix object and assigned dimension labels. The regression weight and R-squared value for the full sample is displayed using the **cat** function and the output matrix for the replication results is output using **print.char.matrix**.

The second program is identical to the first, except that the second half of the sample data is also analyzed with the **lsfit** function instead of just being regressed against the equation developed from the first half. The output of the second program also includes a regression weight for the second half of the sample for comparison. A few of the lines that were not necessary (such as extracting the intercept for the first half of the sample) were omitted in the second program, but they are essentially the same other than the treatment of the second sample half and slightly different output.

CROSS VALIDATION Program Output

Given the following values:

```
bTrue <- .25
aTrue <- 3
sampleSize <- 1000
numReplications <- 5
```

CROSSVALIDATION1

Original Sample: Regression weight = 0.261 , R-Squared = 0.311

	Reg Wt:Sample A	R-Sqr:Sample A	R-Sqr:Sample B
Replication # 1	0.239	0.266	0.259
Replication # 2	0.268	0.324	0.332
Replication # 3	0.265	0.316	0.329
Replication # 4	0.262	0.319	0.31
Replication # 5	0.274	0.333	0.354

CROSSVALIDATION2

Original Sample: Regression weight = 0.254 , R-Squared = 0.317

	Reg Wt:Sample A	R-Sqr:Sample A	Reg Wt:Sample B	R-Sqr:Sample B
Replication # 1	0.255	0.305	0.254	0.331
Replication # 2	0.27	0.352	0.237	0.282
Replication # 3	0.245	0.286	0.263	0.349
Replication # 4	0.234	0.284	0.276	0.354
Replication # 5	0.258	0.318	0.25	0.315

CHAPTER 35 EXERCISES

1. Run the CROSS VALIDATION1 program 5 times for an original sample size of 500. Record the regression weight and the two R-square values for *each* sample of size N = 250. Record the regression weight and R-square value for the original sample.

    a. Original Sample (N = 500): Regression Weight _____   R-Square _____.

    b.

	Sub-sample A (N = 250)		Sub-sample B (N = 250)	
	Regression Weight	R-Square	Regression Weight	R-Square
1.	_____	_____	_____	_____
2.	_____	_____	_____	_____
3.	_____	_____	_____	_____
4.	_____	_____	_____	_____
5.	_____	_____	_____	_____

    c. The regression equation computed for sample A is applied to sample B. Are the R-squared values similar in sample A and sample B for the five replications?

    YES _____NO _____.

2. Run the CROSS VALIDATION1 program 5 times for an original sample size of 1,000.

    a. Compare the regression equation results for the original samples of N = 500 and N = 1000. Record the ORIGINAL SAMPLE regression weights and R-square values.

    N = 500   Regression Weight_____   R-square _____
    N = 1000   Regression Weight_____   R-square _____

    b. Does sample size affect the R-square value?

    YES _____NO _____.

    c. Which sample size would give better estimates of R-square and the regression weight?

    N = 500 _____   N = 1000 _____

3. Run the CROSS VALIDATION2 program 5 times for an original sample size of 500. Record the regression weights and R-square values for *each* sample of size N = 250. Record the regression weight and R-square value for the original sample.

a. Original Sample (N = 500): Regression Weight _____   R-Square _____.

b.

	Sub-sample A (N = 250)		Sub-sample B (N = 250)	
	Regression Weight	R-Square	Regression Weight	R-Square
1.	_____	_____	_____	_____
2.	_____	_____	_____	_____
3.	_____	_____	_____	_____
4.	_____	_____	_____	_____
5.	_____	_____	_____	_____

c. The regression equations for sample A and sample B are computed independently. Are the R-squared values similar in sample A and sample B for the five replications?

YES _____NO _____.

4. Run the CROSS VALIDATION2 program 5 times for an original sample size of 1,000.

a. Compare the regression equation results for the original samples of N = 500 and N = 1000. Record the ORIGINAL SAMPLE regression weights and R-square values.

N = 500   Regression Weight_____   R-square _____
N = 1000 Regression Weight_____   R-square _____

b. Does sample size affect the R-square value?

YES _____NO _____.

c. Which sample size would give better estimates of R-square and the regression weight?

N = 500 _____   N = 1000 _____

TRUE OR FALSE QUESTIONS

T   F   a. Cross-validation techniques verify that the sample statistic is a good estimator
               of the population parameter.

T   F   b. Cross-validation techniques involve splitting a random sample from a
               population into two equal halves.

T   F   c. The cross-validation approach involves computing sample statistics using one
               sub-sample and applying them to the second sub-sample.

T   F   d. Cross-validation techniques require large sample sizes.

T   F   e. A replication of findings generally requires conducting another study using the
               methods and procedures of the original study.

CHAPTER 36

JACKKNIFE

CHAPTER OBJECTIVES

- To understand the jackknife procedure.
- To validate sample estimates of population parameters.
- To assess the stability of the sample statistic as an estimator of the population parameter.
- To establish the accuracy of confidence intervals for sample estimates.

The jackknife procedure involves the use of a single random sample of data drawn from a population of data. Recall that the sample statistic is an estimate of the population parameter. We also learned in previous chapters that how good the sample statistic is as an estimate of the population parameter depends on the sample size. The jackknife procedure is concerned with whether the sample statistic as an estimate of the population parameter is affected by any single data value. For example, we know that the sample mean is affected by extreme data values, which is indicated by the standard deviation of the sample data.

The **jackknife** approach uses a single sample of data, computes the original sample statistic (e.g., sample mean), and then computes the sample statistic for each sample of size $N - 1$. Basically, each sample mean after the original sample mean would be computed based on the omission of one data point. The jackknife approach is therefore useful in determining whether an influential data point exists that dramatically changes the sample statistic. The jackknife procedure can be applied to any sample statistic based on a random sample drawn from a population. The jackknife method computes a jackknife mean based on the exclusion of a different data point each time. The number of jackknife replications therefore typically equals the original sample size so that the influence of each data point on the sample statistic can be determined.

An example might help to better understand the jackknife procedure. A random sample of 10 numbers is drawn from a population. The numbers are 2, 4, 9, 12, 8, 7, 15, 11, 3, and 14. The sum of the numbers is 85. The mean is calculated as 85 divided by 10, which equals 8.5. This sample mean is an estimate of the population mean. The jackknife procedure calculates 10 additional sample means based on $N = 9$, but each time with a different data value omitted. To compute each jackknife mean, the data value omitted is subtracted from the sum of 85 and this new sum is divided by $N = 9$ to yield the jackknife mean. The jackknife procedure for these data values is outlined below.

Sample Size	Mean	Values Used	Value Omitted
10	8.5	2, 4, 9, 12, 8, 7, 15, 11, 3, 14	None
9	9.2	4, 9, 12, 8, 7, 15, 11, 3, 14	2
9	9.0	2, 9, 12, 8, 7, 15, 11, 3, 14	4
9	8.4	2, 4, 12, 8, 7, 15, 11, 3, 14	9
9	8.1	2, 4, 9, 8, 7, 15, 11, 3, 14	12
9	8.5	2, 4, 9, 12, 7, 15, 11, 3, 14	8
9	8.6	2, 4, 9, 12, 8, 15, 11, 3, 14	7
9	7.7	2, 4, 9, 12, 8, 7, 11, 3, 14	15
9	8.2	2, 4, 9, 12, 8, 7, 15, 3, 14	11
9	9.1	2, 4, 9, 12, 8, 7, 15, 11, 14	3
9	7.8	2, 4, 9, 12, 8, 7, 15, 11, 3	14

The jackknife sample means ranged from 7.7 to 9.2 with the original sample mean of 8.5. The omission of a low data value inflated (increased) the sample mean as an estimate of the population mean. The omission of a high data value deflated (lowered) the sample mean as an estimate of the population mean. Both of these outcomes are expected and help us to understand the nature of how extreme data values (**outliers**) affect the sample statistic as an estimate of a population parameter.

Another example of the jackknife procedure will highlight the detection of an influential (outlier) data value. Once again, we randomly sample 10 data values from a population. The sum of the numbers is 158 with an original sample mean of 15.8. The results are summarized below. The jackknife means in this second example ranged from 9.2 to 17.2 with an original sample mean of 15.8. Notice that the original sample mean of 15.8 is less than every other jackknife mean, except the one with an omitted influential data value, i.e., 75. The results indicate how the removal of an influential data value can increase or decrease the sample statistic value.

Sample Size	Mean	Values Used	Value Omitted
10	15.8	75, 4, 9, 12, 8, 7, 15, 11, 3, 14	None
9	9.2	4, 9, 12, 8, 7, 15, 11, 3, 14	75
9	17.1	75, 9, 12, 8, 7, 15, 11, 3, 14	4
9	16.5	75, 4, 12, 8, 7, 15, 11, 3, 14	9
9	16.2	75, 4, 9, 8, 7, 15, 11, 3, 14	12
9	16.6	75, 4, 9, 12, 7, 15, 11, 3, 14	8
9	16.7	75, 4, 9, 12, 8, 15, 11, 3, 14	7
9	15.9	75, 4, 9, 12, 8, 7, 11, 3, 14	15
9	16.3	75, 4, 9, 12, 8, 7, 15, 3, 14	11
9	17.2	75, 4, 9, 12, 8, 7, 15, 11, 14	3
9	16.0	75, 4, 9, 12, 8, 7, 15, 11, 3	14

An important comparison can be made between the first and second example. In the first example, the original sample mean of 8.5 fell between all jackknife means, which ranged from 7.7 to 9.2. In the second example, the jackknife means were all greater than the original sample mean, with the exception of the one influential data value. If we examine the jackknife means for each omitted data value, it points out the presence of an influential data value (outlier or extreme value).

The descriptive information for the jackknife means in both examples also clearly indicates the presence of influential data in the second example. The jackknife means were treated as new data such that the average is the *mean* of the jackknife means. The standard deviation, variance, and 95% confidence interval indicate more data dispersion in the second example. This dispersion is interpreted as less accuracy, more variability, and greater difference between the original sample mean and the jackknife means. The descriptive information is:

Descriptive Information	First Example	Second Example
Sample Size	N = 10	N = 10
Range	7.7 to 9.2	9.2 to 17.2
Mean	8.46	15.77
Standard Deviation	.52	2.35
Variance	.27	5.52
95% Confidence Interval	(7.44, 9.48)	(11.16, 20.38)

SUMMARY

In this chapter, you should learn that:

- The jackknife procedure uses the original sample drawn from a population to estimate additional sample means based on N − 1 sample data points.
- The jackknife procedure is useful for identifying influential, extreme, or outlier data values in a random sample of data.
- The jackknife method can be used with any sample statistic that is computed from a random sample of data drawn from a well-defined population.
- The jackknife approach helps to validate whether a sample of data provides a good sample statistic as an estimator of the population parameter.
- The number of jackknife means is equal to the sample size for the purposes of detecting an influential data value.
- The confidence interval around a set of jackknife means will be smaller when influential data values are not present.

How the JACKKNIFE program works

The JACKKNIFE program utilizes the **jackknife** function incorporated into S-PLUS. The function permits an easy method for calculating the mean and percentiles after jackknifing the samples. The calculations could be done manually instead of using the jackknife function, but it is used here for demonstration purposes. The **jackknife** function doesn't plot the data, so a separate command is used. The plotting of the data alone could indicate influential data points or outliers.

The JACKKNIFE program uses a vector of sample points defined by the user to calculate the mean, standard deviation, and sample size of the sample. Within the main processing loop, a vector of values is created that excludes one sample point at a time [-*i*]. The mean of the remaining sample points is calculated, they are concatenated into a string for output, and the omitted value is identified. The variables are added to an output vector during each iteration of the loop. When the loop finishes, the output vector is moved into a matrix and dimension names are assigned. The jackknife is then performed and assigned to the *jackknifeObj* object, which is plotted for visual inspection. The **jackknife** function is given the vector of values to be jackknifed along with the name of the statistic (which can be any S-PLUS function that accepts a data object as its first parameter, or a user-defined function). The mean and standard deviation for the entire sample are printed out, followed by the matrix that was created within the main processing loop, and finally the summary of the jackknife results.

When the **jackknife** function is used in S-PLUS, it should be assigned to an object as in this program, and then plotted. An outlier will likely be visible in the plot. The **breaks** keyword in this program should be used to assure that divisions along the x-axis are small enough to detect outlier means that are near the edges of the confidence interval. You may want to look back at previous programs to see how to create lines on the **plot** that would correspond to the limits of the confidence interval. Another added function would be to use the $replicates component of the **jackknife** object (which is a vector of the means of all jackknife samples) to test against the values for the confidence interval limits and print out a summary list of influential data points or outliers.

JACKKNIFE Program Output

Given the following values:

```
dataVector <- c(10,20,30,40,50,60,70,80,90,100)
Original mean= 55    Original standard deviation= 30.28
```

Sample Size	Jackknife Mean	Values Used	Value Omitted
9	60	20,30,40,50,60,70,80,90,100	10
9	58.89	10,30,40,50,60,70,80,90,100	20
9	57.78	10,20,40,50,60,70,80,90,100	30
9	56.67	10,20,30,50,60,70,80,90,100	40
9	55.56	10,20,30,40,60,70,80,90,100	50
9	54.44	10,20,30,40,50,70,80,90,100	60
9	53.33	10,20,30,40,50,60,80,90,100	70
9	52.22	10,20,30,40,50,60,70,90,100	80
9	51.11	10,20,30,40,50,60,70,80,100	90
9	50	10,20,30,40,50,60,70,80,90	100

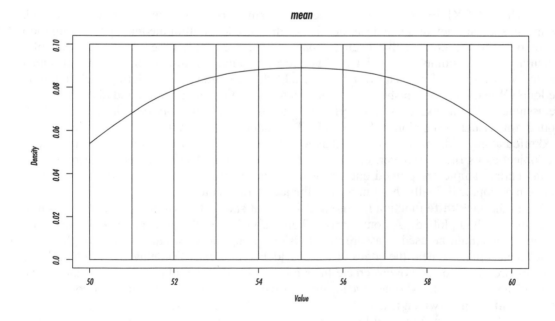

CHAPTER 36 EXERCISES

1. Run the JACKKNIFE program with the following 10 data values as a random Sample A:
   dataVector <- c(1,2,3,4,5,6,7,8,9,10). Print the Graph.

   a. Record the Original mean and standard deviation.

   Original Mean =_____ Original Standard Deviation =_____

   b. Record the following information for the N − 1 data sets.

Run	Sample Size	Jackknife Mean	Value Omitted
1	9		
2	9		
3	9		
4	9		
5	9		
6	9		
7	9		
8	9		
9	9		
10	9		

   c. Calculate the Standard Error of the Mean using Original sample standard deviation and
       the number of replications, N = 10.

   $SE = S / \sqrt{N}$ = _____ = _____.

   d. Calculate the 95% Confidence Interval using the Original sample mean and standard
       deviation.

   $95\%CI = \bar{X} \pm 1.96(S)$ = (_____, _____)

   e. List the Range of Jackknife Means.

   Highest Mean _____ Lowest Mean _____

   f. How many Jackknife means are higher than the Original Sample mean?

   _____

2. Run the JACKKNIFE program with the following 10 data values as a random Sample B: dataVector <- c(1,2,3,4,5,6,7,8,9,100). Print the Graph.

   a. Record the Originial sample mean and standard deviation.

      Original Mean = _____   Original Standard Deviation =_____

   b. Record the following information for the N − 1 data sets

Run	Sample Size	Jackknife Mean	Value Omitted
1	9		
2	9		
3	9		
4	9		
5	9		
6	9		
7	9		
8	9		
9	9		
10	9		

   c. Calculate the Standard Error of the Mean using Original sample standard deviation and the number of replications, N = 10.

$$SE = S / \sqrt{N} = \underline{\hspace{2cm}} = \underline{\hspace{2cm}}.$$

   d. Calculate the 95% Confidence Interval using the Original sample mean and standard deviation.

$$95\% CI = \bar{X} \pm 1.96(S) = (\underline{\hspace{1.5cm}}, \underline{\hspace{1.5cm}})$$

   e. List the Range of Jackknife Means.

      Highest Mean _____ Lowest Mean _____

   f. How many Jackknife means are higher than the Original Sample mean?

      _____

3. List the Original sample means and standard deviations, SE, 95% CI, and range of Jackknife means for Sample A and Sample B above.

	Sample Mean	Sample SD	SE	95%CI		Jackknife Range	
Sample A	_____	_____	_____	(_____,	_____)	High: _____	Low: _____
Sample B	_____	_____	_____	(_____,	_____)	High: _____	Low: _____

a. Does Sample A or Sample B have a higher sample mean?

Sample A _____ Sample B _____

b. Does Sample A or Sample B have a larger standard deviation?

Sample A _____ Sample B _____

c. Does Sample A or Sample B have a larger Standard Error of the Mean?

Sample A _____ Sample B _____

d. Does Sample A or Sample B have a wider 95% Confidence Interval?

Sample A _____ Sample B _____

e. Does Sample A or Sample B have more Jackknife Means higher than the Original

sample mean?

Sample A _____ Sample B _____

f. Which sample has a more accurate sample mean estimator of the population mean?

Sample A _____ Sample B _____

g. Summarize **a** to **e** above in regard to their indicating influential data points.

_____

_____

_____

TRUE OR FALSE QUESTIONS

T   F   a.   The jackknife procedure is useful for detecting influential data values.

T   F   b.   A jackknife mean computed with an influential data value does not fall within the confidence interval of the jackknife means.

T   F   c.   The standard deviation of the jackknife means shows whether more variability is present, hence influential data values.

T   F   d.   The jackknife approach can be used with any sample statistic computed from random samples of data drawn from a population.

T   F   e.   The jackknife procedure repeatedly samples the population data to determine if the sample mean is a good estimate of the population mean.

T   F   f.   The number of jackknife means is typically equal to the original sample size for the purposes of detecting influential data points.

CHAPTER 37

BOOTSTRAP

CHAPTER OBJECTIVES

- To understand the bootstrap procedure.
- To understand resampling as a sampling with replacement method.
- To calculate the bootstrap estimate and standard error.
- To calculate the confidence interval around the bootstrap estimate.
- Use the bootstrap estimate to determine whether the sample statistic is a stable or good estimator of the population parameter.

The bootstrap method differs from the traditional parametric approach to inferential statistics because it uses *sampling with replacement* to create the sampling distribution of a statistic. The bootstrap method doesn't take a random sample from a population in the same way as that used in our previous inferential statistics. The **bootstrap** method is useful for reproducing the sampling distribution of any statistic, e.g., the median or regression weight. The basic idea is that conclusions are made about a population parameter from a random sample of data, but in which a sampling distribution of the statistic is generated based on sampling with replacement. The factors that influence the shape of the sampling distribution are therefore important because it is the bootstrap estimate from the sampling distribution that allows us to make an inference to the population.

The bootstrap procedure uses a random sample of data as a substitute for the population data. The randomly sampled data acts as a "pseudo" population from which the bootstrap method repeatedly samples the data. The repeated sampling of data is done with replacement of each data point after selection. The resampling technique therefore samples from the "pseudo" population using the same set of data values each time. Since each data value is replaced before taking the next random selection, it is possible to have the same data value selected more than once and used in the calculation of the final sample statistic. The probabilities in the earlier chapters of the book were based on randomly sampling *without* replacement where each individual, object, or event had an equally likely chance of being selected. The bootstrap method uses probabilities based upon randomly sampling *with* replacement where each individual, object, or event has an equally likely chance of being selected each time a data value is randomly drawn.

The bootstrap procedure involves the following steps:

Step 1: A random sample of data for a given sample size N is drawn from the population with mean, μ, and standard deviation, σ.

Step 2: The random sample of data size N acts as a "pseudo" population with mean, $\mu *$, and standard deviation, $\sigma*$.

Step 3:   The bootstrap method takes n bootstrap samples of sample size N from the "pseudo" population, each time replacing the randomly sampled data point. For each sample of size N a sample statistic is computed.

Step 4:   A frequency distribution of the n bootstrap sample statistics is graphed which represents the sampling distribution of the statistic. The mean of this sampling distribution is the bootstrap estimate, θ^*, which has a standard error of SE_{θ^*} computed by:

$$SE_\theta = \sqrt{\frac{\sum(\theta_i^* - \theta^*)^2}{n-1}}$$

Step 5:   The amount of bias in the original sample statistic as an estimate of the population parameter is calculated by subtracting: $\mu^* - \theta^*$. If the bootstrap estimate is similar to the corresponding "pseudo" population parameter, then no bias is present. A small difference would still indicate that the original sample statistic is a good estimator of the population parameter.

Step 6:   Calculate a confidence interval around the bootstrap estimate using the standard error of the bootstrap estimate and level of significance, Z. The confidence interval is computed by:

$$CI_\theta = \theta^* \pm Z\ (SE_{\theta^*})$$

The bootstrap method can be based on samples of size N that equal the original sample size N or are larger because it involves sampling data points with replacement. Most applications resample to produce sample sizes equal to the "pseudo" population size. The bootstrap method can also be used to determine the amount of bias between any sample statistic and population parameter. It should be noted that the bootstrap method is only useful for determining the amount of bias in the sample statistic when the original sample is randomly drawn and representative of the population. This makes sense because if the original sample data were not representative of the population, then creating the sampling distribution of this data would erroneously indicate population characteristics.

An example will help to clarify how the bootstrap method is used to determine the amount of bias in the original sample statistic as an estimate of the population parameter. A random sample of 100 data points is drawn from the population. This random sample now becomes a "pseudo" population. The "pseudo" population has a mean, $\mu* = 50$, and standard deviation, $\sigma* = 20$. The bootstrap procedure will randomly sample data points with replacement from this "pseudo" population. The bootstrap sample size will be $n = 10$ and the number of bootstrap samples will be $N = 5$. The resulting data for each bootstrap sample is given below.

Run	Sample Size	Bootstrap Data	Bootstrap Mean	Bootstrap Standard Deviation
1	10	10, 30, 35, 40, 50, 80, 90, 75, 20, 60	49.0	26.75
2	10	15, 25, 75, 40, 55, 55, 95, 70, 30, 65	52.5	24.97
3	10	85, 45, 35, 25, 45, 60, 75, 80, 90, 15	55.5	26.40
4	10	20, 30, 45, 50, 55, 65, 10, 70, 85, 95	52.5	27.41
5	10	50, 50, 20, 45, 65, 75, 30, 80, 70, 30	51.5	20.69

The bootstrap estimate, based on the average of the sampling distribution of bootstrap means is $\theta* = 52.2$. The standard error of the bootstrap estimate, based on the square root of the sum of squares difference between each bootstrap sample mean and the bootstrap estimate, divided by the number of bootstrap samples minus one, is $SE_{\theta*} = 2.33$. To establish a 95% confidence interval, a $Z = 1.96$ value under the normal distribution is used. The 95% confidence interval is therefore computed as:

$$95\% \ CI_\theta = \theta* \pm Z \ (SE_{\theta*})$$

$$95\% \ CI_\theta = 52.2 \pm 1.96 \ (\sqrt{21.80 / 4})$$

$$95\% \ CI_\theta = 52.2 \pm 1.96 \ (2.33)$$

$$95\% \ CI_\theta = 52.2 \pm 4.57$$

$$95\% \ CI_\theta = (47.63, 56.77)$$

The amount of bias is indicated by, $\mu* - \theta*$, which is $50 - 52.2 = -2.2$. On the average, the bootstrap means were 2.2 units higher than the "pseudo" population mean. The sign of the *bootstrap estimate* will be either positive or negative depending upon whether the bootstrap estimate is lower or higher than the "pseudo" population parameter, respectively. Since the *bootstrap confidence interval* captures the "pseudo" population mean, we would conclude that the original sample mean is a good stable estimate of the population mean.

SUMMARY

In this chapter, you should learn that:

- The bootstrap method uses a random sample of data as a "pseudo" population.
- The bootstrap procedure resamples the "pseudo" population with replacement.
- The bootstrap samples of data can contain some of the same data points.
- The bootstrap estimate is the average of the bootstrap sample statistics.
- The bootstrap standard deviation is based on the bootstrap data.
- The bootstrap confidence interval should capture the "pseudo" population parameter when the original sample statistic is a good estimate of the population parameter.
- The bootstrap method is used to determine the amount of bias between the "pseudo" population parameter and the bootstrap estimate. Similar values indicate no bias.
- The bootstrap method can be used with any sample statistic to help determine if the sample statistic is a good or stable estimator of the population parameter.
- The bootstrap method is not useful when the random sample of data is not representative of the population data.

How the BOOTSTRAP program works

The BOOTSTRAP program is perhaps the shortest one in the book because the built-in **bootstrap** function produces the necessary meaningful output. The user defines the sample size, number of bootstrap samples, and size of each bootstrap sample. A random sample of the desired number of points is taken from a normal distribution with a mean of 50 and standard deviation of 10. The **bootstrap** function is then performed with the *sampleData* object as the target and the number of bootstrap samples and size of each bootstrap sample passed as arguments along with the function (**mean**) to be performed. Finally, the results of the bootstrap are plotted and summary information printed to the screen. On the output, the "Observed" mean corresponds to the mean of the "pseudo" population mentioned in this chapter and the "Mean" refers to the bootstrap estimate of the mean. The "Bias" is of course the difference between the two and the SE of the bootstrap estimate is reported. Two different confidence intervals are reported for the 5% and 95% confidence levels. The empirical percentile approach is used in the chapter examples. The BCa percentiles refer to intervals based on bias-correction and acceleration values. If the bias-corrected and accelerated values are zero, then the empirical percentile confidence interval and BCa percentile confidence interval will be the same. Calculations of the bias-corrected and accelerated values are beyond the scope of this book, but BCa confidence intervals are typically reported, so they are reported here. You may wish to run the BOOTSTRAP program and change the **sizeBootstraps** to equal the **sampleSize**, which is commonly done in practice, and compare this to choosing bootstrap samples less than the original sample size.

BOOTSTRAP Program Output

Given the following values:

```
sampleSize <- 100
numBootstraps <- 5
sizeBootstraps <- 10
```

Number of Replications: 5

Summary Statistics:

	Observed	Bias	Mean	SE
mean	48.9	0.2243	49.13	1.077

Empirical Percentiles:
        5%   95%

mean 48 50.47

BCa Percentiles:
        5%   95%

mean 48.26 50.6

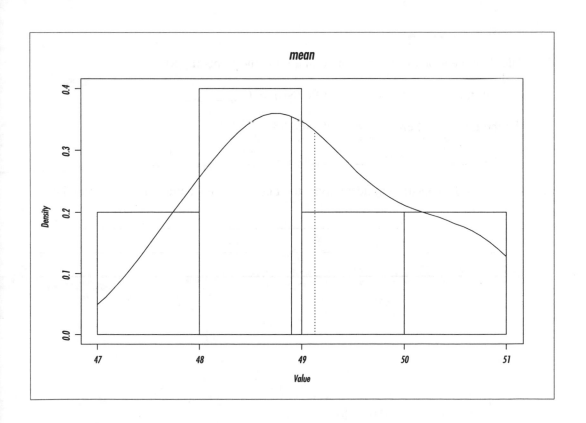

CHAPTER 37 EXERCISES

1. Run the BOOTSTRAP program for a random sample of N = 200, then take 10 bootstrap

    samples of n = 10. Print the Graph. The program settings should be:

    ```
    sampleSize <- 200
    numBootstraps <- 10
    sizeBootstraps <- 10
    ```

    a. Record the Observed Mean, Bias, Bootstrap Mean, and Standard Error.

        Observed Mean _____

        Bootstrap Mean _____

        Bias _____

        SE _____

    b. Calculate the 95% Confidence Interval around the Bootstrap Mean.

        95%CI = Bootstrap Mean +/- 1.96 (SE) = (_____, _____)

    c. List the Empirical Percentiles for 5% and 95%.

        5% _____   95% _____

    d. What does the bootstrap indicate given the bias, confidence interval, and Percentiles?

        _____

        _____

        _____

2. Run the BOOTSTRAP program for a random sample of N = 1000, then take 30 bootstrap
    samples of n = 100. Print the Graph. The program settings should be:

```
sampleSize <- 1000
numBootstraps <- 30
sizeBootstraps <- 100
```

a. Record the Observed Mean, Bias, Bootstrap Mean, and Standard Error.

Observed Mean _____

Bootstrap Mean _____

Bias _____

SE _____

b. Calculate the 95% Confidence Interval around the Bootstrap Mean.
    95%CI = Bootstrap Mean +/- 1.96 (SE) = (_____, _____)

c. List the Empirical Percentiles for 5% and 95%.
    5% _____   95% _____

d. What does the bootstrap indicate given the bias, confidence interval, and Percentiles?

    _____

    _____

    _____

e. Does the number of bootstrap samples provide a better bootstrap estimate?
    YES ____ NO _____

f. Does the size of the samples provide a better bootstrap estimate?
    YES ____ NO _____

g. What would happen if the random sample of data from the population was not
    representative?

    _____

TRUE OR FALSE QUESTIONS

T   F   a.   The bootstrap method is used to determine if the sample statistic is a stable estimator of the population parameter.

T   F   b.   The "Observed Mean" will always fall in the bootstrap confidence interval.

T   F   c.   A random sample of data must be representative of the population before the bootstrap procedure is accurate.

T   F   d.   The bootstrap procedure involves sampling data with replacement.

T   F   e.   No bias between the "observed mean" and the bootstrap mean estimate indicates that the sample statistic is a good estimator of the population parameter.

T   F   f.   The bootstrap method can be used with any sample statistic computed from a random sample of data.

T   F   g.   The bootstrap procedure creates random samples of data where each data value is unique.

T   F   h.   The resampling method draws random samples from the "pseudo" population using the same set of data values each time.

CHAPTER 38

META-ANALYSIS

CHAPTER OBJECTIVES

- To define and explain meta-analysis.
- To compare various approaches using p-values to combine research studies.
- To calculate an effect size estimate.
- To understand a pooled effect size estimate
- To compute r and d effect size estimates.
- To interpret r and d effect size measures.
- To understand how various statistics are converted to a common metric.
- To understand how meta-analysis methods quantitatively combine the results of several research studies.
- To understand how to weight studies by sample size when combining d effect size measures.
- To calculate an unbiased weighted average d effect size estimate.

Much of the research conducted in education, psychology, business, and other disciplines has involved single experiments or studies that rarely provide definitive answers to research questions. We have learned from the previous chapters that researchers seldom replicate their research studies and instead use cross-validation, bootstrap, or jackknife methods to estimate the stability and accuracy of the sample estimate. The world around us is understood better when we discover underlying patterns, trends, and principles, which can result from an accumulation of knowledge gained from several studies on a topic of interest. Consequently, a review of the research literature is invaluable in summarizing and understanding the current state of knowledge about a topic. Rather than rely on subjective judgments or interpretations of the research literature, meta-analysis techniques provide a quantitative objective assessment of the study results.

Meta-analysis is the application of statistical procedures to the empirical findings in research studies for the purpose of summarizing and concluding whether the findings in the studies overall were significant. The meta-analytic approach therefore provides a method to synthesize research findings from several individual studies. It makes sense that if several hundred studies had researched socioeconomic status and achievement in school, that a summarization of the findings in these individual studies would aid our understanding of this relationship. From a scholarly point of view, we might ask, "After twenty years of studying the efficacy of psychotherapy, what have we learned?" At some point in time, it becomes frugal to assess what we have learned from the research that was conducted. Further research in an area may be unproductive, unscientific, or take a wrong direction, if we don't stop from time to time and assess what we have learned. If we view science as an objective activity, then it becomes critical to establish an objective method to integrate and synthesize similar research studies. **Meta-analysis** is therefore an objective analysis of the statistical analyses from several individual studies for the purpose of integrating and summarizing the findings.

Sir Ronald A. Fisher in 1932, **Karl Pearson** in 1933, and **Egon S. Pearson** in 1938 all independently addressed the issue of statistically summarizing the results of research studies. In 1952, **Mordecai H. Gordon**, **Edward H. Loveland**, and **Edward E. Cureton** produced a chi-square table for use in combining the probability values from independent research studies. In 1953, **Lyle V. Jones** and **Donald W. Fiske** further clarified their approaches for testing the significance of results from a set of combined studies. They further demonstrated Fisher's approach of taking a natural logarithm of a p-value to calculate a summary chi-square value. **Gene Glass** in 1976 is credited with using the term *meta-analysis* to describe the statistical analysis of a collection of analysis results from several individual studies. He provided guidelines for converting various statistics into a common metric. **Jacob Cohen** in 1965 and again in 1977 provided measures of effect size for many common statistical tests. An effect size measure indexes the degree of departure from the null hypothesis in standard units. Examples of these various approaches to combining results from several research studies will be presented in this chapter.

A Comparison of Fisher, Log, and Chi-square Approaches

The Fisher approach to combining p-values from several independent research studies was accomplished by using a natural logarithmic transformation of the p-value (The natural log or log base e is equal to 2.7182818). The sum of the log base e values times - 2 resulted in a chi-square value: $\chi^2 = -2 \Sigma (\log_e p)$, with degrees of freedom equal to 2n, where n = the number of studies. Lyle V. Jones and Donald W. Fiske demonstrated that using log base 10 (log p + 10) also yielded a chi-square value: $\chi^2 = -2 (\log_e 10) (\Sigma (\log p + 10) - 10n)$, with degrees of freedom equal to 2n, where n = the number of studies. The following example helps to illustrate Fisher's approach, the Jones and Fiske approach, and the tabled chi-square values provided by Gordon, Loveland, and Cureton.

Research Study	p	Fisher $\log_e p$	Jones & Fiske $\log_{10} p$	Gordon et al. Tabled χ^2
A	.05	-2.9957	8.6990-10	6.4378
B	.01	-4.6052	8.0000-10	9.2103
C	.04	-3.2189	8.6021-10	5.9915
Total		-10.8198	25.3011-30	21.6396

Fisher's approach required multiplying -2 times the sum of the natural log values to calculate the chi-square value: -2 (-10.8198) = 21.6396! The Jones and Fiske approach required multiplying -2 times the natural log base 10 (2.3026) times the difference between the sum of the log base 10 values and the number of studies times ten: -2 (2.3026) (- 4.69895) = 21.6396! (Note: This multiplication of numbers would equal 21.6394 due to the rounding up of the log values, consequently to achieve accurate results, the difference value was carried out to five decimal places). Gordon et al. produced a chi-square table with the chi-square values for various p-values, thus making the task easier!

Converting Various Statistics to a Common Metric

Gene Glass discovered that various test statistics reported in the research literature could be converted to the Pearson Product Moment Correlation Coefficient or r, e.g., the t, chi-square, and F values. This provided a common metric to compare the various statistical values reported in research studies. The formula for transforming r to each statistic is presented below.

t-test

$$r = \sqrt{\frac{t^2}{t^2 + df}}$$

F-test

$$r = \sqrt{\frac{F}{F + df_{error}}}$$

Chi-square

$$r = \sqrt{\frac{\chi^2}{n}}$$

Converting Various Statistics to Effect Size Measures

Jacob Cohen expanded Gene Glass's idea to include a formula that would use an **effect size** measure (d) in the computation of the correlation statistic.   The effect size formula is:

Effect-Size

$$r = \frac{d}{\sqrt{d^2 + 4}}$$

The formula for transformation to an effect size measure d for each statistic is presented below.

t-test

$$d = \frac{2t}{\sqrt{df}}$$

F-test

$$d = \frac{2\sqrt{F}}{\sqrt{df_{error}}}$$

r

$$d = \frac{2r}{\sqrt{1 - r^2}}$$

Comparison and Interpretation of Effect Size Measures

The concept behind an effect size measure, d, was to determine the amount of departure from the null hypothesis in standard units. Consequently, an effect size measure in an experimental-control group study was determined by the following formula:

$$d = \frac{\overline{Y}_{EXP} - \overline{Y}_{CTRL}}{S_{CTRL}}$$

If $d = .50$, then the experimental group scored one-half standard deviations higher than the control group. If the population standard deviation is known, it would be used instead of the control group sample standard deviation estimate. Another alternative was to use the pooled estimate of the standard deviation from both groups in the denominator.

Not all research studies however used an experimental-control group design, so the development of other effect size formulae were very important in being able to compare the results of various studies. A comparison of r and d effect size measures for a set of studies should help to better understand how the two methods are computed and interpreted. A comparison of r and d is listed below for four studies, each with a different statistic reported.

| | | | | | Effect Size Measures | |
Study	Statistic	N	df	p (one-tail)	r	d
A	$t = 2.70$	42	40	.005	.3926	.8538
B	$F = 4.24$	27	1,25*	.025	.3808	.8236
C	$\chi^2 = 3.84$	100	1	.05	.1959	.3995
D	$r = .492$	22	20	.01	.4920	1.1302

In the S-PLUS meta-analysis program only the degree of freedom error is input. This is the second degree of freedom listed.

The calculations are straightforward using the formula for the r and d effect size measures. For example, given that $t = 2.70$, the r effect size is computed as:

$$r = \sqrt{\frac{t^2}{t^2 + df}} = \sqrt{\frac{(2.7)^2}{(2.7)^2 + 40}} = \sqrt{\frac{7.29}{47.29}} = \sqrt{.1542} = .3926$$

The d effect size is computed as:

$$d = \frac{2t}{\sqrt{df}} = \frac{2(2.7)}{\sqrt{40}} = \frac{5.4}{6.3245} = .8538$$

The calculation of the r effect size measure for the chi-square value is straightforward, however, the resulting r effect size value should be used in the formula for computing the corresponding d effect size measure.   Given chi-square $= 3.84$ with a sample size of 100, the r effect size measure is .1959. This r effect size value is used in the d effect size formula to obtain the value of .3995.

Since the various statistics from the different research studies are now on a common metric, they can be compared. Study D had the highest r effect size measure, followed by studies A, B, and C, respectively. The corresponding d effect size measures also indicate the same order, but help our interpretation by indicating how much the dependent variable (Y) changed for unit change in the independent variable (X). Notice this interpretation is directly related to the use of the correlation coefficient as an effect size measure. If we had used the experimental-group effect size measure, our interpretation would be how much the experimental group increased on average over the control group with regard to the dependent variable.

The null hypothesis always implies that the effect size is zero.   If the alternative hypothesis is accepted, then the effect size departs from zero and leads to a standardized interpretation.   Jacob Cohen in 1977 offered basic guidelines for interpreting the magnitude of the d effect size measure ($d = .2 =$ small, $d = .5 =$ medium, and $d = .8 =$ large) and r effect size measure ($r = .10 =$ small, $r = .30 =$ medium, $r = .50 =$ large), however, any interpretation of an effect size measure is relative. Knowledge of the professional discipline and the distribution of effect size measures in similar research studies provide reference points for interpretation. Sometimes, no such distributions of effect size estimates exist, so no standard reference point is available. In this instance, the computation of effect size estimates in several hundred studies can provide the necessary distribution and reference point. Summary statistics in the stem and leaf procedure will facilitate the interpretation of the distribution of d and r effect size measures. Given the standard deviation unit interpretation, it is important to determine whether a one-half, one-third, or one-quarter standard deviation improvement is due to some type of intervention that implies a meaningful effect size for the interpretation of the research study outcome.

A basic approach in conducting a meta-analysis across several related research studies is to combine the results and determine if there was an *overall* significant effect. The use of p-values from research studies (see Fisher, Jones and Fiske, and Gordon et al.) readily lends itself to a summary chi-square value. The chi-square value indicates the significance of the combined research study results. The meta-analysis formula for combining the p-values from individual studies is $\chi^2 = - 2 \Sigma (\log_e p)$. The combined chi-square value reported earlier was 21.6396. This chi-square value is tested for significance using 2n degrees of freedom (df = 6) to determine the overall effect across the different research studies. The tabled chi-square value at p < .01 for 6 degrees of freedom is 16.812. The combined chi-square of 21.6396 exceeds this tabled value and therefore indicates an overall significant effect across the three research studies. In the case of using an *r* effect size measure, the correlation coefficients converted from the various statistics are simply averaged, using the formula:

$$\bar{r} = \frac{\Sigma r}{n}$$

In the previous example, the overall *r* effect size is:

$$\bar{r} = \frac{\Sigma r}{n} = \frac{(.3926 + .3808 + .1959 + .4920)}{4} = \frac{1.4613}{4} = .3653$$

In the case of using a *d* effect size measure, the individual values are also averaged:

$$\bar{d} = \frac{\Sigma d}{n} = \frac{(.8538 + .8236 + .3995 + 1.1302)}{4} = \frac{3.2071}{4} = .8018$$

Sample Size Considerations in Meta-Analysis

An important concern in combining studies using meta-analytic techniques is the influence that different sample sizes may have on the overall interpretation. Some studies may be based on small sample sizes whereas others may be based on larger sample sizes. Since the correlation coefficient is not a function of sample size, procedures were developed to take into account the different sample sizes from the research studies when averaging the *d* effect size estimates. **L. Hedges**, as well as, **R. Rosenthal** and **D. Rubin** separately developed a formula in 1982 for calculating an *unbiased estimate* of the average *d* effect size. The formula was:

$$\bar{d} = \frac{\Sigma wd}{\Sigma w}$$

with w calculated as (N = total sample size):

$$w = \frac{2N}{8 + d^2}$$

The results of applying this unbiased, weighted approach to the previous example are listed below.

Study	N	d	w
A	42	.8538	9.623
B	27	.8236	6.222
C	100	.3995	24.511
D	22	1.1302	4.743

The calculation of the unbiased, weighted average effect estimate is:

$$\bar{d} = \frac{\Sigma wd}{\Sigma w} = \frac{(9.623)(.8538) + (6.222)(.8236) + (24.5111)(.3995) + (4.743)(1.1302)}{9.623 + 6.222 + 24.511 + 4.743} = \frac{28.493}{45.099} = .6318$$

The *unbiased* weighted average d effect size measure of .6318 is then compared to the *biased* weighted average d effect size measure of .8018 reported earlier. The amount of bias, or the value .8018 − .6318 is .17, which is due to the research studies having very different sample sizes. In practice, we would report the unbiased, weighted d effect size.

SUMMARY

In this chapter, you should learn that:

- Meta-analysis is an objective quantitative method for combining the results of several independent research studies.
- One approach to combining research findings uses the log of p-values.
- The overall significant effect using p-values is indicated by a chi-square value.
- The experimental-control group effect size estimate is determined by subtracting the two group means and dividing by the standard deviation of the control group.
- The effect size indicates the departure from the null hypothesis in standard units.
- Other approaches to combining research findings use *r* and *d* effect size estimates, which involve the transformation of several common statistics.
- The overall significant effect from several studies using transformed statistics is obtained by averaging either the *r* or *d* effect size measures.
- Meta-analysis compares the relative importance of findings in several research studies by interpreting effect size measures, which are on a common metric.
- The overall *d* effect size measure can be weighted by sample size to compute an unbiased, average *d* effect size measure.

How the META-ANALYSIS program works

The META-ANALYSIS program is lengthy due to the use of a dialog box and custom controls within that dialog box. The program begins by setting several vectors to **NULL** and the variable *moreTests* to a true value. After that, various controls are created that will be placed into the program's dialog box. The first type of control is a **combobox**, which is a dropdown list of choices from which the user can select. The label is set to "Test type:" and the values within the list are set to "t", "F", "ChiSq", and "r". The **noedit**=T means that the user cannot type in an option that isn't in the list and the position keyword sets the position of the control within the dialog box. The next type of control, the **editfield**, has been used previously and is set with a label equal to "Stat value:", a given size, and position. The next three controls follow the same pattern and then two buttons are created for the options to continue to another set of test values or begin the analysis. After all controls have been created, they are placed into a list and assigned to the *controlList* object to reduce the length of the line defining the dialog box itself. The dialog box is created with a title of "Enter study results", no built-in buttons, controls equal to the *controlList* that was created, and a size of 120 units by 105 units.

The first processing loop of the program continues as long as the *moreTests* variable equates to true, which is guaranteed to be at least one time. Within that loop, the dialog box is displayed and the results of this (which include the values of each control and the button that was pushed to finish the dialog) are assigned to the *studyInfoResults* object for extraction of the various components. Each of the component values are extracted from the results object and added to the appropriate vector. The loop is continued if the "Another Test" button was pressed.

Upon completion of this processing loop, the total number of defined studies is determined, the Fisher chi-square is calculated as well as the probability associated with it, an output matrix of the values is created, and dimension names are assigned. Then a label with the chi-square value and probability is created and a variable used to determine whether to output values for effect sizes is set to false, pending the check to determine whether enough information was provided to create these values.

The following **if** statement is what performs this check by seeing whether the key information needed was supplied for all tests entered, and if so it sets the *runEffects* variable to true and begins the calculations of the effect size measures. The first thing that has to be done is to create numerical values from the vectors extracted from the dialog box, which always outputs string values, for those vectors that require it for calculation. This is accomplished by use of the **as.integer** or **as.single** functions, depending on whether the result should be a whole number or a decimal number. Next, the second processing loop of the program begins, which iterates through the tests entered and determines the *r* value for each based on the type of test statistic. These are added to vectors, which are used to create the corresponding *d* values after the loop completes. The *d* values, along with the associated sample sizes, are used to calculate the *w* values. Then, the total *r* effect size, *d* effect size, and unbiased *d* effect size are calculated. These results are combined into a vector, which is then added to a label vector created by combining the test type with the value of the test statistic for each study, placed into a matrix, and assigned dimension names.

After the completion of this rather long **if** clause, another **if** clause determines whether just the Fisher natural log of p table is output or whether the effect size table is also printed. The use of the **if..else** clause assures that no lines of code are interspersed with the output, making the results cleaner than if the log table was always printed and the **if** clause applied only to whether the effect size table was added. The **cat** function and **print.char.matrix** are used to output the various values and output matrices that were created earlier in the program.

Once you have run the program to obtain the values for the exercises in the chapter, replace the computation of the *d* value with selective computations of *d* for the t-statistic and F-statistic, as reported in the chapter. The calculation of *d* from *r* for the chi-square and calculation of *r* will remain unchanged. Do your results for the *d* values for *t* and *F* remain the same? If you include only *p* values, then only the Fisher log table will be calculated and printed. Entering the p-values in the dialog box, clicking on "Another Test", and entering a second p-value will accomplish this. When the last p-value is entered, click on "Run Analysis". You could create another dialog box that would appear first and ask whether the user wants just the Fisher log calculations or both the Fisher log calculations and the effect size calculations. Dialog boxes permit one to ask for pertinent information. The use of dialog boxes can be very important when creating programs, thus minimizing S-PLUS script code.

META-ANALYSIS Program Output

NOTE: All values are set via dialog boxes.

Note: If only p values are entered, then only Fisher's ln(p) is run.

Research Study	p	Fisher ln(p)
a	0.001	-6.908
b	0.001	-6.908
c	0.001	-6.908
d	0.02	-3.912

Chi-square = 49.271 , df = 8 , p = 0.0001

Note: If statistical values are entered, then effect size measures are run.
(For F values, **only** use the degrees of freedom error or denominator degree of freedom in the dialog box).

Study	Statistic	N	df	r	d	w
a	t = 1.96	62	60	0.05	0.245	0.506
b	F = 4	50	48	0.05	0.277	0.577
c	ChiSq = 45	100	36	0.001	0.671	1.809
d	r = 0.39	60	59	0.02	0.39	0.847

Effect size(r)= 0.396, Effect size(d)= 0.935, Unbiased effect size(d)= 0.996

CHAPTER 38 EXERCISES

1. Run the META-ANALYSIS program for the p-values from the research studies below. Record the corresponding Fisher log base e values, total, and overall chi-square, df, and p.

Research Study	p	Fisher $\log_e p$
A	.05	
B	.001	
C	.20	
D	.01	
E	.025	

Total

Chi-Square = _____, df =_____, p = _____

a. Compute the chi-square value (-2 times the sum of $\log_e p$ values) with 2n degrees of freedom. Note: n = number of studies.

$\chi^2 = -2 \Sigma (\log_e p)$: _____

df = 2n: _____

b. Compare the chi-square above to the tabled chi-square value in Table 4 in the appendix. What would you conclude?

_____

_____

_____

2. Run the META-ANALYSIS program to compute r and d effect size estimates for the statistical values reported in the research studies below. Record the values in the table.

Study	Statistic	N	df	p (one-tail)	Effect Size Measures r	d
A	t = 2.617	122	120	.005		
B	F = 4.000	62	60	.025		
C	χ^2 = 6.635	50	1	.01		
D	r = .296	32	30	.05		

a. What is the overall average r effect size? _____

b. What is the overall average d effect size? _____

c. What would you conclude about the research findings from these results?

_____

_____

_____

3. Run the META-ANALYSIS program again using the p-values from Exercise 2. Record the chi-square value and degrees of freedom. Select a tabled chi-square value for $p < .05$.

$\chi^2 = -2 \Sigma (\log_e p)$: _____   Tabled $\chi^2 =$ _____

df = 2n: _____   df = 2n: _____

a. What would you conclude about the research findings using the p-value approach?

_____

_____

b. Compare the chi-square, r, and d effect size results. What would you conclude?

_____

_____

4. Run the META-ANALYSIS program using the sample sizes from the research studies in
    Exercise 2. Record the *d* effect size measures computed in Exercise 2 and the weight
    values in the table below. (Note: NA equals a weight of 1.0).

Study	N	d	w	wd
A	122			
B	62			
C	50			
D	32			

$$\Sigma w = \underline{\quad\quad} \quad \Sigma wd = \underline{\quad\quad}$$

a. Compute the unbiased, average *d* effect size using the formula:

$$\bar{d} = \frac{\Sigma wd}{\Sigma w}$$

Unbiased Effect Size = _____

b. Compare the bias effect size (d) in Exercise 2 with the unbiased effect size ($\bar{d}$)
    above. How much bias in the overall effect size is due to the research studies having
    different sample sizes? Note: Overall Bias = (Bias Effect Size - Unbiased Effect
    Size) = $d - \bar{d}$.

TRUE OR FALSE QUESTIONS

T   F   a. Meta-analysis uses subjective techniques to combine research studies.

T   F   b. The p value approach combines research findings using chi-square values.

T   F   c. Various statistics are converted to a common metric so research findings across studies can be quantitatively compared.

T   F   d. The r effect size measure can be interpreted by using a standard reference scale.

T   F   e. The d effect size measure is interpreted relative to findings from a large body of research in an academic discipline.

T   F   f. When combining effect size measures, it is important to weight by sample size.

T   F   g. The p value, log(p), and chi-square approach yield similar results.

T   F   h. Gene Glass is recognized as creating the term "Meta-Analysis".

CHAPTER 39

SIGNIFICANCE TESTING VS PRACTICAL IMPORTANCE

CHAPTER OBJECTIVES

- To understand criticisms of statistical significance testing.
- To know how the researcher can manipulate statistical testing to achieve significant results.
- To know that confidence intervals are important to report along with the significance testing of a statistic.
- To know that replication and/or extension of a research study is the most meaningful way to extend knowledge.
- To know that cross validation, jackknife, and bootstrap methods are valuable to explain results in a single study.
- To learn that the effect size helps our practical understanding of the importance of our research results.
- To understand the difference between statistical significance versus practical importance of study results.

In Part V, statistical tests of null hypotheses for different types of data were presented. The statistical tests were the z test, chi-square test, t test, analysis of variance, correlation, and linear regression. The outcomes of the statistical tests were to either retain the null hypothesis or reject the null hypothesis in favor of an alternative hypothesis based on the significance of the statistic computed. Type I and Type II errors were illustrated to better understand the nature of falsely rejecting the null hypothesis or falsely retaining the null hypothesis at a given level of significance for the sample statistic. The level of significance or p value that we choose, i.e., .05 or .01, to test our null hypothesis has come under scrutiny due to the nature of statistical significance testing.

Researchers have criticized significance testing because it can be manipulated to achieve the desired outcome, namely, a significant finding. This can be illustrated by presenting different research outcomes based on only changing the p value selected for the research study. The research study involves fifth-grade boys and girls who took the Texas Assessment of Academic Skills (TAAS) test. The study was interested in testing whether fifth-grade boys on average scored statistically significantly higher than girls on the TAAS test (a directional or one-tailed test of the null hypothesis). The researcher took a random sample of 31 fifth-grade boys and 31 fifth-grade girls and gave them the TAAS test under standard administration conditions. An independent t-test was selected to test for mean differences between the groups in the population at the .01 level of significance with 60 degrees of freedom (df = N - 2). The resultant sample values were:

Group	N	Mean	Standard Deviation	t
Boys	31	85	10	
				1.968
Girls	31	80	10	

The researcher computed the t value as follows:

$$t = \frac{85 - 80}{\sqrt{\dfrac{30(100) + 30(100)}{31 + 31 - 2}\left(\dfrac{1}{31} + \dfrac{1}{31}\right)}} = \frac{5}{2.54} = 1.968$$

The tabled t value that was selected for determining the research study outcome (based on a directional, one-tailed test, with 60 degrees of freedom at the .01 level of significance) was t = 2.39. Since the computed t = 1.968 was not greater than the tabled t value of 2.66 at the .01 level of significance, the researcher would *retain* the null hypothesis. However, if the researcher had selected a .05 level of significance, the tabled t value would equal 1.67, and the researcher would *reject* the null hypothesis in favor of the alternative hypothesis. The two possible outcomes in the research study are due solely to the different levels of significance a researcher could choose for the statistical test. This points out why significance testing has been criticized, namely the researcher can have statistically significant research findings by simply changing the p value.

Researchers could also manipulate whether statistically significant results are obtained from a research study by using a *one-tailed test* rather than a *two-tailed test*. In the previous example, a two-tailed test of significance would have resulted in a tabled t=2.66 at the .01 level of significance or a tabled t = 2.00 at the .05 level of significance. If the researcher had chosen a two-tailed test rather than a one-tailed test, the null hypothesis would have been rejected at either level of significance or p value. This illustrates how changing the directional nature of the hypothesis (one-tailed versus two-tailed test) can result in statistically significant findings.

Researchers can also increase the *sample size*, hence degrees of freedom, and achieve statistically significant research results. If we increase our sample sizes to 100 boys and 100 girls, we enter the t table with infinity degrees of freedom. The resultant tabled t values, given a one-tailed test, would be 1.645 at a .05 level of significance or 2.326 at a .01 level of significance. An examination of the t table further indicates that the tabled t values are larger for smaller degrees of freedom (smaller sample sizes). The bottom row indicates tabled t values that are the same as corresponding z values in the normal distribution given larger sample sizes. This illustrates how increasing the sample size (degrees of freedom greater than 120) can yield a lower tabled t value for making comparisons to the computed t value in determining whether the results are statistically significant.

When significance testing, the researcher obtains a sample statistic or "point estimate" of the population parameter. The researcher could compute *confidence intervals* around the sample statistic thereby providing an additional interpretation of the statistical results. The confidence interval width provides valuable information about capturing the population parameter beyond the statistical significance of a "point estimate" of the population value. If the 95% confidence interval for a sample mean ranged from 2.50 to 3.00, then we could conclude with 95 percent confidence that the interval contained the population mean. Each time we take a random sample of data, the confidence interval would change. If we took all possible samples and computed their confidence intervals, then 95 percent of the intervals would contain the population mean and 5 percent would not; therefore, one should not report that the probability is .95 that the interval contains the population mean. Unfortunately, many researchers either do not report confidence intervals and/or misreport them.

In Part VI, various methods for the replicability of research findings were presented. These chapters highlighted additional methods a researcher could use to present research findings and address the practical importance of the research study findings. The most meaningful technique would be to *replicate* the study and/or *extend the research* based on earlier findings. This provides the best evidence of research findings or outcomes. Researchers could also use their sample data from a single study and *cross-validate*, *jackknife*, or *bootstrap* the results. In some cases, a researcher might synthesis several findings from research studies by conducting a *meta-analysis*. Most researchers however do not take the time to replicate their study, cross-validate, jackknife, bootstrap, or conduct a meta-analysis. These methods are well known, but not available in most mainstream statistical packages and therefore not readily available to researchers. The *S-PLUS* statistical package does make these methods available to the researcher.

Another important consideration above and beyond the significance of a statistical test is the *effect size* or magnitude of difference reported (see Chapter 38). The interpretation of the effect size can directly indicate whether the statistically significant results are of any practical importance. An example will better illustrate the practical importance of research findings based on an effect size. The previous research study reported a five point average difference between boys and girls in the population on the TAAS test. Is this average five-point difference (approximately getting two test questions correct or incorrect) of practical importance? If we retain the null hypothesis of no difference in the population based on our statistical test of significance, then we conclude that fifth-grade boys and girls achieve about the same. Alternatively, if we reject the null hypothesis in favor of an alternative hypothesis based on our statistical test of significance, then we conclude that fifth-grade boys scored statistically significantly higher on average than the girls at a given level of significance. What are the consequences of our decisions based on a statistical test of significance? If we retain the null hypothesis when it is really false, we make the error of not spending additional money for programs to better educate fifth-grade girls. If we reject the null hypothesis when it is really true, we make the error of spending additional money on programs that are not needed to better educate fifth-grade girls. The effect size helps our practical understanding of the magnitude of the difference detected in a research study. The effect size however should be interpreted based upon a synthesis of findings in several other related studies. This comparison provides a frame of reference for interpreting whether the effect size value is small, medium, or large. The r and d effect size measures (see Chapter 38) for the computed t value are computed as follows:

$$r = \sqrt{\frac{t^2}{t^2 + df}}$$

and

$$d = \frac{2t}{\sqrt{df}}$$

A few final words of wisdom can be given when faced with significance testing and issues related to the practical importance of research findings. In conducting basic applied research, one asks a question, analyzes data, and answers the research question. Beyond this task, we need to be reminded of several concerns. How do our research findings relate to the research findings in other related studies? What is the educational importance of our findings? What implications do our research findings have on practice? What recommendations can we make that might affect or modify the underlying theory? What recommendations can we make that might enhance future research efforts?

SUMMARY

In this chapter, you should learn that:

- The researcher, to achieve significant findings, can manipulate the level of significance, directional nature of the test, and sample size in statistical significance testing.
- The confidence interval should be reported along with the statistic and p value to aid in the interpretation of research findings.
- The effect size helps our practical understanding of the importance of our research results.
- Replication and/or the extension of a research study are the most meaningful ways to validate findings in a research study.
- Cross validation, bootstrap, and jackknife methods provide additional information in explaining results from a single study.
- Results can be statistically significant but have little practical importance.

How the PRACTICAL program works

The PRACTICAL program computes an independent t-test and outputs the associated values that a researcher should report. The program begins by setting the **sampleSize** for both groups to n = 30. For the first population, **meanOne** = 50 and **stdDevOne** = 10. For the second population, **meanTwo** =50 and **stdDevTwo** = 10. A random sample of data is then assigned to the vector **sampleOne** and a second random sample of data is assigned to the vector **sampleTwo**. The sample means and standard deviations for the two samples are then input into the **t.test** function. The results of the independent t-test are output to the vector **tResults**. In addition, the t value, degrees of freedom, d and r effect size measures are assigned to variable names. The **outputText** variable is then used to assign different text messages with the t-test results. The **outputMatrix** is created as 6 rows and 2 columns and the **print.char.matrix** command is used to print the **outputText** character strings and associated values in the rows and columns, respectively.

PRACTICAL Program Output

Given the following population values:

```
sampleSize <- 30
meanOne <- 50
stdDevOne <- 10
meanTwo <- 50
stdDevTwo <- 10
```

The independent t-test results that should be reported are:

```
+-------------------------------+-------------------------------------------+
|Two sample independent t-test  |Sample size= 30                            |
+-------------------------------+-------------------------------------------+
|Sample One Mean= 48.82         |Sample One Std Dev= 9.52                   |
+-------------------------------+-------------------------------------------+
|Sample Two Mean= 47.65         |Sample Two Std Dev= 8.24                   |
+-------------------------------+-------------------------------------------+
|t-test= 0.51                   |df= 58                                     |
+-------------------------------+-------------------------------------------+
|p value= 0.614                 |95% Confidence Interval= -3.439 to 5.769|
+-------------------------------+-------------------------------------------+
|r Effect= 0.066                |d Effect= 0.133                            |
+-------------------------------+-------------------------------------------+
```

CHAPTER 39 EXERCISES

1. Run the Practical program 10 times and record the results below.

	t value	p value	95%CI	r effect size	d effect size
1)	_____	_____	_____	_____	_____
2)	_____	_____	_____	_____	_____
3)	_____	_____	_____	_____	_____
4)	_____	_____	_____	_____	_____
5)	_____	_____	_____	_____	_____
6)	_____	_____	_____	_____	_____
7)	_____	_____	_____	_____	_____
8)	_____	_____	_____	_____	_____
9)	_____	_____	_____	_____	_____
10)	_____	_____	_____	_____	_____

a. What conclusions can be drawn about the statistical significance of the computed t value if the tabled t value = 1.671 at the .05 level of significance for a one-tailed test?

_____

_____

b. How many p values are less than the .05 level of significance? _____

c. What percent of the confidence intervals captured the population mean difference of zero? _____

d. What interpretation would you give for the r effect size measures for these 10 replications?

_____

_____

e. What interpretation would you give for the d effect size measures for these 10 replications?

_____

_____

2. The *Journal of Experimental Education* in 1993 criticized statistical significance testing and proposed certain alternatives. List the recommended alternatives below.

3. The *Psychological Science* journal in 1997 wanted to "Ban Significance Testing." What argument and rationale did they give for banning significance testing?

4. The *APA Taskforce on Statistical Inference* in 1999 made several recommendations regarding methodological practice (http://www.apa.org/). List their recommendations below.

5. The *Educational and Psychological Measurement* journal in 2000 discussed the historical growth of statistical significance testing and its future prospects. What did the article conclude about the historical growth of statistical significance testing from 1910 to 2000.

TRUE OR FALSE QUESTIONS

T   F   a. Significance testing is the *only* way to know if your findings are
                important.

T   F   b. Replication is the *least* meaningful way to determine the validity of
                your research findings.

T   F   c. Cross-validation, jackknife, and bootstrap methods provide important
                information about results when analyzing a single sample of data.

T   F   d. Research findings can be statistically significant, but have no practical
                importance to the field of study.

T   F   e. Increasing the sample size can *always* make a statistical test significant at a
                given level of significance.

T   F   f. The sample statistic, p value, confidence interval, and effect size are
                recommended values that should be reported in a research study.

GLOSSARY OF TERMS

Alpha level:	The level of statistical significance selected prior to a test for incorrectly rejecting a true null hypothesis, e.g., .05 alpha level of significance (See Type I error).
Alternative Hypothesis:	A statistical hypothesis that indicates a difference in population parameters. For example, the means of two populations are different, i.e., possible outcomes not stated in the null hypothesis.
Analysis of Variance:	A technique that tests whether the dependent variable means of three or more mutually exclusive groups are statistically significantly different at a specified level of significance. The F-test is a ratio of MS Between Groups divided by MS Within Groups.
Bell Shaped Curve:	Describes a normal or symmetrical distribution of data in which intervals around the mean are known.
Bimodal:	A frequency distribution of data that has two modes, i.e., two scores that occur most frequently in a set of data.
Binomial Distribution:	A probability distribution generated by taking $(a + b)$ to the nth power. Used in a binomial test to determine whether the probability of two outcomes exceed the chance level of occurrence.
Binomial test:	A non-parametric test, which doesn't depend on any population data characteristics and measures whether a distribution of scores results in a binomial distribution (each outcome is equally likely). For example, if you tossed an unbiased coin 1000 times it should land approximately 500 heads and 500 tails.
Bootstrap:	An approach that samples with replacement to generate a sampling distribution of a statistic that serves as the population distribution. The mean of the bootstrap sampling distribution or bootstrap estimate is used to determine the amount of bias in the random sample.

Central Limit
Theorem: A theorem that provides a mathematical basis for using the normal distribution, as a sampling distribution of a statistic for a given sample size, to test a statistical hypothesis. For example, the theorem states that a sampling distribution of means for a given sample size is 1) normally distributed, 2) the sampling distribution mean is equal to the population mean, and 3) the sampling distribution variance is equal to the variance divided by the sample size.

Central Tendency: A concept that implies most scores fall in the middle of a symmetrical distribution with the scores spreading out evenly toward both tails of the distribution.

Chi-Square
Distribution: A probability distribution or family of curves generated by the difference between observed and expected frequencies. The sampling distribution of chi-square values is used in both parametric and non-parametric tests of significance.

Chi-Square
Statistic: A non-parametric test that measures the difference between the observed frequencies and expected frequencies in two or more groups.

Combinations: The number of ways in which different subsets of events or numbers can be selected.

Conditional
Probability: The probability of an event B is based upon the occurrence or non-occurrence of event A.

Confidence Interval: A high and low value which forms an interval around the sample statistic that should contain the population parameter. The interval will be different depending upon the percentage used, i.e., 68%, 95%, or 99%.

Confidence Level: A percentage that indicates how certain we are that the interval around the sample statistic contains the population parameter (see alpha level).

Correlation: A statistic that indicates the strength and direction of association between two sets of scores. The strength is indicated by a correlation value closer to 1.0 and the direction indicated by a +/- sign. A positive correlation indicates that both variables increase in value across the range of scores while a negative correlation indicates that one set of scores increases as the other set of scores decreases.

Cross-validation: An original sample of data is randomly split into two equal samples, then a sample statistic is computed using one sample of data and applied to the other sample of data.

Cumulative
Frequency
Distribution: A frequency distribution of raw scores that indicates successive addition of the number of events, individuals, or objects up to the total number or 100%.

Degrees of Freedom: The number of observations or groups minus the restrictions placed upon them. For example, if four out of five sample means are known, the one remaining unknown sample mean can be determined, hence $df = 5 - 1 = 4$.

Dependent t-test: A statistical test of whether two sample means from the same subjects or group are significantly different. Also called a paired t-test or correlated t-test.

Dichotomous
Population: A population of data that can be divided into two mutually exclusive categories.

Directional
Hypothesis: A hypothesis that states one population parameter is greater than the other. The direction can be stated in a positive or negative direction, e.g., boys' verbal scores will be lower on average than girls' verbal scores. A one-tailed test because the region of rejection is only in one tail of the sampling distribution.

Effect Size: Conveys the magnitude of difference in standard units between the mean of the experimental group and the mean of the control group. Used in conjunction with sample size, alpha level, and direction of the statistical hypothesis to select a value for power.

Equally Likely
Events: Events, individuals, or objects that have the same chance of being selected.

Exponential
Function: A relationship between two sets of data points that does not have a constant rate of change for a random variable X, i.e., $Y = 2^X$.

F-curve: A positively skewed frequency distribution of F values for specific degrees of freedom.

F-distribution: A probability distribution or family of curves that require two degrees of freedom. The normal, t, and chi-square distributions are special cases of the F-distribution.

F-test: In Analysis of Variance, the test to determine if sample means are different beyond chance expectation. The F-test is the ratio of MS Between Groups divided by the MS Within Groups.

Factoring: A product of sequential numbers that indicate the total number of choices possible (see factorial notation).

Factorial notation: Indicated as n!, i.e., $3! = 3 \times 2 \times 1 = 6$.

Finite Distribution: A population of data where the number of individuals, objects, or events is known, hence exact probabilities of occurrence can be computed.

Frequency Distribution: A tabulation of data that indicates the number of times a score or value occurs.

Hartley F-max test: A test of whether three or more sample variances are statistically different. The largest sample variance is divided by the smallest sample variance to form an F-ratio with degrees of freedom from the two sample sizes.

Heterogeneity: Refers to a grouping of dissimilar individuals, objects, or events.

Histogram: A bar chart that indicates the frequency of numbers on the Y axis and the mutually exclusive groups or categories on the X axis. (Also, see Pie Chart).

Homogeneity: Refers to a grouping of similar individuals, objects, or events.

Independent t-test: A statistical test of whether two independent sample means are significantly different implying that the two population means are different.

Infinite Population: A population of data where the number of individuals, objects, or events are too numerous to count, hence exact probabilities of occurrence cannot be computed.

Intercept: The intercept is the point in a linear equation where the line of best fit crosses the Y-axis. The intercept is the predicted value of Y when the X variable equals zero. The value a in the linear regression equation: $Y = a + bX + e$.

Interquartile
Range: A score that represents the distance between the first and third quartile. It
                           indicates the range of scores in the middle 50% of a frequency
                           distribution.

Jackknife: An approach that uses a single sample of data and computes sample
                           statistics based on different n – 1 sample sizes.

Joint Probability: The probability of two events occurring that is determined by multiplying
                           the independent probability of each event.

Kurtosis: A measure that indicates the flatness or peakedness of the frequency
                           distribution of scores. Leptokurtic implies a peaked distribution,
                           mesokurtic a bell-shaped normal distribution, and platykurtic a flattened
                           distribution of scores.

Law of
Complements: Given the probability of event A, P(A), the complement is $1 - P(A)$, or the
                           remaining probability since $P(A) + [1 - P(A)] = 1$.

Leaves: The numbers to the right of the vertical line in a stem-and-leaf plot.

Level of
Significance: The probability of making a Type I error (see alpha level).

Linear
Function: An angled straight line of data points that indicate a constant rate of
                           change for a random variable, X, i.e., $y = bX$.

Linear
Regression
(Equation):   A statistical technique designed to predict values of Y (dependent
                           variable) from one or more X variables (independent predictor variables).
                           The regression equation: $Y = a + bX + e$.

Line of best fit: In linear regression, the line formed by the predicted Y values that pass
                           through the scatterplot of X and Y values. The line indicates the best
                           prediction that minimizes the sum of squared errors of prediction.

Mean: The arithmetic mean computed as the sum of a set of scores divided by the
                           number of scores. Typically referred to as a measure of central tendency.

Mean Square: A variance estimate computed by dividing the sum of squares by the
                           degrees of freedom.

Median:	The middle score in a distribution of odd-numbered scores or the mid-point in an even-numbered set of scores. Typically referred to as a measure of central tendency.
Meta-Analysis:	A statistical procedure that averages the effect sizes across several studies to determine the overall significance of a large number of research studies on the same topic.
Mode:	The most frequently occurring score in a set of scores. It is possible to have a single modal score (unimodal), two scores that occur the most (bimodal), or even three or more scores that occur the most. Typically referred to as a measure of central tendency.
Monte Carlo:	An approach that describes a statistical technique that simulates data and approximates probability density functions of population distributions to study the robustness and properties of statistical tests.
MS Between Groups:	The sum of the squared deviations of group means around the grand mean weighted (multiplied) by the sample size of each group and divided by the number of groups minus one. Indicates whether the group means are similar or different based on how much they vary.
MS Within Groups:	The sum of squared deviations of individual scores around each group mean divided by the number of scores in each group minus the number of groups. Indicates how much the scores vary within each group.
Multiplication Law:	The independent probabilities of two events can be multiplied to obtain their probability of joint occurrence, i.e., $P(J) = P(A) * P(B)$.
Non-directional Hypothesis:	A hypothesis that states two population parameters are different, rather than one population parameter is greater than the other. A two-tailed test because the region of rejection is in both tails of the sampling distribution.
Normal Curve:	A symmetric distribution of data based on a mathematical equation formulated by DeMoivre in 1733 and further developed by Carl Fredrick Gauss.
Normal Distribution:	A frequency distribution of scores that when graphed produces a symmetrical, bell-shaped distribution with skewness and kurtosis of zero. Sometimes referred to as a mesokurtic distribution.

Null Hypothesis: A statistical hypothesis that indicates no difference in population
                          parameters. For example, the means of two populations are equal.
                          The null hypothesis is either retained or rejected in favor of an alternative
                          hypothesis.

Ogive: A graph of the cumulative frequency distribution of data that has a
                          characteristic S-shaped curve.

One-sample
t-test: A statistical test of whether a sample mean is significantly different from a
                          population mean.

One-way Analysis
Of Variance: A statistical test that is an extension of the independent t-test to test
                          whether three or more independent sample means are statistically different
                          implying that the population means are different.

Outlier: An extreme or influential score or data value that affects the sample
                          statistic, e.g., sample mean.

Parameter(s):   Population values or characteristics that are estimated by sample statistics,
                          e.g., population mean or population correlation.

Parametric Statistics: Parametric or inferential statistics are based upon being able to randomly
                          draw a sample from a well defined population, estimate the sample
                          statistic, and make an inference about the population parameter. For
                          example, the sample mean is an estimate of the population mean.

Permutations: A technique used to determine the number of different ways individuals,
                          objects, or events can be ordered.

Pie Chart: A circle with portions or parts of the circle indicated for each mutually
                          exclusive group or category. (Also, see Histogram).

Population: A set of individuals or scores that are well defined and share some
                          characteristic in common.   Typically, population data is randomly
                          sampled and sample statistics computed to estimate the population values
                          because the population is typically too large to measure all the data. (See
                          Parametric Statistics)

Power: The probability of rejecting the null hypothesis when it is false. The
                          expression, $1 - \beta$, is used to indicate the level of power. Values of .80 are
                          typically selected for power; power is a function of sample size, alpha
                          level, effect size, and directional nature of the statistical hypothesis (one-
                          tailed or two-tailed test).

Probability: The ratio of the number of favorable outcomes to the total possible
                            number of outcomes.

Properties of
Estimators: Important characteristics we want sample statistics to possess as estimates
                            of population parameters, i.e., unbiased, consistent, efficient, and
                            sufficient.

Pseudo Random
Numbers: Numerical values typically generated by a random number generator on a
                            computer, but not truly independent or unbiased because they will
                            eventually correlate and repeat.

Quartile: A score that divides a set of data into four equal divisions, i.e., first
                            quartile is a score that separates the bottom 25% of the data in a frequency
                            distribution from the other data values.

Random Assignment: The random process of assigning individuals, objects, or events to a group,
                            i.e., random assignment of individuals to experimental and control groups.

Random Numbers: Independent, unbiased numerical values that have an equally likely chance
                            of being selected.

Random Number
Generator: A mathematical algorithm in a software program that is run on a computer
                            to generate pseudo random numbers.

Random Sample: A sample of data from a well-defined population where every individual,
                            object, or event has an equally likely chance of being selected.

Random Sampling: The process of selecting individuals, objects, or events from a well-
                            defined population in which all members have an equal and independent
                            chance of being selected. Not the same as random assignment.

Range: A score that indicates the distance between the highest and lowest data
                            value in a set of data.

Region of Rejection: The area under a sampling distribution where sample statistics fall that is
                            highly improbable if the null hypothesis is true.

Regression
Weight: In regression analysis, the regression coefficient or slope of the line of
                            best fit that passes through the predicted Y values. The value b in the
                            linear regression equation: $Y = a + bX + e$. A weight computed by the
                            least squares method of minimizing the sum of squared errors of
                            prediction.

| Repeated Measures ANOVA: | A statistical procedure in which subjects are measured two or more times and the total variation of scores is partitioned into three components: 1) variation among subjects, 2) variation among occasions (time), and 3) residual variation. |

Sample:
A random selection of individuals, objects, or events from a well-defined population of data.

Sample Error:
The difference between a sample statistic and the population parameter.

Sampling Error:
The error in using a sample statistic as an estimate of a population parameter.

Sampling Distribution:
A probability frequency distribution of a sample statistic formed for all possible random samples of a given sample size. Examples of sampling distributions include: 1) sampling distribution of means, 2) t-distribution, 3) chi-square distribution, and 4) F-distribution.

Sampling with Replacement:
Each randomly sampled data point is returned to the population before another data point is randomly sampled, therefore it is possible for a data point to be selected more than once.

Sampling without Replacement:
Each randomly sampled data point is not returned to the population before another data point is randomly sampled, therefore each data point is uniquely drawn and can not be selected again.

Scheffe Post-hoc Test:
A type of post-hoc "t-test" for conducting multiple comparisons of group mean differences after an analysis of variance F-test.

Skewness:
A measure of deviation from symmetry in a frequency distribution of scores. Negative skew indicates a distribution with more scores above the mean. Positive skew indicates a distribution with more scores below the mean.

Slope:
The amount of change in Y that corresponds to a change of one unit in X. (See Regression Weight).

Standard Deviation:	The square root of the average squared deviations of scores around the mean. A measure of how much the individual scores deviate from the mean.
Standard Errors of Statistic:	The standard deviation of the sampling distribution of the statistic that indicates the amount of error in estimating the population parameter.
Standard Score:	A score computed by taking the deviation of the raw score from the group mean divided by the group standard deviation, i.e., z-score.
Statistic:	A sample value that estimates a population parameter.
Stem and Leaf:	A graphical display that illustrates the shape of a distribution of scores.
Sum of Squared Deviations:	The deviations of each score from the group mean that is squared and then summed for all scores.
Symmetric Distribution:	A sampling distribution or frequency distribution of scores that is the same on either side of the median value. The normal distribution is an example of a symmetric distribution.
Tchebysheff Inequality Theorem:	A theorem that indicates the percentage of data between intervals around the mean regardless of the shape of the frequency distribution of data.
t-distribution:	A probability distribution or family of t-curves for different degrees of freedom that is used to determine whether an obtained t value between two sample means is statistically significant at a specified alpha level.
Type I error:	The rejection of the null hypothesis of no difference in population parameters when it is true, i.e., the probability that a null hypothesis would be rejected in favor of an alternative hypothesis. The probability is set by selection of an alpha level (see Alpha level). If the alpha level is set at .05, then 5% of the time a true null hypothesis would be incorrectly rejected in favor of the alternative hypothesis. The symbol, α, is used to refer to this type of error.
Type II error:	The retention of a null hypothesis of no difference in population parameters when it is false, i.e., the probability that we failed to reject the null hypothesis in favor of an alternative hypothesis. The symbol, β, is used to refer to this type of error.

Uniform
Distribution: A rectangular distribution of scores that are evenly distributed in the range
                                 of possible values.

Unimodal
Distribution: A symmetrical distribution with a single mode.

Variance: A positive value that measures how scores vary around a group mean. If
                                 all scores are the same, then the variance is zero. Calculated as the sum of
                                 squared deviations around the group mean divided by the number of
                                 scores.

z-score: Sometimes called a standard score. A frequency distribution of raw scores
                                 that have been standardized to a mean of zero and a standard deviation of
                                 one. A z score indicates the direction and degree to which a score deviates
                                 from the mean of a distribution of scores.

z-test: A statistical test for the significant difference in independent or dependent
                                 population proportions.

ABOUT THE AUTHORS

Dr. Randall E. Schumacker is a Professor of Educational Research at the University of North Texas (UNT) and an adjunct Professor of Medical Education at the UNT Health Sciences Center. Randall was the 1996 recipient of the outstanding scholar award at UNT and 1998 recipient of the Charn Oswachoke International award. He has written and co-edited several books including *A Beginner's Guide to Structural Equation Modeling*, *Advanced Structural Equation Modeling*: *Issues and Techniques*, *Interaction and Non-Linear Effects in Structural Equation Modeling*, and *New Developments and Techniques in Structural Equation Modeling*. Randall was the founder and now Emeritus Editor of the *Structural Equation Modeling*: *A Multidisciplinary Journal*, and established the Structural Equation Modeling Special Interest Group within the American Educational Research Association. Dr. Schumacker currently conducts international and national workshops, serves on the editorial board of several journals, and pursues his research interests in measurement, statistics, structural equation modeling, and medical education. His homepage on the Internet is: *http://www.coe.unt.edu/schumacker*.

Allen Akers is a doctoral student in the Educational Research program at the University of North Texas. He has taught a basic statistics course and completed doctoral coursework in measurement, statistics, and research design. His current job position, as a programmer analyst, involves interfacing the UNT web site with mainframe data for access to student information, including registration, student account information, and financial aid. Allen has a bachelor's degree in Kinesiology Exercise Science and a master's degree from UNT in Exercise Physiology. Allen had the primary responsibility of programming the S-PLUS script files for the various chapters.

APPENDIX

Tables were copied from John T. Roscoe, *Fundamental Research Statistics for the Behavioral Sciences* (2nd Edition). New York, NY: Holt, Rinehart and Winston, Inc., 1975.

NOTE: Tables 2 to 4 originally adapted from R. A. Fisher and F.Yates: *Statistical Tables for Biological, Agricultural, and Medical Research.* Published by Oliver and Boyd, Ltd, Edinburgh. Tables 5 and 6 are abridged from Tables 18 and 31, respectively, in *Biometrika Tables for Statisticians*, vol. 1, 2nd ed. New York: Cambridge University Press, 1958. Edited by E. S. Pearson and H. O. Hartley.

Table 1: Areas under the Normal Curve (z-scores)

Table 2: Distribution of t for Given Probability Levels

Table 3: Distribution of r for Given Probability Levels

Table 4: Distribution of Chi-Square for Given Probability Levels

Table 5: Distribution of F for Given Probability Levels

Table 6: Distribution of Hartley F for Given Probability Levels

Table 1: Areas Under the Normal Curve (z-scores)

z	.00	.01	.02	.03	.04	.05	.06	.07	.08	.09
				Second decimal place in z						
.0	.0000	.0040	.0080	.0120	.0160	.0199	.0239	.0279	.0319	.0359
.1	.0398	.0438	.0478	.0517	.0557	.0596	.0636	.0675	.0714	.0753
.2	.0793	.0832	.0871	.0910	.0948	.0987	.1026	.1064	.1103	.1141
.3	.1179	.1217	.1255	.1293	.1331	.1368	.1406	.1443	.1480	.1517
.4	.1554	.1591	.1628	.1664	.1700	.1736	.1772	.1808	.1844	.1879
.5	.1915	.1950	.1985	.2019	.2054	.2088	.2123	.2157	.2190	.2224
.6	.2257	.2291	.2324	.2357	.2389	.2422	.2454	.2486	.2517	.2549
.7	.2580	.2611	.2642	.2673	.2704	.2734	.2764	.2794	.2823	.2852
.8	.2881	.2910	.2939	.2967	.2995	.3023	.3051	.3078	.3106	.3133
.9	.3159	.3186	.3212	.3238	.3264	.3289	.3315	.3340	.3365	.3389
1.0	.3413	.3438	.3461	.3485	.3508	.3531	.3554	.3577	.3599	.3621
1.1	.3643	.3665	.3686	.3708	.3729	.3749	.3770	.3790	.3810	.3830
1.2	.3849	.3869	.3888	.3907	.3925	.3944	.3962	.3980	.3997	.4015
1.3	.4032	.4049	.4066	.4082	.4099	.4115	.4131	.4147	.4162	.4177
1.4	.4192	.4207	.4222	.4236	.4251	.4265	.4279	.4292	.4306	.4319
1.5	.4332	.4345	.4357	.4793	.4382	.4394	.4406	.4418	.4429	.4441
1.6	.4452	.4463	.4474	.4484	.4495	.4505	.4515	.4525	.4535	.4545
1.7	.4554	.4564	.4573	.4582	.4591	.4599	.4608	.4616	.4625	.4633
1.8	.4641	.4649	.4656	.4664	.4671	.4678	.4686	.4693	.4699	.4706
1.9	.4713	.4719	.4726	.4732	.4738	.4744	.4750	.4756	.4761	.4767
2.0	.4772	.4778	.4783	.4788	.4793	.4798	.4803	.4808	.4812	.4817
2.1	.4821	.4826	.4830	.4834	.4838	.4842	.4846	.4850	.4854	.4857
2.2	.4861	.4826	.4868	.4871	.4875	.4878	.4881	.4884	.4887	.4890
2.3	.4893	.4896	.4898	.4901	.4904	.4906	.4909	.4911	.4913	.4916
2.4	.4918	.4920	.4922	.4925	.4927	.4929	.4931	.4932	.4934	.4936
2.5	.4938	.4940	.4941	.4943	.4945	.4946	.4948	.4949	.4951	.4952
2.6	.4953	.4955	.4956	.4957	.4959	.4960	.4961	.4962	.4963	.4964
2.7	.4965	.4966	.4967	.4968	.4969	.4970	.4971	.4972	.4973	.4974
2.8	.4974	.4975	.4976	.4977	.4977	.4978	.4979	.4979	.4980	.4981
2.9	.4981	.4982	.4982	.4983	.4984	.4984	.4985	.4985	.4986	.4986
3.0	.4987	.4987	.4987	.4988	.4988	.4989	.4989	.4989	.4990	.4990
3.1	.4990	.4991	.4991	.4991	.4992	.4922	.4992	.4992	.4993	.4993
3.2	.4993	.4993	.4994	.4994	.4994	.4994	.4994	.4995	.4995	.4995
3.3	.4995	.4995	.4995	.4996	.4996	.4996	.4996	.4996	.4996	.4997
3.4	.4997	.4997	.4997	.4997	.4997	.4997	.4997	.4997	.4997	.4998
3.5	.4998									
4.0	.49997									
4.5	.499997									
5.0	.4999997									

Table 2: Distribution of t for Given Probability Levels

df	Level of significance for one-tailed test					
	.10	.05	.025	.01	.005	.0005
	Level of significance for two-tailed test					
	.20	.10	.05	.02	.01	.001
1	3.078	6.314	12.706	31.821	63.657	636.619
2	1.886	2.920	4.303	6.965	9.925	31.598
3	1.638	2.353	3.182	4.541	5.841	12.941
4	1.533	2.132	2.776	3.747	4.604	8.610
5	1.476	2.015	2.571	3.365	4.032	6.859
6	1.440	1.943	2.447	3.143	3.707	5.959
7	1.415	1.895	2.365	2.998	3.499	5.405
8	1.397	1.860	2.306	2.896	3.355	5.041
9	1.383	1.833	2.262	2.821	3.250	4.781
10	1.372	1.812	2.228	2.764	3.169	4.587
11	1.363	1.796	2.201	2.718	3.106	4.437
12	1.356	1.782	2.179	2.681	3.055	4.318
13	1.350	1.771	2.160	2.650	3.012	4.221
14	1.345	1.761	2.145	2.624	2.977	4.140
15	1.341	1.753	2.131	2.602	2.947	4.073
16	1.337	1.746	2.120	2.583	2.921	4.015
17	1.333	1.740	2.110	2.567	2.898	3.965
18	1.330	1.734	2.101	2.552	2.878	3.992
19	1.328	1.729	2.093	2.539	2.861	3.883
20	1.325	1.725	2.086	2.528	2.845	3.850
21	1.323	1.721	2.080	2.518	2.831	3.819
22	1.321	1.717	2.074	2.508	2.819	3.792
23	1.319	1.714	2.069	2.500	2.807	3.767
24	1.318	1.711	2.064	2.492	2.797	3.745
25	1.316	1.708	2.060	2.485	2.787	3.725
26	1.315	1.706	2.056	2.479	2.779	3.707
27	1.314	1.703	2.052	2.473	2.771	3.690
28	1.313	1.701	2.048	2.467	2.763	3.674
29	1.311	1.699	2.045	2.462	2.756	3.659
30	1.310	1.697	2.042	2.457	2.750	3.646
40	1.303	1.684	2.021	2.423	2.704	3.551
60	1.296	1.671	2.000	2.390	2.660	3.460
120	1.289	1.658	1.980	2.358	2.617	3.373
∞	1.282	1.645	1.960	2.326	2.576	3.291

Table 3: Distribution of r for Given Probability Levels

df	Level of significance for one-tailed test			
	.05	.025	.01	.005
	Level of significance for two-tailed test			
	.10	.05	.02	.01
1	.988	.997	.9995	.9999
2	.900	.950	.980	.990
3	.805	.878	.934	.959
4	.729	.811	.882	.917
5	.669	.754	.833	.874
6	.622	.707	.789	.834
7	.582	.666	.750	.798
8	.540	.632	.716	.765
9	.521	.602	.685	.735
10	.497	.576	.658	.708
11	.576	.553	.634	.684
12	.458	.532	.612	.661
13	.441	.514	.592	.641
14	.426	.497	.574	.623
15	.412	.482	.558	.606
16	.400	.468	.542	.590
17	.389	.456	.528	.575
18	.378	.444	.516	.561
19	.369	.433	.503	.549
20	.360	.423	.492	.537
21	.352	.413	.482	.526
22	.344	.404	.472	.515
23	.337	.396	.462	.505
24	.330	.388	.453	.496
25	.323	.381	.445	.487
26	.317	.374	.437	.479
27	.311	.367	.430	.471
28	.306	.361	.423	.463
29	.301	.355	.416	.486
30	.296	.349	.409	.449
35	.275	.325	.381	.418
40	.257	.304	.358	.393
45	.243	.288	.338	.372
50	.231	.273	.322	.354
60	.211	.250	.295	.325
70	.195	.232	.274	.303
80	.183	.217	.256	.283
90	.173	.205	.242	.267
100	.164	.195	.230	.254

Table 4: Distribution of Chi-Square for Given Probability Levels

Probability

df	.99	.98	.95	.90	.80	.70	.50	.30	.20	.10	.05	.02	.01	.001
1	.00016	.00663	.00393	.0158	.0642	.148	.455	1.074	1.642	2.706	3.841	5.412	6.635	10.827
2	.0201	.0404	.103	.211	.446	.713	1.386	2.408	3.219	4.605	5.991	7.824	9.210	13.815
3	.115	.185	.352	.584	1.005	1.424	2.366	3.665	4.642	6.251	7.815	9.837	11.345	16.266
4	.297	.429	.711	1.064	1.649	2.195	3.357	4.878	5.989	7.779	9.488	11.668	13.277	18.467
5	.554	.752	1.145	1.610	2.343	3.000	4.351	6.064	7.289	9.236	11.070	13.388	15.086	20.515
6	.872	1.134	1.635	2.204	3.070	3.828	5.348	7.231	8.558	10.645	12.592	15.033	16.812	22.457
7	1.239	1.564	2.167	2.833	3.822	4.671	6.346	8.383	9.803	12.017	14.067	16.622	18.475	24.322
8	1.646	2.032	2.733	3.490	4.594	5.527	7.344	9.524	11.030	13.362	15.507	18.168	20.090	26.125
9	2.088	2.532	3.325	4.168	5.380	6.393	8.343	10.656	12.242	14.684	16.919	19.679	21.666	27.877
10	2.558	3.059	3.940	4.865	6.179	7.267	9.342	11.781	13.442	15.987	18.307	21.161	23.209	29.588
11	3.053	3.609	4.575	5.578	6.989	8.148	10.341	12.899	14.631	17.275	19.675	22.618	24.725	31.264
12	3.571	4.178	5.226	6.304	7.807	9.034	11.340	14.011	15.812	18.549	21.026	24.054	26.217	32.909
13	4.107	4.765	5.892	7.042	8.634	9.926	12.340	15.119	16.985	19.812	22.362	25.472	27.688	34.528
14	4.660	5.368	6.571	7.790	9.467	10.821	13.339	16.222	18.151	21.064	23.685	26.873	29.141	36.123
15	5.229	5.985	7.261	8.547	10.307	11.721	14.339	17.322	19.311	22.307	24.996	28.259	30.578	37.697
16	5.812	6.614	7.962	9.312	11.152	12.624	15.338	18.418	20.465	23.542	26.296	29.633	32.000	39.252
17	6.408	7.255	8.672	10.085	12.002	13.531	16.338	19.511	21.615	24.769	27.587	30.995	33.409	40.790
18	7.015	7.906	9.390	10.865	12.857	14.440	17.338	20.601	22.760	25.989	28.869	32.346	34.805	42.312
19	7.633	8.567	10.117	11.651	13.716	15.352	18.338	21.689	23.900	27.204	30.144	33.687	36.191	43.820
20	8.260	9.237	10.851	12.443	14.578	16.266	19.337	22.775	25.038	28.412	31.410	35.020	37.566	45.315
21	8.897	9.915	11.591	13.240	15.445	17.182	20.337	23.858	26.171	29.615	32.671	36.343	38.932	46.797
22	9.542	10.600	12.338	14.041	16.314	18.101	21.337	24.939	27.301	30.813	33.924	37.659	40.289	48.268

Note: For larger values of df, the expression $\sqrt{(X^2)^2} - \sqrt{2df - 1}$ may be used as a normal deviate with unit variance, remembering that the probability for X^2 corresponds with that of a single tail of the normal curve.

Table 4: Distribution of Chi-Square for Given Probability Levels (Continued)

df	.99	.98	.95	.90	.80	.70	Probability .50	.30	.20	.10	.05	.02	.01	.001
23	10.196	11.293	13.091	14.848	17.187	19.021	22.337	26.018	28.429	32.007	35.172	38.968	41.638	49.728
24	10.856	11.992	13.848	15.659	18.062	19.943	23.337	27.096	29.553	33.196	36.415	40.270	42.980	51.179
25	11.524	12.697	14.611	16.473	18.940	20.867	24.337	28.172	30.675	34.382	37.652	41.566	44.314	52.620
26	12.198	13.409	15.379	17.292	19.820	21.792	25.336	29.246	31.795	35.563	38.885	42.856	45.642	54.052
27	12.879	14.125	16.151	18.114	20.703	22.719	26.336	30.319	32.912	36.741	40.113	44.140	46.963	55.476
28	13.565	14.847	16.928	18.939	21.588	23.647	27.336	31.391	34.027	37.916	41.337	45.419	48.278	56.893
29	14.256	15.574	17.708	19.768	22.475	24.577	28.336	32.461	35.139	39.087	42.557	46.693	49.588	58.302
30	14.953	16.306	18.493	20.599	23.364	25.508	29.336	33.530	36.250	40.256	43.773	47.962	50.892	59.703
32	16.362	17.783	20.072	22.271	25.148	27.373	31.336	35.665	38.466	42.585	46.194	50.487	53.486	62.487
34	17.789	19.275	21.664	23.952	26.938	29.242	33.336	37.795	40.676	44.903	48.602	52.995	56.061	65.247
36	19.233	20.783	23.269	25.643	28.735	31.115	35.336	39.922	42.879	47.212	50.999	55.489	58.619	67.985
38	20.691	22.304	24.884	27.343	30.537	32.992	37.335	42.045	45.076	49.513	53.384	57.969	61.162	70.703
40	22.164	23.838	26.509	29.051	32.345	34.872	39.335	44.165	47.269	51.805	55.759	60.436	63.691	73.402
42	23.650	25.383	28.144	30.765	34.147	36.755	41.335	46.282	49.456	54.090	58.124	62.892	66.206	76.084
44	25.148	26.939	29.787	32.487	35.974	38.641	43.335	48.396	51.639	56.369	60.481	65.337	68.710	78.750
46	26.657	28.504	31.439	34.215	37.795	40.529	45.335	50.507	53.818	58.641	62.830	67.771	71.201	81.400
48	28.177	30.080	33.098	35.949	39.621	42.420	47.335	52.616	55.993	60.907	65.171	70.197	73.683	84.037
50	29.707	31.664	34.764	37.689	41.449	44.313	49.335	54.723	58.164	63.167	67.505	72.613	76.154	86.661
52	31.246	33.256	36.437	39.433	43.281	46.209	51.335	56.827	60.332	65.422	69.832	75.021	78.616	89.272
54	32.793	34.856	38.116	41.183	45.117	48.106	53.335	58.930	62.496	67.673	72.153	77.422	81.069	91.872
56	34.350	36.464	39.801	42.937	46.955	50.005	55.335	61.031	64.658	69.919	74.468	79.815	83.513	94.461
58	35.913	38.078	41.492	44.696	48.797	51.906	57.335	63.129	66.816	72.160	76.778	82.201	85.950	97.039
60	37.485	39.699	43.188	46.459	50.641	53.809	59.335	65.227	68.972	74.397	79.082	84.580	88.379	99.607
62	39.063	41.327	44.889	48.226	52.487	55.714	61.335	67.322	71.125	76.630	81.381	86.953	90.802	102.166
64	40.649	42.960	46.595	49.996	54.336	57.620	63.335	69.416	73.276	78.860	83.675	89.320	93.217	104.716
66	42.240	44.599	48.305	51.770	56.188	59.527	65.335	71.508	75.424	81.085	85.965	91.681	95.626	107.258
68	43.838	46.244	50.020	53.548	58.042	61.436	67.335	73.600	77.571	83.308	88.250	94.037	98.028	109.791
70	45.442	47.893	51.739	55.329	59.898	63.346	69.335	75.689	79.715	85.527	90.531	96.388	100.425	112.317

Table 5: The F-Distribution for Given Probability Levels (.05 Level)

df₁ \ df₂	1	2	3	4	5	6	7	8	9	10	12	15	20	24	30	40	60	120	∞
1	161.4	199.5	215.7	224.6	230.2	234.0	236.8	238.9	240.5	241.9	243.9	245.9	248.0	249.1	250.1	251.1	252.2	253.3	254.3
2	18.51	19.00	19.16	19.25	19.30	19.33	19.35	19.37	19.38	19.49	19.41	19.43	19.45	19.45	19.46	19.47	19.48	19.49	19.50
3	10.13	9.55	9.28	9.12	9.01	8.94	8.89	8.85	8.81	8.79	8.74	8.70	8.66	8.64	8.62	8.59	8.57	8.55	8.53
4	7.71	6.94	6.59	6.39	6.26	6.15	6.09	6.04	6.00	5.96	5.91	5.86	5.80	5.77	5.75	5.72	5.69	5.66	5.63
5	6.61	5.79	5.41	5.19	5.05	4.95	4.88	4.82	4.77	4.74	4.68	4.62	4.56	4.53	4.50	4.46	4.43	4.40	4.36
6	5.99	5.14	4.76	4.53	4.39	4.28	4.21	4.15	4.10	4.06	4.00	3.94	3.87	3.84	3.81	3.77	3.74	3.70	3.67
7	5.59	4.74	4.35	4.12	3.97	3.87	3.79	3.73	3.68	3.64	3.57	3.51	3.44	3.41	3.38	3.34	3.30	3.27	3.23
8	5.32	4.46	4.07	3.84	3.69	3.58	3.50	3.44	3.39	3.35	3.28	3.22	3.15	3.12	3.08	3.04	3.01	2.97	2.93
9	5.12	4.26	3.86	3.63	3.48	3.37	3.29	3.23	3.18	3.14	3.07	3.01	2.94	2.90	2.86	2.83	2.79	2.75	2.71
10	4.96	4.10	3.71	3.48	3.33	3.22	3.14	3.07	3.02	2.98	2.91	2.85	2.77	2.74	2.70	2.66	2.62	2.58	2.54
11	4.84	3.98	3.59	3.36	3.20	3.09	3.01	2.95	2.90	2.85	2.79	2.72	2.65	2.61	2.57	2.53	2.49	2.45	2.40
12	4.75	3.89	3.49	3.26	3.11	3.00	2.91	2.85	2.80	2.75	2.69	2.62	2.54	2.51	2.47	2.43	2.38	2.34	2.30
13	4.67	3.81	3.41	3.18	3.03	2.92	2.83	2.77	2.71	2.67	2.60	2.53	2.46	2.42	2.38	2.34	2.30	2.25	2.21
14	4.60	3.74	3.34	3.11	2.96	2.85	2.76	2.70	2.65	2.60	2.53	2.46	2.39	2.35	2.31	2.27	2.22	2.18	2.13
15	4.54	3.68	3.29	3.06	2.90	2.79	2.71	2.64	2.59	2.54	2.48	2.40	2.33	2.29	2.25	2.20	2.16	2.11	2.07
16	4.49	3.63	3.24	3.01	2.85	2.74	2.66	2.59	2.54	2.49	2.42	2.35	2.28	2.24	2.19	2.1	2.11	2.06	2.01
17	4.45	3.59	3.20	2.96	2.81	2.70	2.61	2.55	2.49	2.45	2.38	2.31	2.23	2.19	2.15	2.10	2.06	2.01	1.96
18	4.41	3.55	3.16	2.93	2.77	2.66	2.58	2.51	2.46	2.41	2.34	2.27	2.19	2.15	2.11	2.06	2.02	1.97	1.92
19	4.38	3.52	3.13	2.90	2.74	2.63	2.54	2.48	2.42	2.38	2.31	2.23	2.16	2.11	2.07	2.03	1.98	1.93	1.88
20	4.35	3.49	3.10	2.87	2.71	2.60	2.51	2.45	2.39	2.35	2.28	2.20	2.12	2.08	2.04	1.99	1.95	1.90	1.84
21	4.32	3.47	3.07	2.84	2.68	2.57	2.49	2.42	2.37	2.32	2.25	2.18	2.10	2.05	2.01	1.96	1.92	1.87	1.81
22	4.30	3.44	3.05	2.82	2.66	2.55	2.46	2.40	2.34	2.30	2.23	2.15	2.07	2.03	1.98	1.94	1.89	1.84	1.78
23	4.28	3.42	3.03	2.80	2.64	2.53	2.44	2.37	2.32	2.27	2.20	2.13	2.05	2.01	1.96	1.91	1.86	1.81	1.76
24	4.26	3.40	3.01	2.78	2.62	2.51	2.42	2.36	2.30	2.25	2.18	2.11	2.03	1.98	1.94	1.89	1.84	1.79	1.73
25	4.24	3.39	2.99	2.76	2.60	2.49	2.40	2.34	2.28	2.24	2.16	2.09	2.01	1.96	1.92	1.87	1.82	1.77	1.71
26	4.23	3.37	2.98	2.74	2.59	2.47	2.39	2.32	2.27	2.22	2.15	2.07	1.99	1.95	1.90	1.85	1.80	1.75	1.69
27	4.21	3.35	2.96	2.73	2.57	2.46	2.37	2.31	2.25	2.20	2.13	2.06	1.97	1.93	1.88	1.84	1.79	1.73	1.67
28	4.20	3.34	2.95	2.71	2.56	2.45	2.36	2.29	2.24	2.19	2.12	2.04	1.96	1.91	1.87	1.82	1.77	1.71	1.65
29	4.18	3.33	2.93	2.70	2.55	2.43	2.35	2.28	2.22	2.18	2.10	2.03	1.94	1.90	1.85	1.81	1.75	1.70	1.64
30	4.17	3.32	2.92	2.69	2.53	2.42	2.33	2.27	2.21	2.16	2.09	2.01	1.93	1.89	1.84	1.79	1.74	1.68	1.62
40	4.08	3.23	2.84	2.61	2.45	2.34	2.25	2.18	2.12	2.08	2.00	1.92	1.84	1.79	1.74	1.69	1.64	1.58	1.51
60	4.00	3.15	2.76	2.53	2.37	2.25	2.17	2.10	2.04	1.99	1.92	1.84	1.75	1.70	1.65	1.59	1.53	1.47	1.39
120	3.92	3.07	2.68	2.45	2.29	2.17	2.09	2.02	1.96	1.91	1.83	1.75	1.66	1.61	1.55	1.50	1.43	1.35	1.25
∞	3.84	3.00	2.60	2.37	2.21	2.10	2.01	1.94	1.88	1.83	1.75	1.67	1.57	1.52	1.46	1.39	1.32	1.22	1.00

Table 5: The Distribution of F for Given Probability Levels (.01 Level)

df₂ \ df₁	1	2	3	4	5	6	7	8	9	10	12	15	20	24	30	40	60	120	∞
1	4052	4999.5	5403	5625	5764	5859	5928	5982	6022	6056	6106	6157	6209	6235	6261	6287	6313	6339	6366
2	98.5	99.00	99.17	99.25	99.30	99.33	99.36	99.37	99.39	99.40	99.42	99.43	99.45	99.46	99.47	99.47	99.48	99.49	99.50
3	34.12	30.82	29.46	28.71	28.24	27.91	27.67	27.49	27.25	27.23	27.05	26.87	26.69	26.60	26.50	26.41	26.32	26.22	26.13
4	21.20	18.00	16.69	15.98	15.52	15.21	14.98	14.80	14.66	14.55	14.37	14.20	14.02	13.93	13.84	13.75	13.65	13.56	13.46
5	16.26	13.27	12.06	11.39	10.97	10.67	10.46	10.29	10.16	10.05	9.89	9.72	9.55	9.47	9.38	9.29	9.20	9.11	9.02
6	13.75	10.92	9.78	9.15	8.75	8.47	8.26	8.10	7.98	7.87	7.72	7.56	7.40	7.31	7.23	7.14	7.06	6.97	6.88
7	12.25	9.55	8.45	7.85	7.46	7.19	6.99	6.84	6.72	6.62	6.47	6.31	6.16	6.07	5.99	5.91	5.82	5.74	5.65
8	11.26	8.65	7.59	7.01	6.63	6.37	6.18	6.03	5.91	5.81	5.67	5.52	5.36	5.28	5.20	5.12	5.03	4.95	4.86
9	10.56	8.02	6.99	6.42	6.06	5.80	5.61	5.47	5.35	5.26	5.11	4.96	4.81	4.73	4.65	4.57	4.48	4.40	4.31
10	10.04	7.56	6.55	5.99	5.64	5.39	5.20	5.06	4.94	4.85	4.71	4.56	4.41	4.33	4.25	4.17	4.08	4.00	3.91
11	9.65	7.21	6.22	5.67	5.32	5.07	4.89	4.74	4.63	4.54	4.40	4.25	4.10	4.02	3.94	3.86	3.78	3.69	3.60
12	9.33	6.93	5.95	5.41	5.06	4.82	4.64	4.50	4.39	4.30	4.16	4.01	3.86	3.78	3.70	3.62	3.54	3.45	3.36
13	9.07	6.70	5.74	5.21	4.86	4.62	4.44	4.30	4.19	4.10	3.96	3.82	3.66	3.59	3.51	3.43	3.34	3.25	3.17
14	8.86	6.51	5.56	5.04	4.69	4.46	4.28	4.14	4.03	3.94	3.80	3.66	3.51	3.43	3.35	3.27	3.18	3.09	3.00
15	8.68	6.36	5.42	4.89	4.56	4.32	4.14	4.00	3.89	3.80	3.67	3.52	3.37	3.29	3.21	3.13	3.05	2.96	2.87
16	8.53	6.23	5.29	4.77	4.44	4.20	4.03	3.89	3.78	3.69	3.55	3.41	3.26	3.18	3.10	3.02	2.93	2.84	2.75
17	8.40	6.11	5.18	4.67	4.34	4.10	3.93	3.79	3.68	3.59	3.46	3.31	3.16	3.08	3.00	2.92	2.83	2.75	2.65
18	8.29	6.01	5.09	4.58	4.25	4.01	3.84	3.71	3.60	3.51	3.37	3.23	3.08	3.00	2.92	2.84	2.75	2.66	2.57
19	8.18	5.93	5.01	4.50	4.17	3.94	3.77	3.63	3.52	3.43	3.30	3.15	3.00	2.92	2.84	2.76	2.67	2.58	2.49
20	8.10	5.85	4.94	4.43	4.10	3.87	3.70	3.56	3.46	3.37	3.23	3.09	2.94	2.86	2.78	2.69	2.61	2.52	2.42
21	8.02	5.78	4.87	4.37	4.04	3.81	3.64	3.51	3.40	3.31	3.17	3.03	2.88	2.80	2.72	2.64	2.55	2.46	2.36
22	7.95	5.72	4.82	4.31	3.9	3.76	3.59	3.45	3.35	3.26	3.12	2.98	2.83	2.75	2.67	2.58	2.50	2.40	2.31
23	7.88	5.66	4.76	4.26	3.94	3.71	3.54	3.41	3.30	3.21	3.07	2.93	2.78	2.70	2.62	2.54	2.45	2.35	2.26
24	7.82	5.61	4.72	4.22	3.90	3.67	3.50	3.36	3.26	3.17	3.03	2.89	2.74	2.66	2.58	2.49	2.40	2.31	2.21
25	7.77	5.57	4.68	4.18	3.85	3.63	3.46	3.32	3.22	3.13	2.99	2.85	2.70	2.62	2.54	2.45	2.36	2.27	2.17
26	7.72	5.53	4.64	4.14	3.82	3.59	3.42	3.29	3.18	3.09	2.96	2.81	2.66	2.58	2.50	2.42	2.33	2.23	2.13
27	7.68	5.49	4.60	4.11	3.78	3.56	3.39	3.26	3.15	3.06	2.93	2.78	2.63	2.55	2.47	2.38	2.29	2.20	2.10
28	7.64	5.45	4.57	4.07	3.75	3.53	3.36	3.23	3.12	3.03	2.90	2.75	2.60	2.52	2.44	2.35	2.26	2.17	2.06
29	7.60	5.42	4.54	4.04	3.73	3.50	3.33	3.20	3.09	3.00	2.87	2.73	2.57	2.49	2.41	2.33	2.23	2.14	2.03
30	7.56	5.39	4.51	4.02	3.70	3.47	3.30	3.17	3.07	2.98	2.84	2.70	2.55	2.47	2.39	2.30	2.21	2.11	2.01
40	7.31	5.18	4.31	3.83	3.51	3.29	3.12	2.99	2.89	2.80	2.66	2.52	2.37	2.29	2.20	2.11	2.02	1.92	1.80
60	7.08	4.98	4.13	3.65	3.34	3.12	2.95	2.82	2.72	2.63	2.50	2.35	2.20	2.12	2.03	1.94	1.84	1.73	1.60
120	6.85	4.79	3.95	3.48	3.17	2.96	2.79	2.66	2.56	2.47	2.34	2.19	2.03	1.95	1.86	1.76	1.66	1.53	1.38
∞	6.63	4.61	3.78	3.32	3.02	2.80	2.64	2.51	2.41	2.32	2.18	2.04	1.88	1.79	1.70	1.59	1.47	1.32	1.00

Table 6: Distribution of Hartley F for Given Probability Levels

$df = $ n-1	a	k = number of variances										
		2	3	4	5	6	7	8	9	10	11	12
4	.05	9.60	15.5	20.6	25.2	29.5	33.6	37.5	41.4	44.6	48.0	51.4
	.01	23.2	37.	49.	59.	69.	79.	89.	97.	106.	113.	120.
5	.05	7.15	10.8	13.7	16.3	18.7	20.8	22.9	24.7	26.5	28.2	29.9
	.01	14.9	22.	28.	33.	38.	42.	46.	50.	54.	57.	60.
6	.05	5.82	8.38	10.4	12.1	13.7	15.	16.3	17.5	18.6	19.7	20.7
	.01	11.1	15.5	19.1	22.	25.	27.	30.	32.	34.	36.	37.
7	.05	4.99	6.94	8.44	9.70	10.8	11.8	12.7	13.5	14.3	12.2	15.8
	.01	8.89	12.1	14.5	16.5	18.4	20.	22.	23.	24.	19.8	27.
8	.05	4.43	6.00	7.18	8.12	9.03	9.78	10.5	11.1	11.7	10.3	12.7
	.01	7.50	9.9	11.7	13.2	14.5	15.8	16.9	17.9	18.9	16.0	21.
9	.05	4.03	5.34	6.31	7.11	7.80	8.41	8.95	9.45	9.91	9.01	10.7
	.01	6.54	8.5	9.9	11.1	12.1	13.1	13.9	14.7	15.3	13.4	16.6
10	.05	3.72	4.85	5.67	6.34	6.92	7.42	7.87	8.28	8.66	9.01	9.34
	.01	5.85	7.4	8.6	9.6	10.4	11.1	11.8	12.4	12.9	13.4	13.9
12	.05	3.28	4.16	4.79	5.30	5.72	6.09	6.42	6.72	7.00	7.25	7.48
	.01	4.91	6.1	6.9	7.6	8.2	8.7	9.1	9.5	9.9	10.2	10.6
15	.05	2.86	3.54	4.01	4.37	4.68	4.95	5.19	5.40	5.59	5.77	5.93
	.01	4.07	4.9	5.5	6.0	6.4	6.7	7.1	7.3	7.5	7.8	8.0
20	.05	2.46	2.95	3.29	3.54	3.76	3.94	4.10	4.24	4.37	4.49	4.59
	.01	3.32	3.8	4.3	4.6	4.9	5.1	5.3	5.5	5.6	5.8	5.9
30	.05	2.07	2.40	2.61	2.78	2.91	3.02	3.12	3.21	3.29	3.36	3.39
	.01	2.63	3.0	3.3	3.4	3.6	3.7	3.8	3.9	4.0	4.1	4.2
60	.05	1.67	1.85	1.96	2.04	2.11	2.17	2.22	2.26	2.30	2.33	2.36
	.01	1.96	2.2	2.3	2.4	2.4	2.5	2.5	2.6	2.6	2.7	2.7
∞	.05	1.00	1.00	1.00	1.00	1.00	1.00	1.00	1.00	1.00	1.00	1.00
∞	.01	1.00	1.00	1.00	1.00	1.00	1.00	1.00	1.00	1.00	1.00	1.00

ANSWERS TO CHAPTER EXERCISES

Chapter 1

a.   T
b.   F
c.   T
d.   T
e.   F

Chapter 2

a.   F
b.   F
c.   F
d.   T
e.   T

Chapter 3

a.   T
b.   T
c.   F
d.   T
e.   T

Chapter 4

a.   F
b.   T
c.   T
d.   F
e.   T

Chapter 5

a.   T
b.   T
c.   T
d.   F
e.   T

Chapter 6

a.   T
b.   F
c.   F
d.   T
e.   T

Chapter 7

a.   F
b.   T
c.   F
d.   F
e.   T

Chapter 8

a.   F
b.   F
c.   F
d.   T
e.   T

Chapter 9

a.   T
b.   T
c.   F
d.   F
e.   T

Chapter 10

a.   F
b.   T
c.   F
d.   F
e.   T

Chapter 11

a.   F
b.   T
c.   F
d.   T
e.   T

Chapter 12

a.   T
b.   F
c.   T
d.   F
e.   T

Chapter 13

a.   F
b.   T
c.   F
d.   T
e.   F

Chapter 14

a.   T
b.   T
c.   F
d.   F
e.   F

Chapter 15

a.   T
b.   T
c.   T
d.   F
e.   T

Chapter 16

a.   F
b.   T
c.   T
d.   F
e.   F

Chapter 17

a.   F
b.   F
c.   T
d.   T
e.   T
f.   T
g.   T
h.   T
i.   T

Chapter 18

a.   F
b.   T
c.   F
d.   T
e.   F
f.   T

Chapter 19

a.   F
b.   F
c.   T
d.   T
e.   T
f.   T

Chapter 20

a.   F
b.   T
c.   T
d.   T
e.   T
f.   T

Chapter 21

a.   F
b.   F
c.   F
d.   T
e.   F

Chapter 22

a.   T
b.   T
c.   T
d.   F
e.   T
f.   T
g.   T
h.   F

Chapter 23

a.   F
b.   T
c.   F
d.   T
e.   F
f.   T

Chapter 24

a.   T
b.   T
c.   T
d.   F
e.   T

Chapter 25

a.   T
b.   T
c.   T
d.   F
e.   T
f.   F

Chapter 26

a.   F
b.   T
c.   F
d.   T
e.   F
f.   T
g.   F
h.   T
i.   T

Chapter 27

a.   T
b.   T
c.   T
d.   T
e.   T
f.   T
g.   T

Chapter 28

a.   T
b.   T
c.   F
d.   T
e.   T
f.   T
g.   T
h.   T
i.   T
j.   T
k.   F
l.   T
m.   T

Chapter 29

a.	F
b.	F
c.	T
d.	T
e.	F
f.	F
g.	T

Chapter 30

a.	F
b.	T
c.	T
d.	T
e.	T
f.	F
g.	T

Chapter 31

a.	T
b.	T
c.	F
d.	T
e.	T
f.	F
g.	T
h.	F

Chapter 32

a.	F
b.	T
c.	T
d.	T
e.	F
f.	T
g.	T
h.	F

Chapter 33

a.	T
b.	F
c.	F
d.	T
e.	F
f.	T
g.	F
h.	T
i.	T

Chapter 34

a.	F
b.	T
c.	T
d.	T
e.	T

Chapter 35

a.	T
b.	T
c.	T
d.	T
e.	T

Chapter 36

a.	T
b.	F
c.	T
d.	T
e.	F
f.	T

Chapter 37

a.	T
b.	F
c.	T
d.	T
e.	T
f.	T
g.	F
h.	T

Chapter 38

a.	F
b.	F
c.	T
d.	T
e.	T
f.	T
g.	T
h.	T

Chapter 39

a.	F
b.	F
c.	T
d.	T
e.	F
f.	T

AUTHOR INDEX

SUBJECT INDEX